BARCODE ON NEXT PAGE

P9-EEN-845

My New iPhone

My New iPhone

52 Simple Projects to Get You Started

WALLACE WANG

no starch
press

12 11 10 09   1 2 3 4 5 6 7 8 9

ISBN-10: 1-59327-195-6
ISBN-13: 978-1-59327-195-4

SUSTAINABLE FORESTRY INITIATIVE

Certified Fiber Sourcing

www.sfiprogram.org

Publisher: William Pollock
Managing Editor: Megan Dunchak
Production Editor: Kathleen Mish
Cover and Interior Design: Octopod Studios
Developmental Editor: Tyler Ortman
Copyeditor: Lisa Theobald
Compositor: Riley Hoffman
Proofreaders: Cristina Chan and Megan Dunchak
Indexer: Jan Wright

For information on book distributors or translations, please contact No Starch Press, Inc. directly:

No Starch Press, Inc.
555 De Haro Street, Suite 250, San Francisco, CA 94107
phone: 415.863.9900; fax: 415.863.9950; info@nostarch.com; http://www.nostarch.com/

Library of Congress Cataloging-in-Publication Data

```
Wang, Wally.
  My new iPhone : 52 simple projects to get you started / Wallace Wang.
      p. cm.
  Includes index.
  ISBN-13: 978-1-59327-195-4
  ISBN-10: 1-59327-195-6
  1.  iPhone (Smartphone) 2.  Cellular telephones. 3.  Digital music players. 4.  Pocket computers.  I. Title.
  TK6570.M6W36 2009
  621.3845'6--dc22
                                              2009012721
```

Dedication

This book is dedicated to everyone who has ever used a mobile phone and found it too limited, too confusing, and ultimately too frustrating. Welcome to the world of the iPhone, which acts as a mobile phone and handheld computer capable of playing games, browsing the Internet, playing music and video, retrieving and sending email, and much more, while being easy to use at the same time. You'll find that your iPhone is one of the most sophisticated handheld computers on the market today. With a little guidance from this book, you'll be able to master all the features crammed and buried in your iPhone. Get ready for a mobile phone experience that you'll never receive from any other phone. The iPhone is in a class by itself, and you're about to find out how to make it uniquely your own.

Acknowledgments

This book owes its life to Bill Pollock, the publisher at No Starch Press, who pretty much lets me write anything I want, as long as he thinks there's a market for it. Thanks also go to Kathleen Mish, Riley Hoffman, and Tyler Ortman for keeping this entire project together and making sure everything in the book made sense and really worked.

Additional thanks also go to Jack Dunning at ComputorEdge Online (*http://webserver.computoredge.com/online.mvc*) for giving me a weekly Macintosh column, where I can write about Macintosh computers, iPhones, and anything else related to Apple and personal computers. Thanks also goes to Monish Bhatia for giving me a chance to write Macintosh hardware and software reviews for MacNN (*http://www.macnn.com/*), one of the best little websites for tracking the latest Apple news and rumors.

I'd also like to thank all the people I've met during my 18-year career as a stand-up comedian: Steve Schirripa (who appeared on HBO's hit show *The Sopranos*) and Don Learned for giving me my first break performing in Las Vegas at the Riviera Hotel & Casino, Russ Rivas, Dobie "The Uranus King" Maxwell, Darrell Joyce, and Leo "The Man, the Myth, the Legend" Fontaine.

I'd also like to thank my radio comedy co-hosts on *CyberSports Today* (*http://www.cybersportstoday.com/*), which airs on ESPN Radio (800 AM) in San Diego: Dane Henderson and Alexia Lunaria. Dane and I are refugees from 103.7 FreeFM, where we ran a show focusing on the unusual and supernatural. This let us chat with folks who believed they were in contact with space aliens, as well as a tugboat museum captain and a group of paramilitary, die-hard nationalists. We may not have always known what we were doing, but every night was a complete blast until the station switched to an all-music format and kicked us off the air.

Finally, I'd like to acknowledge my wife, Cassandra, my son, Jordan, and my three cats, Bo, Scraps, and Nuit, for putting up with all my time spent sitting in front of the computer instead of doing anything else, like cleaning the house or putting books back where they belong.

Brief Contents

Part 6: Using Email

Part 7: Business Stuff

Part 8: Fun Stuff

Part 9: Safety and Privacy

Part 10: Cool Things You Can Do with Apps

Contents in Detail

Part 3: Making Phone Calls

Part 8: Fun Stuff

Part 9: Safety and Privacy

Part 10: Cool Things You Can Do with Apps

Introduction

When most people see an iPhone, their first reaction is awe with a little bit of covetousness thrown in for good measure. After most people buy an iPhone, their feelings of awe and envy soon change to a desire to show off and start using their new handheld computer. However, the iPhone offers so many cool features that you may feel overwhelmed, wondering how to get started and how to get the most out of your new tool.

If you're feeling overwhelmed by your new iPhone, this is the book you'll need to gently guide you through the basics of using your new phone, browsing the Internet, and performing all kinds of personal and business tasks. This book will show you how to make the iPhone work best for you.

If you already know how to use a smart phone made by another company, you'll discover that moving to the iPhone represents a new-generation technology that's as dramatic as moving from an abacus to a personal computer. If you're new to smart phones, you'll find that the iPhone can be a friendly, forgiving, and fun tool that will make you wonder why anybody would ever want to use another mobile phone.

By the way, if you have an iPod touch, you basically have an iPhone without the telephone feature. Although you can't make telephone calls with an iPod touch, it offers many of the same features as the iPhone. So whether you have an iPhone or iPod touch, you can learn something from this book.

To avoid having to mention both the iPhone and iPod touch all the time, the rest of this book will use the phrase *iPhone* to represent both the iPhone and iPod touch. Just keep in mind that some tasks, such as making phone calls, sending text messages, and taking pictures, apply only to the iPhone.

How This Book Is Organized

To help you get started using your iPhone right away, this book is divided into short projects that act like recipes in a cookbook. Each project states a common goal, explains how your iPhone can help you reach that goal, and then lists all the steps you need to follow to accomplish it in a way that only an iPhone can.

By learning how to perform fun and useful tasks via hands-on instructions, you'll discover how to achieve specific results using your iPhone. You don't have to go through this book in any particular order. Just bounce around, follow the projects that catch your interest, and ignore the projects that you don't care about.

Although your iPhone comes packed with plenty of features, don't bother trying to learn them all if you don't need to. Just learn the features that you need now so you can be productive right away. By following the projects in this book, your iPhone will become a useful and indispensable tool that you can rely on every day.

To help you expand the capabilities of your iPhone, this book includes short descriptions of some of the more popular apps you can download and install for free (you'll learn how to find and install them in Project 11). These apps can help you do things like make free phone calls, edit pictures you've captured with your iPhone's built-in camera, or tune in to Internet radio stations. The huge library of free apps available lets you expand your iPhone's capabilities so it can help you accomplish what you need to do right now.

PART 1

Getting Started

1 Turning Your iPhone On and Off

Turning an iPhone on and off should be easy—and it is. However, the iPhone can be in one of four states: *on*, *off*, *sleep*, or *airplane mode*. If all of this sounds more confusing than just turning your iPhone on and off, relax. There are actually valid reasons for putting your iPhone into different states. The trick is learning the advantages of each state and how best to put your iPhone into each state.

When your iPhone is on, you can use it to make calls, browse the Internet, listen to music, or perform a multitude of other tasks.

After you've turned on your iPhone, you can switch it to sleep, off, or airplane mode. When your iPhone is in sleep mode, you'll conserve its battery power while keeping it ready to receive calls. Most of the time, when you're not actually using your iPhone, you'll want to put it in sleep mode to conserve its battery power.

Airplane mode turns off your iPhone's ability to make calls, send text messages, access email, or surf the Web. This essentially cuts off your iPhone from the rest of the world while letting you do most other tasks, such as play music, check your calendar, use the calculator, or take pictures. As the name suggests, airplane mode is used when you're in an airplane and can't risk having your iPhone interfere with the airplane's navigation systems.

Turning your iPhone off stops you from receiving any calls or text messages altogether. You might turn off your iPhone to keep it from running down its battery, or to keep it from accessing your telephone company's network and vibrating or ringing when you receive a call and possibly disturbing others around you (such as in a crowded movie theatre).

Project goal: Learn how to turn on your iPhone, put it to sleep, put it in airplane mode, and shut it off completely.

What You'll Be Using

To turn an iPhone on and off, you need to use the following:

▸ The Sleep/Wake button

 The Settings application

Turning On Your iPhone

When your iPhone is off, you can turn it on by following these steps:

1. Press and hold down the Sleep/Wake button at the top of your iPhone, as shown in Figure 1-1, until the Apple logo appears on the screen.

✳ **NOTE:** If you see a blank screen after pressing the Sleep/Wake button, your iPhone doesn't have enough power to turn on.

Courtesy of Apple

FIGURE 1-1: *The Sleep/ Wake button is located on the upper-right corner of the iPhone.*

2. Wait a few seconds until the Home screen appears, as shown in Figure 1-2. This tells you that your iPhone is now on.

Turning Off Your iPhone

When your iPhone is on, you can turn it off by following these steps:

1. Hold down the Sleep/Wake button until a red arrow slider appears at the top of the screen.
2. Drag the slider to the right (or tap **Cancel** if you don't want to turn off your iPhone after all).

Putting Your iPhone to Sleep

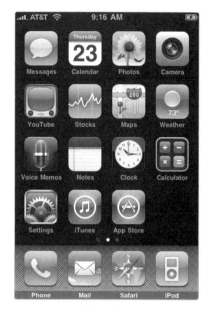

FIGURE 1-2: *The Home screen contains icons for accessing various features.*

After you've turned on your iPhone, you can change it from on to sleep mode to conserve battery power while still receiving phone calls or text messages. To put an iPhone that is already turned on to sleep, do this:

1. Press the Sleep/Wake button once. The screen darkens.

✳ **NOTE:** At a glance, you cannot tell whether an iPhone is turned off or in sleep mode. If you press the Home or Sleep/Wake button and your iPhone turns on, then you'll know it was asleep. If you press either button and nothing happens, then you'll know that it's turned off.

Putting Your iPhone to Sleep Automatically

Since sleep mode is critical in conserving your iPhone's battery, you may be happy to know that if you leave an iPhone on, it will put itself into sleep mode automatically after a fixed period of time. To specify this period of time, follow these steps:

1. From the Home screen, tap **Settings**. The Settings screen appears, as shown in Figure 1-3.
2. Tap **General**. The General screen appears, as shown in Figure 1-4.

FIGURE 1-3: *The Settings screen*

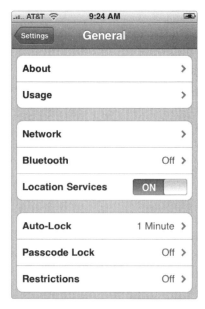

FIGURE 1-4: *The General screen*

3. Tap **Auto-Lock**. The Auto-Lock screen appears, as shown in Figure 1-5.
4. Tap one of the available options: **1 Minute**, **2 Minutes**, **3 Minutes**, **4 Minutes**, **5 Minutes**, or **Never**.
5. Press the Home button to return to the Home screen.

Waking Up Your iPhone from Sleep

When you put your iPhone to sleep, you must wake it up to change its state from sleep to on. To wake up your iPhone in sleep mode, do this:

1. Press the Sleep/Wake button on top of the iPhone (or press the Home button). An arrow slider appears at the bottom of the screen.
2. Drag the slider to the right. The Home screen appears.

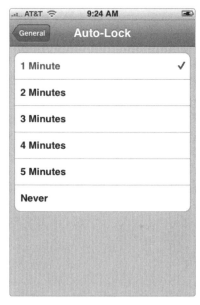

FIGURE 1-5: *The Auto-Lock screen lets you define a fixed inactivity time before your iPhone goes to sleep automatically.*

The slider forces you to slide your finger to unlock your iPhone. That way your iPhone won't accidentally turn on if you press its Sleep/Wake button in your pocket or purse.

∗ *NOTE:* **If you fail to use the slider to unlock your iPhone after a few seconds, your iPhone will automatically go back into sleep mode.**

Turning On Airplane Mode

On most airlines, you are not allowed to make phone calls or send or receive text messages; this prevents cellular phones from interfering with the plane's navigational systems. To avoid this problem but still use your iPhone for other tasks, such as jotting down notes or using its calculator, you can place your iPhone in airplane mode by following these steps:

1. Make sure your iPhone is turned on.
2. From the Home screen, tap **Settings**. The Settings screen appears (see Figure 1-3).
3. Tap the **ON/OFF** button next to Airplane Mode to turn this option on or off. An orange airplane icon will appear in the upper-left corner of the screen when this option is turned on, as shown in Figure 1-6.

FIGURE 1-6: An orange airplane icon appears when an iPhone is in airplane mode.

∗ *NOTE:* **When in airplane mode, a white airplane icon appears in the upper-left corner of the Home screen.**

Additional Ideas for Turning Your iPhone On and Off

The four states of an iPhone are on, off, sleep, and airplane mode. When an iPhone is off, it can only be switched on. When an iPhone is on, it can be switched to off, sleep, or airplane mode.

In sleep mode, the iPhone can only be switched to on. In airplane mode, you can switch an iPhone to sleep or off.

As a general rule, turn off your iPhone whenever you don't want to be bothered with incoming calls or text messages, such as at night when you're sleeping or if you're busy on a hot date.

Airplane mode is most useful when you're stuck in an airplane and don't feel like interacting with any of your fellow passengers, preferring to let your iPhone amuse you instead.

Sleep mode is generally used during the day when you need to accept incoming calls and text messages, but you want to conserve battery power.

Now that you understand the basics of turning your iPhone on and off (and everything in between), the rest of this book will teach you how to use all the other features of your iPhone so you can do something useful.

Turn Your iPhone into a Flashlight

If you ever get caught in the dark, just turn your iPhone on—the illumination from the screen can give you a little bit of light. In case you need a more sophisticated flashlight, download the myLite Flashlight app, which turns your iPhone into a flashlight and a whole lot more.

Besides letting you adjust the color and brightness of your light, this app also lets you choose from several types of lights such as Strobe, Emergency, and Caution Flare. Now you can use your iPhone as an emergency signaling light to warn oncoming drivers of an accident ahead, attract the attention of the police if you need to signal for help, or flash an SOS signal so your rescuers can find you in case you're lost somewhere in the wilderness. With this free app, your iPhone can literally save your life one day.

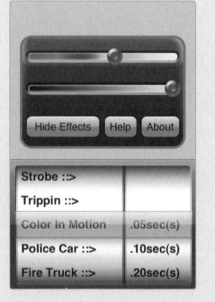

The myLite Flashlight app can turn your iPhone into a flashlight.

myLite Flashlight   *http://www.doapps.com/products/iPhone/myLite/*

2 Charging and Conserving Battery Power

Nothing is more frustrating than wanting to use your iPhone and finding that it has run out of battery power. To help prevent this problem, this chapter explains how your iPhone's battery works and how you can modify your iPhone settings to minimize power usage, thereby extending the daily life of your battery.

Your iPhone runs on an internal, non-removable lithium-ion battery, which you'll need to recharge periodically, depending on how often you use your iPhone. Unlike other mobile phones, you cannot remove your iPhone's battery and replace it with a spare, fully charged one.

Like all batteries, your iPhone's battery will eventually wear out, but by then you'll probably have a new iPhone model anyway (or you can take your iPhone to an Apple store and pay for a replacement battery).

Project goal: Learn how to maximize the charge of your battery to allow your iPhone to run as long as possible.

What You'll Be Using

To maximize your iPhone's battery life, you need to use the following:

 The iPhone USB cable

 The Settings application

▶ The iPhone USB power adapter

Recharging Your iPhone

Your iPhone comes with a USB cable and a power adapter that provide two ways to recharge your iPhone. First, you can plug the USB cable into the bottom of your iPhone and then plug the other end directly into the USB port of any computer. This not only recharges your iPhone, but it lets you transfer files from your computer to your iPhone (and vice versa).

✳ *NOTE:* **Always plug the USB cable directly into your computer and not into the USB port of your keyboard. The keyboard's USB port doesn't provide enough power to recharge your iPhone.**

A second way to recharge your iPhone is to plug the USB cable directly into the power adapter, which you can plug into a wall socket. This can be handy if you don't have access to a computer with an open USB port.

To ensure a full battery, most people plug their iPhone into a computer or wall outlet overnight. That way, the iPhone will be fully charged the next morning. If you don't use your iPhone every day, you should fully charge and discharge your iPhone's battery at least once a month by following these steps:

1. Charge your iPhone by plugging it into the USB port of a computer or into the USB power adapter that's plugged into an electrical outlet.
2. Unplug the iPhone from the USB cable.
3. Leave the iPhone turned on until its battery power completely drains away.
4. Recharge the iPhone.

✳ *WARNING:* **Hot weather (above 95°F or 35°C) can irreversibly harm your iPhone's battery. Avoid storing your iPhone in direct sunlight. If your iPhone feels excessively warm while it's recharging inside a carrying case, take it out of its case before recharging. Cold weather will only temporarily prevent your iPhone's battery from holding a charge. Once you move your iPhone to a warmer area, its battery will hold its charge normally.**

Turning Off Bluetooth

Bluetooth is primarily used to connect an iPhone wirelessly to a headset so you can listen to music or make phone calls without holding the iPhone. If you don't use Bluetooth devices such as hands-free headsets, turning off Bluetooth can save power and increase your iPhone's battery life. To turn off Bluetooth, follow these steps:

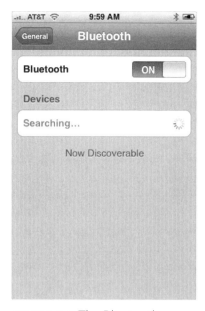

1. From the Home screen, tap **Settings**. The Settings screen appears.
2. Tap **General**. The General screen appears.
3. Tap **Bluetooth**. The Bluetooth screen appears, as shown in Figure 2-1.
4. Tap the **ON/OFF** button next to Bluetooth to turn this option off.
5. Press the Home button to return to the Home screen.

FIGURE 2-1: The Bluetooth screen

Turning Off Wi-Fi and 3G

If you frequently surf the Internet to look up map directions, watch YouTube videos, or browse your favorite web pages, you'll want to leave Wi-Fi turned on. If you turn Wi-Fi off and access the Internet, the iPhone uses your cellular telephone network, which requires more energy and drains your iPhone's battery in the process.

To make Internet surfing fast over cellular telephone networks, the iPhone uses a technological standard known as *3G*. You can turn off 3G to reduce your iPhone's power consumption.

To turn off Wi-Fi and 3G, follow these steps:

1. From the Home screen, tap **Settings**. The Settings screen appears.
2. Tap **General**. The General screen appears.
3. Tap **Network**. The Network screen appears, as shown in Figure 2-2.
4. Tap the **ON/OFF** button next to Enable 3G to turn this option off.
5. Tap **Wi-Fi**. The Wi-Fi Networks screen appears, as shown in Figure 2-3.

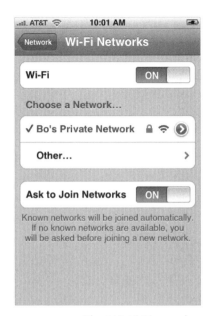

FIGURE 2-2: *The Network screen displays 3G and Wi-Fi options.*

FIGURE 2-3: *The Wi-Fi Networks screen*

6. Tap the **ON/OFF** button next to Wi-Fi to turn this option off.
7. Press the Home button to return to the Home screen.

✳ **NOTE:** You can also put your iPhone into airplane mode (see Project 1) to save energy.

Turning Off Push Accounts

Another handy feature of the iPhone is the *push account*. If you have a supported email account, your email server can deliver new messages to your iPhone automatically and quickly, so you receive the information almost the instant someone sends it to you (see Project 32 on how to set this up).

Since a push account requires that your iPhone periodically accesses your email account over the Internet, it uses energy. If you don't need or care to receive email messages as quickly as possible, you can turn off the push account by following these steps:

1. From the Home screen, tap **Settings**. The Settings screen appears.
2. Tap **Mail, Contacts, Calendars**. The Mail, Contacts, Calendars screen appears.
3. Tap **Fetch New Data**. The Fetch New Data screen appears, as shown in Figure 2-4.

4. Tap the **ON/OFF** button next to Push to turn this option off.

5. Press the Home button to return to the Home screen.

* NOTE: **If you want to keep the push account turned on, tap an option under the Fetch category to define how often you want your iPhone to check for new messages. The longer the time interval, the less power your iPhone will consume.**

Turning Off Location Services

Location Services is a fancy term that means some iPhone programs, such as the Maps program, rely on GPS (global positioning system) and triangulation of cellular phone towers to identify the physical location of your iPhone. If it knows your physical location in the world, an iPhone application can then help you find the nearest restaurant or gas station, for example.

Naturally, Location Services burns up battery energy, so if you don't need this type of service, you can turn it off to reduce power consumption by following these steps:

1. From the Home screen, tap **Settings**. The Settings screen appears.

2. Tap **General**. The General screen appears, as shown in Figure 2-5.

3. Tap the **ON/OFF** button next to Location Services to turn this option off.

4. Press the Home button to return to the Home screen.

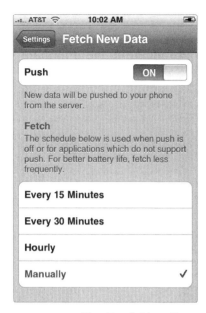

FIGURE 2-4: *The Fetch New Data screen*

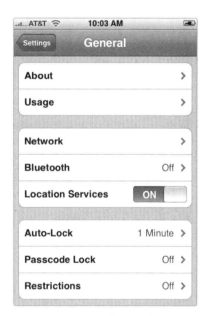

FIGURE 2-5: *The General screen displays the Location Services option.*

Additional Ideas for Conserving Power

Two ways to increase your iPhone's battery life involve conservation and additional power sources. If you're sure that you don't need (or want) to receive phone calls or text messages, you can turn off your iPhone completely instead of putting it in sleep mode. Conserving power can help you get the most out of your battery, but another solution is to keep your iPhone charged at all times.

Many third-party companies sell power packs that plug into your iPhone. The moment your iPhone runs out of power, you can slap a power pack on it and continue using your iPhone. Of course, this means lugging around a spare power pack and remembering to keep it charged, but it can be handy in an emergency to help you avoid being stranded somewhere with a dead iPhone battery.

Another solution is to buy special adapter cables that let you recharge your iPhone through the cigarette lighter in your car. You can even connect a solar panel to your iPhone to recharge it with sunlight.

Carry your iPhone's USB cable and you'll be able to recharge it from any computer with a USB port. If you lug around a laptop computer, use the laptop as a spare power source to keep your iPhone charged. (Of course, remember that this will drain your laptop's battery if it's not plugged into the wall.)

✳ *WARNING:* **If you connect an iPhone to a computer through its USB cable, make sure the computer doesn't go to sleep and don't turn it off. If this happens, your iPhone can't recharge its battery, and staying connected to a computer that's asleep or turned off can actually drain the iPhone's battery.**

Don't forget that your iPhone is actually an iPod too, so you can recharge your iPhone by plugging it into any iPod-compatible device such as a stereo charging dock.

If you combine conservation techniques with additional power sources, there's no reason you should ever run out of power for your iPhone—unless, of course, you forget to charge your power packs or laptop, forget to bring along your cigarette lighter adapter cable, or forget to carry a solar panel charger with your iPhone.

Find Your Lost iPhone

It's easy to plug your iPhone into an electric outlet in a library or coffeehouse and then walk away without it. To make sure you don't lose your iPhone, use the free app, If Found, Please..., which lets you customize your wallpaper to include a phone number and email address.

Even if your iPhone is locked, anyone can turn it on and see the wallpaper message that appears. Then if you're lucky, someone will contact you so you can get your iPhone back.

If Found, Please... *http://www.polka.com/*

If you subscribe to MobileMe, you can use the built-in Find My iPhone feature to locate a misplaced phone. (You must activate this feature through the MobileMe screen, in the Mail, Contacts, Calendars screen in the Settings app.) In the event that you lose your iPhone, just sign in to your MobileMe account with any web browser, click the Account icon, and enter your password again. In the list of information that appears, click **Find My iPhone**. A map will appear showing the general location of your iPhone. From here, you can choose to display a message on your iPhone's screen, have it play a sound, or erase all the data on your iPhone. For more detailed instructions on how to do this, download the bonus chapter at *http://www .nostarch.com/newiphone.htm*.

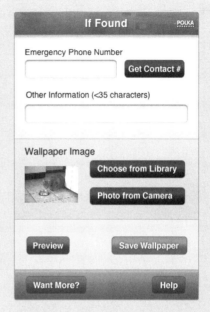

Use If Found, Please... to display contact information on your wallpaper.

Through MobileMe, you can display a custom message to appear on your lost iPhone.

3 Controlling the User Interface

The iPhone may be one of the easiest mobile phones to use. While other mobile phones waste space with cluttered and cryptic keypads that force you to press the same button multiple times just to type a single character, or display clumsy menus that more closely resemble a computer operating system, the iPhone offers its unique Multi-Touch interface, which lets you control your entire iPhone with the tip of your finger.

The Multi-Touch screen forms the basis of the iPhone. By tapping or sliding your finger across the screen, you can select items or scroll across the screen.

Of course, the iPhone offers ordinary buttons on the front, top, and side that you can press. These buttons typically control the basic functions of the iPhone (such as turning it on or off), while the Multi-Touch screen handles the dedicated features such as letting you type messages on the screen or display web pages.

Project goal: Learn how to control your iPhone using its physical buttons and Multi-Touch screen.

What You'll Be Using

To learn how to control your iPhone, you need to use the following:

- ▶ The Ring/Silent switch
- ▶ The Volume Up and Volume Down buttons

 The Calculator application

 The App Store application

The Maps application

Viewing the Home Screen

After the Sleep/Wake button at the top of the iPhone, the physical button you'll use most often is the Home button, which appears at the bottom of the iPhone, on the front. No matter what program you may be using at the time, pressing the Home button immediately displays the Home screen, which displays icons that represent all the different programs you can run on your iPhone, as shown in Figure 3-1. (Try it now!)

Modifying the Home Button

Press the Home button once and you'll always see the Home screen. Press the Home button twice and you can view one of five screens:

- ▶ The Home screen
- ▶ The Search screen
- ▶ The Phone Favorites screen
- ▶ The Camera screen
- ▶ The iPod screen

The Home screen displays icons for all the programs available on your iPhone such as Maps and Safari. The Search screen lets you search for information stored on your iPhone, such as a name in the Contacts program or a song title.

Courtesy of Apple

FIGURE 3-1: *The Home button*

The Phone Favorites screen displays the names of people you call most often. The Camera screen allows you to take photos with the iPhone's built-in camera. The iPod screen lets you start listening to music stored on your iPhone. By default, pressing the Home button twice displays the Phone Favorites screen, but you can change this by following these steps:

1. From the Home screen, tap **Settings**. The Settings screen appears.
2. Tap **General**. The General screen appears.
3. Scroll down and tap **Home Button**. The Home Button screen appears, as shown in Figure 3-2.
4. Tap **Home**, **Search**, **Phone Favorites**, **Camera**, or **iPod**. A checkmark appears next to the option you choose. From now on, pressing the Home button twice will display the screen you choose in this step. (Try it now!)

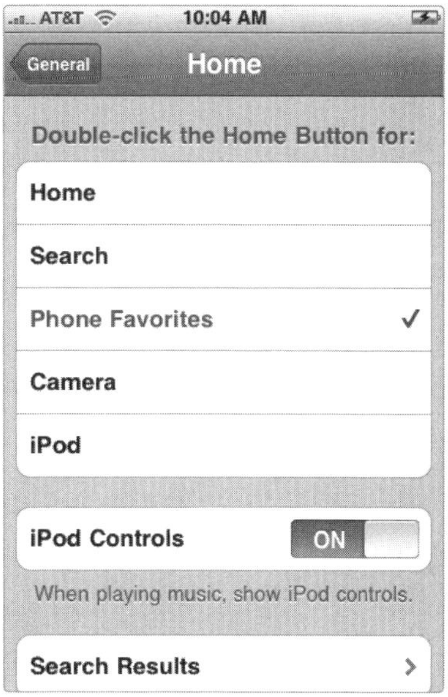

FIGURE 3-2: *The Home Button screen lets you choose which screen appears when you press the Home button twice.*

Turning the Ringer On and Off

Like most mobile phones, the iPhone can vibrate to alert you when you receive a phone call, or it can vibrate and play a ringtone. In most cases, you'll want to let the iPhone vibrate and play a ringtone to make sure you don't miss an incoming call. However, you may sometimes want to turn off the sound to avoid annoying others in a public area.

The Ring/Silent switch appears on the left side of the iPhone, as shown in Figure 3-3.

Unlike the other buttons on the iPhone that you press, the Ring/Silent button slides up and down toward the front and back of the iPhone. Sliding it

Ring/ Silent

Courtesy of Apple

FIGURE 3-3: *The Ring/Silent switch*

up (toward the screen) turns the ringer on. Sliding it down (toward the back of the iPhone) turns the ringer to vibrate mode only.

Adjusting the Volume

To make it easy for you to increase or decrease the volume, the iPhone includes Volume Up and Volume Down buttons on its left side, as shown in Figure 3-4.

You can adjust the volume by pressing and releasing a Volume button or by holding it down. When you adjust the volume, the iPhone displays a ringer icon with a horizontal bar underneath that visually displays the current volume level, as shown in Figure 3-5.

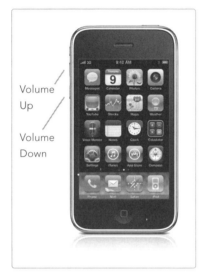

Courtesy of Apple

FIGURE 3-4: *The Volume Up and Volume Down buttons*

FIGURE 3-5: *A ringer icon appears on the screen to show you the current volume level.*

Using the Multi-Touch Screen

The Multi-Touch screen functions as both a display and a user interface that you can control with your fingertip. You can perform three main touch commands:

► Select (tap)

► Scroll (drag)

► Zoom (pinch or double tap)

＊ **NOTE:** The Multi-Touch screen lets you rotate the iPhone vertically or horizontally to make it easy to view data. No matter how you rotate your iPhone, the select, scroll, and zoom touch commands work the same.

Using the Select Command

The simplest command is *select*, which lets you tap an item that you want to select. To use the select command, point at an icon or button, press it lightly, and lift your finger off the screen again. When done correctly, the select command involves nothing more than tapping the screen.

✻ *NOTE:* **The Multi-Touch screen works only when it detects your fingertip touching the screen. If you tap the screen with your fingernail or while wearing gloves, the Multi-Touch screen won't recognize this physical contact.**

To see how the select command works, follow these steps to use the built-in calculator:

1. Hold the iPhone vertically.
2. From the Home screen, tap **Calculator**. The four-function Calculator screen appears, as shown in Figure 3-6.
3. Rotate the iPhone horizontally. Notice that the Calculator screen now expands and changes orientation to display the Scientific Calculator screen shown in Figure 3-7.

FIGURE 3-6: *The Calculator screen*

FIGURE 3-7: *The Scientific Calculator screen*

4. Tap number keys to perform a calculation.
5. Press the Home button. The Home screen appears again.

✳ **NOTE:** Not all programs change orientation when you rotate the iPhone vertically or horizontally. To find out whether your favorite program can automatically change orientation, just rotate your iPhone while running a specific program and see what happens.

Using the Scroll Command

Since the iPhone's tiny screen can't always display everything at once, you may need to scroll to see more information. You can actually choose between three different scrolling commands: controlled scroll, quick scroll, and scroll to top of the page.

The *controlled scroll* lets you scroll horizontally or vertically by sliding or dragging your finger across the screen. To practice the controlled scroll, quick scroll, and scroll to top of the page commands, try the following to acquaint you with the App Store, where you can buy and download new programs for your iPhone:

1. From the Home screen, tap **App Store**.
2. Tap **Featured**. The App Store screen appears, as shown in Figure 3-8.
3. Near the bottom of the screen, slide your finger up and down the screen. Notice that the screen scrolls up and down as your finger slides up and down the screen. As soon as you lift your finger off the screen, it stops scrolling. This is a controlled scroll.
4. Near the bottom (or top) of the screen, slide your finger up or down quickly, and lift your finger off the screen in a quick flicking motion. Even after you lift your finger off the screen, the screen should continue scrolling in the direction you flicked your finger. This is a *quick scroll*.

FIGURE 3-8: *The App Store screen*

5. (Optional) Repeat the last step, except before the screen can stop scrolling, tap your finger on the screen. This immediately stops the scrolling and is known as a *quick scroll stop*.
6. Scroll down and then tap the top bar that displays the time and battery life of your iPhone. The top of the page suddenly scrolls into view. This is a *scroll to top of the page*.
7. Press the Home button. The Home screen appears again.

Sliding your finger across the screen lets you control the scrolling rate (the controlled scroll). Flicking your finger across the screen lets you scroll quickly (the quick scroll). Flick your finger and then tap your finger on the screen to stop a scrolling screen. Tap the top bar of any screen to display the top of the page.

Since the iPhone's tiny screen can barely display one window of information, programs can't display multiple, overlapping windows like an ordinary computer screen. Instead, some programs display multiple windows as individual, side-by-side *panes*. One pane is always visible, but other panes are tucked out of sight to the left or right of the screen.

To let you know that a screen consists of multiple panes, two or more dots are displayed at the bottom of the screen—each dot represents a pane. A bright dot represents the current screen, while dimmed dots represent hidden screens. To view these additional screens, you need to slide the current screen left or right with your finger.

The Home screen actually consists of multiple panes (up to a maximum of nine). To practice scrolling horizontally to view other panes, follow these steps to get acquainted with the Home screen:

1. From the Home screen, slide your finger to the left across the screen. Another Home screen pane fills the screen, as shown in Figure 3-9.
2. Slide your finger to the right across the screen, and the original Home screen pane appears again.

The first pane of the Home screen

Sliding the pane to the left reveals part of the second Home screen pane.

The second pane of the Home screen

FIGURE 3-9: *Sliding your finger horizontally to the left displays another Home screen pane.*

Using the Zoom Command

The iPhone's tiny screen can actually display entire web pages. Of course, the images and text appear so small that they may be nearly impossible to read, so the iPhone gives you the option to zoom in and zoom out. To enlarge or shrink an image, you can use two fingers in a pinching motion. Touch the screen with your fingers spread out and bring them closer together to cause the iPhone image to shrink. If you start with your fingers close together and slide them apart, the iPhone image enlarges.

A second way to zoom in and out is to tap the screen. To zoom in, tap one finger twice on the screen in rapid succession. To zoom out, tap two fingers on the screen once at the same time.

✳ *NOTE:* Not all programs allow you to zoom in and out.

To practice zooming in and out, try the following steps to get acquainted with the Maps program:

1. From the Home screen, tap **Maps**. The Map screen appears, as shown in Figure 3-10.
2. Zoom in using the pinching gesture: Place two fingers close together and slide them apart while maintaining contact with the iPhone screen. Notice that the Map screen zooms in.
3. Zoom out using the pinching gesture: Place two fingers apart and slide them together while maintaining contact with the iPhone screen. Notice that the Map screen zooms out.
4. Zoom in by tapping one finger on the screen twice in rapid succession. Notice that the Map screen zooms in.
5. Zoom out by tapping two fingers on the screen at the same time. Notice that the Map screen zooms out.
6. Press the Home button. The Home screen appears again.

FIGURE 3-10: *The Map screen*

Additional Ideas for Controlling Your iPhone

By using both the physical buttons on the iPhone and the Multi-Touch screen, you can control all aspects of your iPhone. After the Sleep/Wake button, you'll find that your most commonly used physical buttons are the Home button and the Volume Up and Volume Down buttons, so be sure you're familiar with their locations.

Also practice using the select, scroll, and zoom commands on the Multi-Touch screen. By knowing these three commands, you'll be able to control and get the most use out of your iPhone.

4

Typing on the Virtual Keyboard

Primitive mobile phones include a fixed keypad used for typing both numbers and letters. This standard telephone numeric keypad may be optimal for typing numbers, but unfortunately, it can be clumsy for typing letters, punctuation marks, and symbols. To overcome the drawbacks of trying to cram multiple characters onto a miniature keyboard, the iPhone offers a virtual keyboard.

When you need to type something like a website address (such as *http://www.nostarch.com/*), a text message, a note to yourself, a calendar appointment, a stock to watch, or any other item that requires typing in letters, numbers, and symbols, you'll be using the iPhone virtual keyboard. In this chapter, you'll get comfortable using this keyboard in different programs.

Project goal: Get familiar with how the virtual keyboard works.

What You'll Be Using

To learn how to use the iPhone virtual keyboard, you need to use the following:

 The YouTube application   The Safari application

 The Settings application

Switching Between Keyboards

If you look at a typical computer keyboard, you'll see that some keys represent letters, while others represent numbers and symbols. Since the iPhone screen is far smaller than a computer keyboard, the iPhone virtual keyboard can't display all of these characters at once. Instead, the virtual keyboard displays characters on one keyboard, numbers and symbols on a second keyboard, and another group of symbols on a third keyboard:

▶ The Character keyboard is for typing uppercase and lowercase letters.

▶ The Numeric keyboard is for typing numbers, symbols, and punctuation marks.

▶ The Symbol keyboard is for typing mathematical symbols such as + or =, seldom used symbols such as square brackets [ ] and curly brackets { }, and even currency symbols such as €.

To get to the Symbol keyboard from the Character keyboard, you'll first need to go into the Numeric keyboard. To practice switching between these three keyboards, follow these steps:

1. From the Home screen, tap **YouTube**. The YouTube screen appears. (If you have previously searched for a YouTube video, you'll see a list of your last displayed videos. Otherwise, the screen will be blank.)
2. Tap the Search icon at the bottom of the screen. The YouTube search text box appears at the top of the screen.
3. Tap the **YouTube** search text box. The Character keyboard appears at the bottom of the screen, as shown in Figure 4-1.
4. Type any word or letters.

FIGURE 4-1: *The Character keyboard*

5. Now tap the **.?123** button. The Numeric keyboard appears, as shown in Figure 4-2.
6. Type any symbol or number.

✳ **NOTE:** If all you need is a period (.) while you're using the Character keyboard, try tapping the spacebar twice. You'll stay on the Character keyboard and get a period with a space after it.

7. Tap **#+=**. The Symbol keyboard appears, as shown in Figure 4-3.
8. From the Symbol keyboard, you can switch to the Character or Numeric keyboard. Tap **ABC** or **123**. The Character or Numeric keyboard appears.
9. Press the Home button to return to the Home screen.

FIGURE 4-2: The Numeric keyboard

FIGURE 4-3: The Symbol keyboard

By switching between the Character, Numeric, and Symbol keyboards, you can type practically all the letters, numbers, and symbols available on a full-size computer keyboard.

✳ **NOTE:** If all you need to do is type one digit or symbol from the Numeric keyboard (such as a comma or the number 3), try pressing and holding the .?123 button, sliding your finger to the character you want, and then releasing. You'll be back at the Character keyboard, and you've saved yourself some taps.

Using the Virtual Keyboard

Since the virtual keyboard is so tiny, you'll probably need to type on it using your thumb or fingertip. Each time you tap a key, you'll see the character you chose pop up on the screen. If you accidentally hit the wrong key, just slide your finger across the screen until your finger touches the character you really meant to type. Then lift your finger off the screen.

Beyond tapping keys to choose the characters you want to type, the virtual keyboard offers four additional features:

▶ Moving the cursor

▶ Deleting characters

▶ Typing uppercase and lowercase letters

▶ Accepting word suggestions

Moving the Cursor

On a computer, you can move the cursor by pointing and clicking the mouse or pressing the arrow keys on the keyboard. The iPhone's keyboard doesn't have room for arrow keys and there's no mouse, so you have to point and move the cursor using your finger.

To learn how to move the cursor, try this:

1. From the Home screen, tap **YouTube**. The YouTube screen appears.
2. Tap the Search icon at the bottom of the screen. The YouTube search text box appears at the top of the screen.
3. Tap the **YouTube** search text box. The Character keyboard appears at the bottom of the screen.
4. Type the name of your favorite band, such as *Coldplay* or *Wilco*.
5. Press and hold your finger on the text you just typed. A magnifying glass appears, enlarging your text and showing the exact position of the cursor, as shown in Figure 4-4.
6. Slide your finger left or right to move the cursor.
7. Remove your fingertip from the screen when the cursor appears in the position that you want. The magnifying glass disappears, allowing you to type again.

FIGURE 4-4: *The magnifying glass enlarges text so you can see where the cursor appears.*

Editing Text

New text will appear at the cursor's current location. Instead of typing new text, you can also tap the Backspace key to delete the character that appears immediately to the left of the cursor.

To learn how to edit text, try this:

1. From the Home screen, tap **YouTube**. The YouTube screen appears.
2. Tap the Search icon at the bottom of the screen. The YouTube search text box appears at the top of the screen.
3. Tap the **YouTube** search text box. The Character keyboard appears at the bottom of the screen.
4. Type the name of your favorite band, such as *U2* or *Nirvana*.
5. Tap the Backspace key, as shown in Figure 4-5. Notice that each time you tap the Backspace key, you erase one character to the left of the current cursor location.

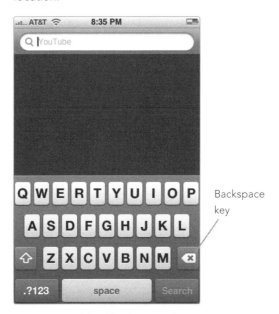

FIGURE 4-5: *The Backspace key*

6. Move the cursor to the middle of the text that you typed. (See "Moving the Cursor" on page 30.)
7. Type any character. Notice that when you type a character, it appears at the location where the cursor appears.
8. Tap the Backspace key. Notice that each time you tap the Backspace key, you erase one character to the left of the cursor's location.

Using Cut, Copy, and Paste

When typing and editing text, you always have the option of cutting, copying, and pasting text. There are four main steps for cutting or copying text and then pasting it afterward:

▶   Selecting text

▶   Choosing the Cut or Copy command

▶   Moving the cursor to where you want to paste your text

▶   Choosing the Paste command

To select and cut text, do this:

1. From the Home screen, tap **Safari**. The Safari screen appears.
2. Tap the address text box at the top of the screen. The virtual keyboard appears.
3. Type **www.nostarch.com**.
4. Tap in the address text box to the right of *nostarch.com*. The Select and Select All commands appear, as shown in Figure 4-6. (If you've previously cut or copied text, the Paste command will also appear.)
5. Tap **Select**. (If you tap Select All, you'll select all the text on the screen.)
6. Place your fingertip over the start selection marker and drag your fingertip left and right. As you drag the start marker, you'll see a magnifying glass highlight the text, as shown in Figure 4-7. Move your fingertip off the screen when you're happy with the position of the start or end marker. After you are done selecting text, the Cut and Copy commands appear, as shown in Figure 4-8. (If you've previously cut or copied text, the Paste command will also appear.)

FIGURE 4-6: *Tapping text displays the Select and Select All commands.*

FIGURE 4-7: *Dragging the start or end marker lets you select text.*

FIGURE 4-8: *After selecting text, you can choose the Cut or Copy command.*

7. Tap **Cut**. Your selected text disappears. (If you tap Copy, your selected text remains.)

8. Tap in the address text box near the top of the screen so the cursor appears. The Paste command appears, as shown in Figure 4-9.

9. Tap **Paste**. Your iPhone inserts the selected text.

＊ **NOTE:** You can cut or copy text from one app (such as Safari) and paste it into another app (such as Notes or Contacts).

＊ **NOTE:** Make a mistake? Just shake your iPhone to undo a cut, copy, or paste.

FIGURE 4-9: *The Paste command*

Shift key

FIGURE 4-10: *The Shift key*

Typing Uppercase Letters

Normally when you type on the Character keyboard, all letters appear in lowercase. To type an uppercase letter, you must first tap the Shift key, as shown in Figure 4-10.

When the Shift key appears clear, typing creates a lowercase letter. When the Shift key appears to "glow," the next character you type will be an uppercase letter. Immediately after typing an uppercase letter, the Shift key switches back to typing lowercase letters until you tap the Shift key again.

Typing Words Automatically

Since typing on the small virtual keyboard isn't always easy, the iPhone offers an auto-correction feature. As you type, the iPhone displays a word that it thinks you're trying to type, as shown in Figure 4-11.

Each time you see a word suggestion pop up on the screen, you have two choices:

▶ Tap the spacebar to make your iPhone finish typing the suggested word automatically.

▶ Tap the displayed suggested word to make it go away.

The more you type on the virtual keyboard, the more the auto-correction feature adapts to the words you're most likely to type. Eventually, you'll find that the word suggestions offered will actually be the words that you'll want to type,

FIGURE 4-11: *As you type, your iPhone suggests words you might want to use.*

so you can save time by typing part of a word, waiting for the suggested word to appear, and then tapping the spacebar.

To try out the auto-correction feature, do this:

1. From the Home screen, tap **YouTube**. The YouTube screen appears.
2. Tap the Search icon at the bottom of the screen. The YouTube search text box appears at the top of the screen.
3. Tap the **YouTube** search text box. The Character keyboard appears at the bottom of the screen.
4. Type **Id**. A window suggests the word *I'd*.
5. Tap the spacebar to watch the word *I'd* magically appear in place of the word you typed.

Customizing the Virtual Keyboard

To make typing even easier and faster, the virtual keyboard offers four additional shortcuts that you can customize:

▶ **Auto-Correction** This feature turns auto-correction on or off. When turned on, auto-correction will suggest a word such as *I'd* whenever you type a similar phrase such as *id*. When auto-correction is turned off, you won't see any word suggestions pop up as you type.

▶ **Auto-Capitalization** This feature automatically turns on the Shift key when starting a new sentence.

▶ **Enable Caps Lock** This feature allows you to lock the Shift key by tapping it twice so you can type in uppercase without constantly having to tap the Shift key.

▶ **"." Shortcut** This feature allows you to tap the spacebar twice to insert a period and a space automatically.

To turn these features on or off, do the following:

1. From the Home screen, tap **Settings**. The Settings screen appears.
2. Tap **General**. The General screen appears.
3. Scroll down the General screen until you see the Keyboard button.
4. Tap **Keyboard**. The Keyboard screen appears, as shown in Figure 4-12.

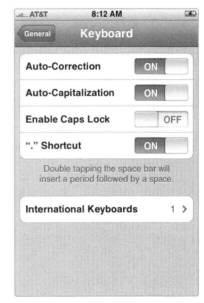

FIGURE 4-12: The Keyboard screen lets you customize the virtual keyboard.

5. Tap the **ON/OFF** button next to Enable Caps Lock to turn this option on.
6. Press the Home button to return to the Home screen.

After you've turned on the Enable Caps Lock option, you can turn on the caps lock by tapping the Shift key twice in rapid succession. This turns the Shift key blue to let you know that everything you type from now on will appear in uppercase. To turn the caps lock feature off temporarily, tap the Shift key once. To experiment with the caps lock feature, make sure you have turned on this feature through the Keyboard screen, and then try this:

1. From the Home screen, tap **YouTube**. The YouTube screen appears.
2. Tap the Search icon at the bottom of the screen. The YouTube search text box appears at the top of the screen.
3. Tap the **YouTube** search text box. The Character keyboard appears at the bottom of the screen.
4. Tap the Shift key twice in rapid succession so that it appears in blue.
5. Type the name of your favorite band. Notice that as you type, all letters appear in uppercase.
6. Tap the Shift key once. The Shift key no longer appears in blue, which means all characters you type will appear in lowercase.
7. Type a few characters. Notice that the characters now appear in lowercase.

Resetting the Keyboard Dictionary

The more you type on the keyboard, the more words your iPhone will recognize and store in its dictionary. However, if you want to return your iPhone to its original factory settings, you can do that by following these steps:

1. From the Home screen, tap **Settings**. The Settings screen appears.
2. Tap **General**. The General screen appears.
3. Scroll down the General screen until you see the Reset button.
4. Tap **Reset**. The Reset screen appears, as shown in Figure 4-13.

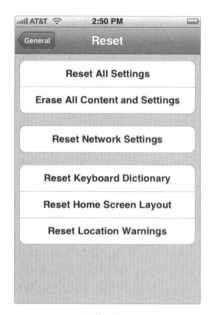

FIGURE 4-13: *The Reset screen*

5. Tap **Reset Keyboard Dictionary**. A dialog appears, warning that you will delete all custom words that your iPhone has recognized from the iPhone's dictionary, as shown in Figure 4-14.
6. Tap **Reset Dictionary**.
7. Press the Home button to return to the Home screen.

Using Safari's Keyboard

The virtual keyboard appears whenever you need to type text in any program, such as typing names and addresses in the Contacts program or names of videos you want to watch in the YouTube screen.

When typing a website address in Safari, the virtual keyboard appears in a slightly different way to help you type website addresses more easily. The most prominent difference is the .com key, which lets you type the common .com extension at the touch of a single button rather than typing the period and the letters *com* in four separate key taps.

The Safari keyboard consists of a Character keyboard and a Numeric keyboard. To switch to the Numeric keyboard, tap the **@123** key that appears in the lower-left corner of the Character keyboard, as shown in Figure 4-15.

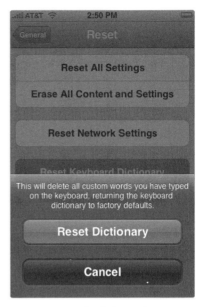

FIGURE 4-14: *A dialog gives you one last chance to change your mind before resetting your keyboard dictionary.*

FIGURE 4-15: *The Safari Character keyboard*

To switch to the Character keyboard from the Numeric keyboard, tap the **ABC** button in the lower-left corner of the Numeric keyboard, as shown in Figure 4-16.

When you tap the .com key, you'll insert the entire *.com* portion of a website address. However, many website addresses use different endings such as *.net*, *.edu*, or *.org*. Rather than typing these letter-by-letter, you can also type them automatically using the .com key. Just hold down the .com key until a list of alternatives pops up, as shown in Figure 4-17. Then tap the option you want to use, such as .net or .edu.

FIGURE 4-16: *The Safari Numeric keyboard*

FIGURE 4-17: *Holding down the .com key displays alternative website address suffixes.*

Rotating the Keyboard

Many people find typing on the virtual keyboard difficult. To fix this problem, you can rotate your iPhone sideways and display the virtual keyboard horizontally. To rotate the virtual keyboard while using Safari, do this:

1. From the Home screen, tap **Safari**. The Safari screen appears.
2. Rotate your iPhone horizontally. The Safari screen now appears horizontally.

3. Tap in the address text box. The virtual keyboard appears horizontally on the screen, as shown in Figure 4-18. Notice how the horizontal virtual keyboard displays its keys in a larger size, making it convenient to type with your thumbs.

FIGURE 4-18: *Rotating the iPhone lets you display the virtual keyboard horizontally.*

✱ **NOTE:** The virtual keyboard can appear horizontally in other apps such as Notes, Messages, or Mail. However, it may not appear horizontally in all apps, so if you rotate your iPhone and nothing happens, you may not be able to use the virtual keyboard in a horizontal position within that particular app.

Additional Ideas for Typing on Your iPhone

Typing on your iPhone can take some getting used to, especially since the keys on the virtual keyboard are so tiny that your fingers may accidentally press the wrong ones. The only solution to this problem is to practice typing on the virtual keyboard as often as possible so you get used to the quirks and size of these keys.

Get familiar with the virtual keyboard now, since you'll always need it for a variety of programs. If you need to type text, you'll have to use the virtual keyboard, so spending a little time learning it now will save you time later when you need to type text and can't figure out how the virtual keyboard works.

Use Your iPhone to Check Your Spelling

Since the iPhone's virtual keyboard is so tiny, you may find typing to be clumsy. To protect yourself from spelling mistakes, download the free Speller app, which checks your spelling as you type. Unlike the iPhone's built-in feature that tries to guess which word you're typing, Speller displays an entire list of possible spelling variations.

Instead of trying to tap every word out, just type a few characters, wait for Speller to list the most likely words, and then tap the word that you want. Now you'll be able to type faster and more accurately using less tapping so you don't wear out your fingers and thumbs.

Speller   *http://www.trancreative.com/*

Use Speller to check the spelling of your words automatically.

5 Searching Your iPhone

After you've stored something on your iPhone (such as contact information for your friends, songs, podcasts, and third-party apps downloaded from the App Store), you'll probably want to find it again.

The best way to do this is to use the Search feature, which lets you type the name (or part of the name) of an item that you want to find. Type **Al**, and you'll suddenly see a list of all names and song titles that begin with *Al*, such as the name *Albert* or the song title *All Out of Love*. The Search feature lets you look for words or phrases stored in Mail (to find messages or names), Calendar (to find appointments), Notes (to find ideas), and iPod (to find song titles). By using the Search feature, you'll be able to find your data whenever you need it.

Project goal: Learn how to search for data stored on your iPhone.

What You'll Be Using

To search on your iPhone, you need to use the following:

    The Search screen

Using the Search Feature

The Search screen displays the virtual keyboard so you can type the name (or part of the name) of an item you want to find. As you type, your iPhone displays a list of items that match what you've typed so far. The Search screen is located to the left of the first Home screen pane.

To use the Search screen, do this:

1.   Place your finger on the Home screen and slide it to the right to access the left pane. The Search screen and the virtual keyboard appear, as shown in Figure 5-1.
2.   (Optional) If text already appears in the search text box, tap the clear button (the white *X* in a gray circle to the far right of the search text box).
3.   Type the letter **A**. If you've stored anything on your iPhone, you'll see a list of items that match your search criteria, as shown in Figure 5-2. To help identify where a particular item is stored on your iPhone, you'll see an icon in the left column, such as the iPod, Contacts, or App Store icon.

✳ *NOTE:* **The exact items that appear on your screen will depend on the items (such as names, apps, and songs) you've stored on your iPhone. If you haven't stored anything on your iPhone yet, the Search feature will only find the apps that come with your iPhone.**

4.   Tap the item you want to view, such as a person's name or a song title. Your iPhone loads the app where your selected item is stored. For example, if you select a song title, the iPod application will open and play the song.

FIGURE 5-1: *The Search screen*

FIGURE 5-2: *As you type, your iPhone displays matching items.*

Additional Ideas for Searching Your iPhone

The most obvious way to use the Search feature is to search for a person's name stored in the Contacts app. Another way is to use the Search feature to find a specific song or a list of songs from your favorite recording artist.

Just type part of a song name, and your iPhone will display all matching song titles right away. Type part of a recording artist's name, and you can see all songs by that artist stored on your iPhone. Tap the song you want to hear, and your iPhone starts playing it immediately. By using the Search feature to help you sort through your music library, you can hear the exact song you want without scrolling through every song stored on your iPhone.

If you've loaded a bunch of apps on your iPhone, you may have screens full of app icons. You could try searching through these multiple screens (you can have up to 11), but a faster way is to use the Search feature and type part of the app name that you want. When the Search feature finds your app, just tap the icon to start it up.

The Search feature can be great for finding all the goodies you have stored on your iPhone. The more stuff you store on your iPhone, the more useful the Search feature will be. Now all you have to remember is where to find the Search feature (to the left of the Home screen).

PART 2

Modifying Your iPhone

6 Rearranging Icons on the Home Screen

The Home screen displays icons for all the applications and features available on your iPhone. To view the Home screen, press the Home button on the front of the iPhone.

Since you'll often be starting at the Home screen when using your iPhone, you may want to customize its appearance by rearranging icons on the screen, moving them off of (or on to) the main home screen pane, or deleting certain programs altogether.

Project goal: Learn how to customize the Home screen of your iPhone.

What You'll Be Using

To customize your iPhone's Home screen, you need to use the following:

 The Settings application

Rearranging Icons

The Home screen displays icons that represent the features and apps on your iPhone, such as Calendar or iTunes. If you find yourself using some features or apps more often than others (or ignoring some features altogether), you may want to rearrange the icons on the Home screen so that they appear in the order you prefer.

For example, suppose you use the Calendar and iTunes programs every day, but you rarely use the Camera or Text messaging programs. To make it easy to access the Calendar and iTunes programs, you could put these icons in the corners of the screen (to make it easy to tap them with your thumbs) and place seldom-used program icons in the middle of the screen.

To rearrange icons on the Home screen, follow these steps:

1. From the Home screen, point to the icon that you want to move and hold your finger on that icon until all icons on the Home screen start jiggling.
2. Slide your finger to a spot where you want to move the icon. A "ghost" image of the icon will appear to show you where the icon will land, as shown in Figure 6-1. When you move an icon in between two others, those two icons glide out of the way.

* **NOTE: The bottom of the Home screen can display your four most commonly used application icons, such as Phone or iPod. You can move any icon off this bottom bar and move another icon in its place. You can store a maximum of four icons on the bottom bar.**

FIGURE 6-1: *An icon appears as a "ghost" image when you move it across the Home screen.*

3. Lift your finger off the screen when you're happy with the new location of the icon. Then move any other icons you'd like to rearrange.

＊ **NOTE: At this time, you can tap the close button (the white X) in the upper-left corner of any application icon you installed on your iPhone, as shown in Figure 6-2. Tapping the close button deletes the app entirely from your iPhone. (You cannot delete the standard iPhone apps such as Phone or Safari.)**

4. Press the Home button to stop all the Home screen icons from jiggling and end your rearranging session.

＊ **NOTE: Remember that the Home screen actually consists of at least two panes. To move an icon off one pane and onto another, hold your finger on the icon and slide it to the left or right until the other pane appears. You can have up to 11 separate panes full of icons.**

FIGURE 6-2: A close button appears in the upper-left corner of apps you can delete off your iPhone.

Resetting Your Home Screen

You can rearrange the icons on the Home screen to customize your iPhone, but if you get carried away and wind up making a mess out of your icons, don't worry. At any time, you can return the Home screen to its original factory settings. To reset the appearance of the Home screen, follow these steps:

1. From the Home screen, tap **Settings**. The Settings screen appears.
2. Tap **General**. The General screen appears.
3. Scroll down the General screen until you see the Reset button.

4. Tap **Reset**. The Reset screen appears, as shown in Figure 6-3.
5. Tap **Reset Home Screen Layout**. A dialog appears, asking if you really want to reset your Home screen.
6. Tap **Reset Home Screen** (or tap **Cancel** if you've changed your mind).

✳ *NOTE:* Resetting the Home screen **rearranges icons but does not delete any icons, such as those programs you've installed since getting your iPhone. They may appear on another Home screen pane, however.**

7. Press the Home button. The Home screen appears. Notice that your Home screen has now returned to its original appearance.

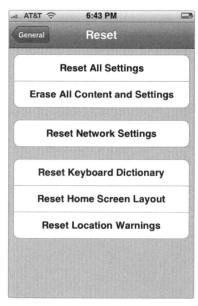

FIGURE 6-3: *The Reset screen displays a button for resetting your Home screen layout.*

Additional Ideas for Customizing Your Home Screen

Since you can have up to 11 panes for your Home screen, try moving all your seldom-used program icons to another pane and keeping all your favorite programs on the first pane. That way, each time you open the Home screen, you'll see only your favorite program icons. When you need to use a seldom-used program, slide your finger over the screen from right to left to reveal the other Home screen panes with additional application icons.

As a rule, try to keep your Home screen as uncluttered as possible. One day when you're in a hurry and see a clean, uncluttered Home screen instead of a cluttered one with icons for programs you haven't used in months, you'll be thankful you followed this advice.

Turn Your iPhone into a Remote Control

If you have a Wi-Fi network and iTunes on your computer or Apple TV, you can turn your iPhone into a remote control so you can choose the music or movies to play without having to get up out of your chair. Now you can forget about all those cheap remote control devices that you'll probably lose within a few days anyway, and put all that functionality on your iPhone (which you'll probably keep better track of than a regular remote).

Remote *http://www.apple .com/itunes/remote/*

Select your computer's iTunes library to access it and start controlling your music from your iPhone.

7

Customizing Your iPhone

Every new iPhone is nearly identical in appearance, so you may want to take some time to modify your iPhone and make it uniquely your own. The two most common ways to customize your iPhone involve changing sounds and pictures. You can use customized sounds so that your iPhone plays different noises to alert you of incoming calls or text messages. Customizing pictures simply makes your iPhone look just the way you like it.

In addition to modifying the way your iPhone plays audio or displays pictures, you can also change the regional settings of your iPhone to view dates and times in a format common in your part of the world.

Project goal: Learn how to customize the sounds and appearance of your iPhone.

What You'll Be Using

To learn how to customize your iPhone, you need to use the following:

 The Settings application

Turning Vibrate Mode On and Off

When you receive a phone call, your iPhone can vibrate and/or play a sound called a *ringtone*. You can silence the ringtone by using the Ring/Silent switch (see Project 3). You can also turn off both vibrate and ring mode in case you don't want a vibrating or ringing iPhone disturbing you, such as when you're trying to sneak out of the house without your parents/spouse/boyfriend/girlfriend hearing you.

To turn vibrate mode on or off, follow these steps:

1. From the Home screen, tap **Settings**. The Settings screen appears.
2. Tap **Sounds**. The Sounds screen appears, as shown in Figure 7-1.
3. (Optional) Tap the **ON/OFF** button next to Vibrate under the Silent category. This turns the vibrate mode on or off when the ringer is off. If you turn vibrate mode off in this category, your iPhone won't vibrate or play a sound when you receive a phone call. This can be useful if you want to keep your iPhone from disturbing you while you're watching a movie at a theatre, for example.
4. (Optional) Tap the **ON/OFF** button next to Vibrate under the Ring category. This turns the vibrate mode on or off when the ringer is on. If you turn vibrate mode off in this category, your iPhone won't vibrate but will play a sound when you receive a phone call.
5. Press the Home button to return to the Home screen.

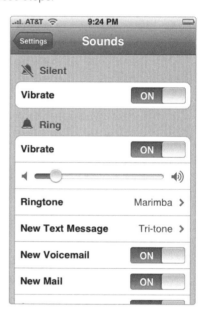

FIGURE 7-1: *The Sounds screen lets you choose sounds for your iPhone.*

Changing Sounds

To alert you of incoming calls or text messages or to provide audio feedback when you type on the screen, your iPhone can play various sounds. You can get as quirky as you want with sounds, although you should choose sounds that you won't mind hearing periodically, or else you'll risk driving yourself crazy.

The two most common uses for sound are for ringtones and text messages. A ringtone plays when you receive a phone call, and a text message sound plays when you receive a text message.

Changing Ringtones

Most people like customizing their ringtone to play something unique or different when they receive a call. To choose a ringtone, follow these steps:

1. From the Home screen, tap **Settings**. The Settings screen appears.
2. Tap **Sounds**. The Sounds screen appears (see Figure 7-1).
3. Tap **Ringtone**. The Ringtone screen appears, as shown in Figure 7-2.
4. Tap a ringtone sound to select and hear it. (You may need to scroll down the list of ringtones to see them all.)
5. Press the Home button to return to the Home screen.

＊ **NOTE:** See Project 18 to see how to create a ringtone from your favorite song.

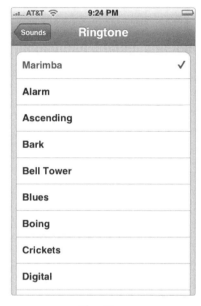

FIGURE 7-2: The Ringtone screen lets you choose a different ringtone.

Changing Text Message Sounds

Every time you receive a text message, your iPhone can play a sound to alert you. To choose a sound to play for incoming text messages, follow these steps:

1. From the Home screen, tap **Settings**. The Settings screen appears.
2. Tap **Sounds**. The Sounds screen appears (see Figure 7-1).

3. Tap **New Text Message**. The New Text Message screen appears, as shown in Figure 7-3.
4. Tap a sound (such as **Bell** or **Chime**) to hear and select it.
5. Press the Home button to return to the Home screen.

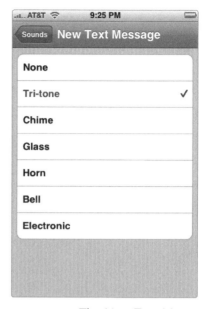

Turning Audio Feedback On and Off

Since most controls on an iPhone involve touching its screen, you don't receive any tactile feedback like you would when you press a button on a regular keyboard or a mouse. To compensate for this, your iPhone can play audio to let you know when you've done something, such as tapping a letter on the keyboard or sending an email message. You can modify audio feedback for the following iPhone features on the Sounds screen:

FIGURE 7-3: *The New Text Message screen lets you choose a sound for incoming text messages.*

▸ **New Voicemail**   Your iPhone can play a sound when you receive new voicemail.

▸ **New Mail**   Your iPhone can play a sound when you receive a new email message.

▸ **Sent Mail**   Your iPhone can play a sound when you send an email message.

▸ **Calendar Alerts**   Your iPhone can play a sound to alert you of a calendar event.

▸ **Lock Sounds**   Your iPhone can play a sound when you wake it from sleep mode.

▸ **Keyboard Clicks**   Your iPhone can play a sound when you type a character on the keyboard.

To turn these audio feedback options on or off, follow these steps:

1. From the Home screen, tap **Settings**. The Settings screen appears.
2. Tap **Sounds**. The Sounds screen appears (see Figure 7-1).
3. Tap the **ON/OFF** button next to an option such as Keyboard Clicks or Sent Mail.
4. Press the Home button to return to the Home screen.

Changing the Screen Brightness

The iPhone's screen is useless if you can't see it, so you can adjust its brightness to make it brighter or dimmer. (Just remember that the brighter the screen, the more power it consumes, reducing the battery life of your iPhone.)

You have two options for modifying the screen brightness. You can modify the brightness manually, or you can rely on the Auto-Brightness feature, which tries to adjust the screen's brightness in changing lighting conditions.

To adjust the screen brightness of your iPhone, follow these steps:

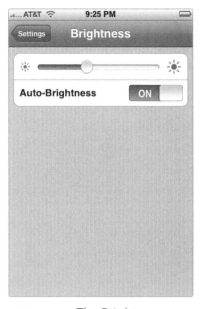

FIGURE 7-4: *The Brightness screen lets you manually adjust the screen brightness.*

1. From the Home screen, tap **Settings**. The Settings screen appears.
2. Tap **Brightness**. The Brightness screen appears, as shown in Figure 7-4.
3. (Optional) Drag the Brightness slider to change the screen brightness. To increase the brightness, move the slider to the right. To decrease, slide left.
4. (Optional) Tap the **ON/OFF** button next to Auto-Brightness to turn the Auto-Brightness feature on or off.
5. Press the Home button. The Home screen appears.

Changing the Wallpaper

Wallpaper is typically an interesting picture that appears every time you wake your iPhone from sleep mode. You can choose from a library of wallpaper images or use the iPhone's built-in camera to capture your own image.

＊ *NOTE:* **The wallpaper won't appear when you are recharging your iPhone.**

To change your iPhone's wallpaper, follow these steps:

1. From the Home screen, tap **Settings**. The Settings screen appears.
2. Tap **Wallpaper**. The Wallpaper screen appears, as shown in Figure 7-5. (If you have not stored any pictures on your iPhone, tapping Wallpaper will bring you directly to the wallpaper images that come with your iPhone.)

FIGURE 7-5: *This screen lets you choose a different wallpaper image.*

FIGURE 7-6: *The Wallpaper screen displays available wallpaper images.*

3. Tap **Wallpaper** to view all available wallpaper images, as shown in Figure 7-6. (If you tap Camera Roll, you can choose from an image you've captured using the iPhone's built-in camera.)

4. Tap the image you want to use. The Wallpaper Preview screen appears to show how the image actually looks on your screen, as shown in Figure 7-7.

5. Tap **Set Wallpaper** (or tap **Cancel** if you don't want to use the image).

6. Press the Home button. The Home screen appears.

FIGURE 7-7: *The Wallpaper Preview screen shows you how the image actually looks.*

Customizing the Regional Settings

Different parts of the world have accepted ways to display times, dates, and telephone numbers. To make your iPhone display this information correctly for your part of the world, your iPhone lets you choose your current location. Based on the region you choose, your iPhone then automatically displays information common to that particular region. (To learn how to change the language your iPhone uses and how to type in that language, see Project 9.)

To change the regional settings for your iPhone, follow these steps:

1. From the Home screen, tap **Settings**. The Settings screen appears.
2. Tap **General**. The General screen appears.
3. Scroll down and tap **International**. The International screen appears, as shown in Figure 7-8.
4. Tap **Region Format** to display the Region Format screen shown in Figure 7-9.

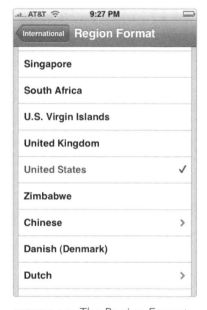

FIGURE 7-8: *The International screen lets you modify your iPhone for your part of the world.*

FIGURE 7-9: *The Region Format screen lets you choose your location.*

5. Tap a button, such as **Canada** or **New Zealand**, which represents the country where you live.
6. Tap **International** to return to the International screen, which displays the format for dates, times, and telephone numbers for your current region.
7. Press the Home button to return to the Home screen.

Additional Ideas for Customizing Your iPhone

Customizing your iPhone can be a fun way to express yourself—you can use a picture of your significant other as wallpaper or play unique sounds as ringtones.

You may also want to customize your iPhone if you move to another part of the world and take your iPhone with you. By modifying the way your iPhone displays dates, times, and telephone numbers, you can blend right into your new culture and act like a native.

As an alternative, you can leave your iPhone settings the way they work in another country and spend your time feeling like a rebel in your land. As long as you're happy with the way your iPhone displays information, you'll be more productive, so don't worry about what anyone else may think.

Keep Track of Your Expenses with Your iPhone

If you need to keep track of your daily expenses, grab iXpenselt, which has both a free and a paid version. The free version only lets you store up to 50 items, while the paid version lets you store an unlimited number of items. Using this app, you can keep track of all those minor, daily expenses that often slip your mind such as tips, books and magazines, or a cup of coffee.

The more you can track your expenses, the better you'll be able to see where your money is going. That way you'll be able to budget your money. (Now if the government would only get this app on its iPhone, maybe it could find a way to balance the budget.)

iXpenselt *http://www.fyimobileware.com/*

iXpenselt tracks your daily expenses.

8

Updating Your iPhone

The iPhone is nothing more than a fancy, powerful computer that happens to fit in your hand. Like most computers, the iPhone comes with built-in software known as *firmware*. The firmware controls the basic functions that make the iPhone actually work.

The problem with computers is that all software contains problems (known as *bugs*). To fix any bugs in the iPhone's firmware, or to add new features to the iPhone, Apple periodically issues *firmware updates*. By ensuring that your iPhone runs the latest firmware, you can keep your iPhone working and using the latest features possible.

Project goal: Learn how to update the firmware on your iPhone.

What You'll Be Using

To update the firmware on your iPhone, you need to use the following:

 iTunes (on your Mac or PC)

 The iPhone USB cable

Downloading iTunes

The only way you can update your iPhone's firmware is to connect your iPhone to a computer and use the iTunes program. Every Macintosh comes with iTunes installed, but Windows PCs do not. If you use a PC running Windows XP, Vista, or Windows 7, you must download iTunes from Apple's website at *http://www.apple.com/itunes/download/*.

After you've installed iTunes on your Windows PC, you'll be ready to connect your iPhone and start working. (Mac users should periodically click the Apple menu and choose Software Update to download the latest version of iTunes.)

Getting Updates

To update the firmware on your iPhone, you need to use iTunes. The first time you follow these steps, iTunes may ask you to register your iPhone. After following this registration process, you won't see the registration screen again.

To update your iPhone firmware, follow these steps:

1. Open iTunes on your computer.
2. Make sure your computer is connected to the Internet.
3. Plug your iPhone into your computer using the USB cable that came with your phone. The iTunes window displays your iPhone under the DEVICES category in the left pane, as shown in Figure 8-1.

✳ **NOTE:** Depending on what's installed on your computer, programs such as iPhoto, Image Capture, and Adobe Photoshop Elements may try to access pictures, video, or music stored on your iPhone. You may need to exit these program windows after plugging your iPhone into a computer.

4. Click **Check for Updates**. If updates to your iPhone's firmware are available, iTunes will automatically download and install them on your iPhone.

✳ **WARNING:** Don't unplug your iPhone while the update process is occurring, or you could temporarily wreck your iPhone. To fix this problem, you'll have to restore it and start the firmware update all over again.

FIGURE 8-1: *Your iPhone appears under the DEVICES category of the iTunes window.*

5. When you see a message at the top of the iTunes window stating that it's safe to disconnect the iPhone, you can click the eject button that appears to the right of your iPhone's name in the left panel. This tells your computer to stop accessing your iPhone.

6. Unplug your iPhone from your computer.

Additional Ideas for Updating Your iPhone

As a rule, you should keep your iPhone updated with the latest firmware. This not only makes your iPhone more stable and reliable, but it can also add new features that make your iPhone easier or faster to use.

Just be aware that you may not always want to update your iPhone the second Apple announces a new firmware update. Sometimes, firmware updates can actually cause more trouble than good, so when iTunes tells you there's a new firmware update, take a moment to browse the Internet and look for reports of problems with the latest update. If you don't see anything about problems and the firmware has been available for a few days, then it's probably safe to download the latest firmware and update your iPhone.

The iPhone is remarkably stable, but like any computer, you never know when it might crash or act erratically at the worst possible moment. By updating your iPhone periodically, you can make sure that your iPhone will work reliably when you need it.

Read an Electronic Book on Your iPhone

The next time you're bored, you could call someone, send a text message, listen to music, or just watch a TV show or movie that you've downloaded. For another way to keep yourself amused with your iPhone, grab an ebook reading program like Stanza or Kindle.

Both programs let you access a variety of free books including classic literature. If you want the latest best-sellers, you can pay to get the electronic versions and read them on your iPhone. With either Stanza or Kindle, you can turn your iPhone into an endless library that's only limited by the storage space available for saving your electronic books.

Stanza *http://www.lexcycle.com/*

Kindle *http://www.amazon.com/*

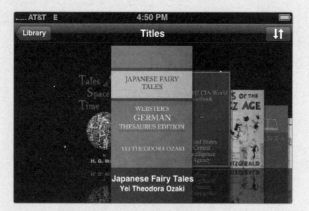

An electronic book reader like Stanza can give you access to the latest best-sellers.

9

Changing Your iPhone's Language

By default, every iPhone uses a language based on where you bought it. So, for example, if you bought your iPhone in the United States, the default language is English; if you bought your iPhone in France, the default language is French.

If you move to another country, or you just like practicing your language skills by using another language, you can make all icons and menus appear in the language of your choice. To complete the language experience, you can also change the keyboard settings to another language. That way, as you type, your iPhone will suggest words in that particular language.

Project goal: Learn to change the default language used for typing and displaying icons and buttons.

What You'll Be Using

To change the language used by the iPhone and practice typing in a foreign language, you need to use the following:

 The YouTube application

 The Settings application

Choosing a Default Language

The default language determines how your iPhone communicates with you. To choose a default language, do this:

1. From the Home screen, tap **Settings**. The Settings screen appears.
2. Tap **General**. The General screen appears. Scroll down the General screen until you see the International button.
3. Tap **International**. The International screen appears, as shown in Figure 9-1.
4. Tap **Language**. The Language screen appears, as shown in Figure 9-2.

FIGURE 9-1: The International screen lets you choose a language and keyboard.

FIGURE 9-2: The Language screen lets you choose your iPhone's default language.

5. Tap the language you want to use, such as **English** or **Italiano**.
6. Tap **Done**.
7. Press the Home button to view the Home screen with icons displayed in the new language, as shown in Figure 9-3.

Using International Keyboards

After you've set your iPhone to display a particular language, your next step is to get the iPhone to recognize any text that appears in that language. To do this, you must configure the keyboard to display characters in that language. You can type in French, English, Finnish, or any other supported language.

Using these international keyboards takes two steps. First, you need to turn on the particular language keyboard. Second, you need to switch to that language keyboard when you want to type in that particular language.

Defining a Foreign Language Keyboard

You can turn on as many foreign language keyboards as you want, but the iPhone can display only one keyboard at a time. By default, the iPhone has only one keyboard turned on (the native language of your country), but if you want to add more, do this:

1. From the Home screen, tap **Settings**. The Settings screen appears.
2. Tap **General**. The General screen appears. Scroll down the General screen until you see the Keyboard button.
3. Tap **Keyboard**. The Keyboard screen appears.
4. Tap **International Keyboards**. A screen displaying all the available language keyboards appears.
5. Tap the **ON/OFF** button next to the language you want to use, such as Italian, German, or Danish, as shown in Figure 9-4.
6. Press the Home button to return to the Home screen.

FIGURE 9-3: You can customize the Home screen to use another language.

FIGURE 9-4: You can set the virtual keyboard to display different languages.

Switching to a Foreign Language Keyboard

After you've chosen two or more foreign language keyboards, you can use the International key on the keyboard to switch between your chosen languages. The International key appears as a wire-frame globe to the left of the spacebar.

When you switch from one language keyboard to another, the actual characters on the keys may remain identical or display characters for that particular language, such as Korean, as shown in Figure 9-5. The automatic word suggestion feature will now recognize words typed in that particular language.

To switch between foreign language keyboards, do this:

1. From the Home screen, tap **YouTube**. The YouTube screen appears. (If you've previously searched for a YouTube video, you'll see a list of your last displayed videos. Otherwise, the screen will be blank.)
2. Tap **Search** at the bottom of the screen.
3. Tap the search text box at the top of the screen. A keyboard appears at the bottom of the screen.
4. Tap the International key, as shown in Figure 9-6. Notice that each time you tap the International key, it displays a different foreign language that lists terms for *space* and *search*.
5. Type a word in the language you chose. Notice that the automatic word suggestion feature now offers words in that language.
6. To type foreign language characters with accent marks (such as é or ç), tap and hold down the appropriate letter on the keyboard until a menu of characters with accent marks appears, as shown in Figure 9-7. Slide your fingertip over the character with the accent mark that you need. (If you lift your fingertip off the screen, this pop-up menu of foreign language characters will disappear.)
7. Press the Home button to return to the Home screen.

FIGURE 9-5: *Some languages, such as Korean, display completely different characters on the virtual keyboard.*

FIGURE 9-6: *When you tap the International key, foreign language terms will appear on the spacebar and search key.*

* **NOTE:** Some languages, such as Chinese and Japanese, let you draw characters or display a menu of characters you can tap, as shown in Figure 9-8.

FIGURE 9-7: *Tapping and holding down a letter key displays variations of that letter with accent marks.*

FIGURE 9-8: *Languages such as Chinese and Japanese offer unique ways to input characters.*

Additional Ideas for Changing Your iPhone's Language

If you're learning a foreign language, turn on the keyboard for that language and practice writing in the language that you're studying. By using the automatic word suggestion feature, you can learn common words in another language.

Students of other languages can also help themselves learn by changing the default language of the iPhone. By making yourself read buttons and icons in Japanese, Spanish, or Portuguese, your iPhone can get you to start thinking in that other language. Now all you have to worry about is learning to speak and understand that language when dealing with an actual human being.

Convert Your Money into Local Currency with Your iPhone

If you're traveling in another country, you may wonder how much your money is really worth. With the Currency app, you can easily compare dollars to yen, euros, or pounds. Now you can see whether you can afford to stay in another country or whether you need to get out of there before your money completely runs out.

Currency *http://www .currencyapp.com/*

Currency can convert your money into the local currency.

10 Resetting and Troubleshooting

If your iPhone starts acting like a bad PC and seems to be hopelessly fouled up, you may need to reset it to its original factory settings. This will wipe out any private information you've stored on your iPhone, but it will also wipe out any potential conflicts that may be causing your iPhone to crash, freeze, or behave erratically. Sometimes you can fix an erratic iPhone by updating its firmware (see Project 8). Firmware is the program that makes your iPhone actually work. It performs functions such as displaying icons on the screen. Apple constantly updates the iPhone's firmware to fix problems iPhone users may be experiencing.

You can reset your iPhone in several ways, ranging from the mild to the drastic. Sometimes programs may freeze or hang, just as they can on any computer. When that happens, you can often shut down the offending program, restart it, and everything works just fine again. If you run into persistent problems, you can also try updating specific apps on your iPhone that may be causing the problem. One way or another, you can find a way to keep your iPhone working properly.

Project goal: Learn how to reset your iPhone.

What You'll Be Using

To reset your iPhone, you need to use the following:

▶ The Sleep/Wake button The iPhone USB cable

 The Settings application iTunes (on your Mac or PC)

Shutting Down a Frozen Program

Occasionally a program may freeze and be unresponsive to anything you may do (including screaming and cursing). If this happens, you can shut down (also known as *force quit*) the frozen program by doing the following:

1. Press and hold down the Home button for approximately 10 seconds.
2. Release the Home button when the program closes by disappearing from the screen.

Try running the same program again to see if it works. If not, you may either need an updated version of that app or you may need to restart your entire iPhone, as explained in the following section.

Restarting Your iPhone

Restarting an iPhone is similar to rebooting a computer. Restarting essentially clears out the iPhone's memory and allows it to start all over again. To restart an iPhone, follow these steps:

1. Press and hold down both the Sleep/Wake button and the Home button for approximately 10 seconds. The red arrow slider may appear at the top of the screen, but you can ignore it.
2. When the Apple logo appears in the middle of the screen, release the Sleep/Wake button and the Home button.

Resetting Your iPhone

Sometimes when you change the settings on an iPhone or install new programs, these changes interfere with one another and cause your iPhone to act erratically or cause programs to freeze or hang. If this happens, you may need to reset one or more of the following parts of your iPhone from the Reset screen:

▸ **Reset All Settings**   This option leaves your data (songs, video, pictures, and so on) alone but restores your iPhone to its original factory settings.

▸ **Erase All Content and Settings**   This option wipes out your entire iPhone and restores it to its original factory settings.

▸ **Reset Network Settings**   This option resets all your network settings including passwords for accessing Wi-Fi networks.

▸ **Reset Keyboard Dictionary**   This option wipes out any words you may have stored in the iPhone's dictionary and returns the virtual keyboard to its original factory settings.

▸ **Reset Home Screen Layout**   This option returns your Home screen to its original factory layout.

▸ **Reset Location Warnings**   This option wipes out any stored information about your current location.

To reset all or some of these settings, follow these steps:

1.   From the Home screen, tap **Settings**. The Settings screen appears.
2.   Tap **General**. The General screen appears.
3.   Scroll down the General screen to find the Reset button, as shown in Figure 10-1.
4.   Tap **Reset**. The Reset screen appears, as shown in Figure 10-2.
5.   Tap a Reset button (such as **Reset All Settings** or **Reset Network Settings**). A dialog appears, warning that you are about to reset your iPhone to its original factory settings, as shown in Figure 10-3.
6.   Tap **Reset All Settings** (or tap **Cancel** if you change your mind).
7.   Press the Home button to return to the Home screen.

FIGURE 10-1: *The Reset button appears at the bottom of the General screen.*

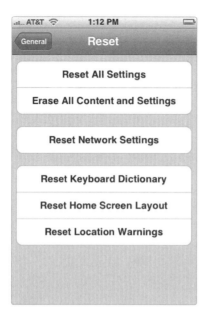

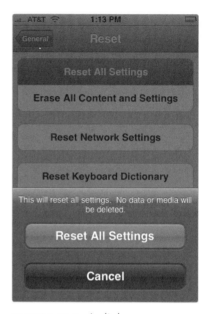

FIGURE 10-2: *The Reset screen displays all the available reset options.*

FIGURE 10-3: *A dialog warns when you are about to reset your iPhone settings.*

Restoring Your iPhone

If you've used a PC, you're probably familiar with the problems that occur when the computer acts up for no apparent reason. When this happens, you might have to reinstall the operating system and start all over again. Since the iPhone is nothing more than a miniature computer, it's possible that your iPhone may start acting up, and you might have to resort to restoring it to its original factory settings. When you do this, you'll wipe out all data that you've added to it, such as music or new apps.

✳ *NOTE:* **Restore your iPhone only as a last resort when you can't get it to work any other way.**

To restore an iPhone and wipe out everything on it in the process, follow these steps:

1. Open iTunes on your computer.
2. Plug your iPhone into your computer with the iPhone USB cable.
3. Click the iPhone icon under the DEVICES category in the left pane of the iTunes window. If the Summary tab, doesn't appear, you may need to click it to display its contents, as shown in Figure 10-4.

FIGURE 10-4: *The Restore button appears under the Summary tab in the iTunes window.*

4. Click the **Encrypt iPhone Backup** checkbox. A Set Password dialog appears, as shown in Figure 10-5.

FIGURE 10-5: *The Set Password dialog lets you encrypt your backup.*

5. Type your password in the Set Password dialog and click **Set Password**.
6. Click **Restore**. A dialog appears, asking if you want to back up all your data.
7. Click **Backup**. After the backup process is complete, iTunes will restore your iPhone. You may need to resynchronize your data on your computer (see Project 12).

Additional Ideas for Troubleshooting Your iPhone

Restarting programs can often cure their erratic behavior, but sometimes you need to go nuclear and wipe out everything so you can start all over again. Resetting all parts of your iPhone can be especially useful if you're getting rid of your iPhone and want to erase any private information stored on it.

For the most part, you'll find your iPhone reliable and ready to use at all times. However, if problems occur and resetting your iPhone doesn't stop them, try updating the firmware on your iPhone (see Project 8). As a last resort, bring your iPhone in to your nearest Apple store and let the experts worry about making the reluctant hardware work again.

Diagnose Yourself with Your iPhone

After you get done fixing minor problems with your iPhone, you may be curious how to fix minor problems with yourself. That's where WebMD Mobile can come to your rescue, helping you identify symptoms and offer possible solutions.

Just keep in mind that this free app won't turn your iPhone into a doctor, but it can give you information on what might be ailing you so you can seek qualified medical advice. Then again, you can use this app to see what kinds of problems different people may have so you can be thankful that you don't experience those symptoms.

WebMD Mobile *http://www .webmd.com/*

WebMD Mobile can turn your iPhone into a source for health advice.

 11 Installing and Uninstalling Applications

Even though the iPhone is a full-fledged computer disguised as a mobile phone, you can't buy programs at your local computer store and install them like software on an ordinary computer. The only way you can install new programs on your iPhone is to go through Apple's App Store.

The reason for this is security. When you install programs from any source, there's always a chance of malicious software (known as *malware*) sneaking on to your computer and damaging it. That's why Apple requires that software developers offer programs only through the App Store. After Apple examines a program to ensure that it's safe, it can be installed on your iPhone.

Project goal: Learn how to install (and uninstall) programs on your iPhone using your iPhone and the iTunes program on your computer.

What You'll Be Using

To install and uninstall programs on your iPhone, you need to use the following:

 The App Store application

 iTunes (on your Mac or PC)

 The iPhone USB cable

Finding Software for Your iPhone

Before you can install software on the iPhone, you need to visit the App Store to find a program you want. Since so many people sell iPhone applications, the App Store consists of five different areas to help you choose what you need:

▶ **Featured**   Lists the newest released apps (New) or the current batch of apps that are most popular (What's Hot)

▶ **Categories**   Lets you search for an iPhone program based on its function, such as Education, Finance, Games, or Productivity

▶ **Top 25**   Lists the 25 most popular iPhone applications that others have downloaded

▶ **Search**   Lets you type a descriptive word or phrase to search for an application that matches your criteria

▶ **Updates**   Shows if any of your currently installed apps have updates available

To find an application for your iPhone, you have two choices. First, you can install an app directly through your iPhone. Second, you can find an app using iTunes on your computer. We'll first discuss installation via your iPhone.

To find an app through your iPhone, follow these steps:

1. From the Home screen, tap **App Store**. The App Store screen appears.
2. Tap **Featured** at the bottom of the screen. The Featured list of iPhone applications appears, as shown in Figure 11-1.

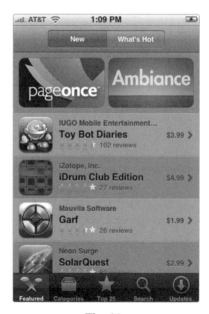

FIGURE 11-1: *The New category on the Featured screen lists the newest apps available.*

3. Tap **New** or **What's Hot** at the top of the screen. The New category lists the latest applications, while What's Hot lists the most popular of the new applications.

4. Tap **Categories**. A list of categories appears, as shown in Figure 11-2.

5. Tap a category, such as **Games** or **Utilities**. A list of applications that fit that category appears.

6. Scroll down to view all the apps in that category, or tap **Categories** to return to the list of categories.

7. Tap **Top 25** at the bottom of the screen. The Top 25 screen appears, as shown in Figure 11-3. At the top of the screen, tap **Top Paid** to see applications you can purchase or **Top Free** to see a list of free applications.

FIGURE 11-2: *The Categories screen organizes applications into groups.*

FIGURE 11-3: *The Top 25 Screen*

8. Tap **Search**. The search text box appears. Tap in the text box and a virtual keyboard appears.

9. Type a word or phrase that describes the type of program you want to find, such as *horoscope,* and then tap **Search** in the lower-right corner of the screen. A list of applications that match your criteria appears.

Reading and Writing Software Reviews

After you find a program that you want to install, you can check its *star rating*, which ranges from one to five stars. As a general rule, you'll find five-star apps more useful than one-star apps.

To read reviews from other people about a particular app, beyond the simplistic one-to-five-star rating system, do this:

1. Follow the steps in the section "Finding Software for Your iPhone" on page 78 to find an application. Tap the name of the app to see to its Info page.
2. Scroll down until you see the Reviews button that lists the app's current rating (one to five stars) and how many reviews are available; Figure 11-4 shows a 9 Reviews button. (The bottom of each app's Info screen also lists general information about that app, such as the version number, the company that made it, and the company's web address.)
3. Tap the **Reviews** button. The Reviews screen appears, letting you see reviews from other people, as shown in Figure 11-5.

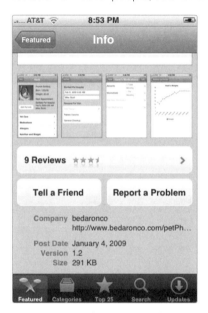

FIGURE 11-4: *The Reviews button appears on the app's Info screen.*

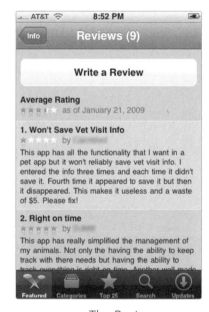

FIGURE 11-5: *The Reviews screen shows reviews from other users.*

4. Scroll down to read the reviews for the app.
5. (Optional) Tap **Write a Review**. Type your iTunes Store password, and then use the virtual keyboard to type your review.

Installing a Program

After browsing through the App Store, you're sure to find a program that you want to install on your iPhone. To install a program, do this:

1. Find the program you want to install, and then tap the blue button to the right of the program name displaying the program's price. Some apps are free, and some cost a few dollars. Once you tap it, the Price button changes into a green INSTALL button, as shown in Figure 11-6.

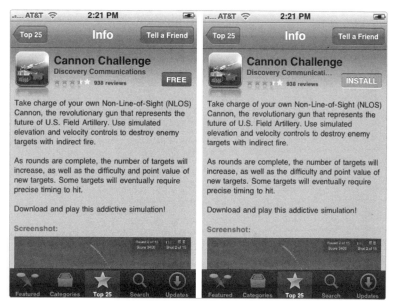

FIGURE 11-6: *Tap the program's price to display the green INSTALL button.*

* **NOTE:** If you tap INSTALL, you'll install the program right away, and the cost of the program will be charged to your iPhone cellular phone account, so make sure you really want to pay for a program before you tap that button.

2. Tap **INSTALL**. An iTunes Password dialog appears, asking you to type your password, as shown in Figure 11-7.
3. Type your password and tap **OK**. The application icon appears on the Home screen with a loading message, as shown in Figure 11-8.
4. When the app's icon appears on your Home screen, you can tap it to run the app.

FIGURE 11-7: *You must type a password before you can download and install a program.*

FIGURE 11-8: *A loading message appears on the Home screen.*

Updating Programs

Software developers frequently update their programs, which may offer new features or eliminate problems with a previous program. To check whether any of your programs need updating, the App Store provides a handy Updates icon. This feature compares the applications installed on your iPhone to the latest versions of the same programs offered in the App Store. If you have an older version of a program, you can install the updated version through the App Store.

To check for and install updates on your iPhone, do this:

1. From the Home screen, you can check whether updates for your installed programs are available. If a number appears in the upper-right corner of the App Store icon, as shown in Figure 11-9, you know that updates are available.

FIGURE 11-9: *The App Store icon on the Home screen alerts you to how many updates are available.*

2. Tap **App Store**. The App Store screen appears.
3. Tap **Updates** at the bottom of the screen. The Updates screen appears, listing any applications that can be updated.
4. Tap the updates you want to install.

Deleting a Program

If you've installed programs on your iPhone, you can always delete the program icons and uninstall those programs. (You cannot, however, uninstall any programs that came preinstalled on the iPhone, such as iTunes, Maps, or Calendar.)

To delete an icon and uninstall the program that the icon represents, do this:

1. From the Home screen, press and hold your finger on the program icon that you want to delete. A close button (an X in a red circle) appears in the upper-left corner of the icon. (If a close button does not appear, it means you cannot delete that icon and uninstall that program.)

* **NOTE:** Press the Home button if you decide you don't want to delete the icon after all. The close button disappears from the appropriate icon.

2. Tap the close button. A Delete dialog appears, as shown in Figure 11-10.
3. Tap **Delete**. The chosen icon disappears from the Home screen, and the application is removed from your iPhone.

FIGURE 11-10: *The Delete dialog alerts you that you're uninstalling a program.*

Installing and Deleting Software with iTunes

While you can install and delete apps directly on your iPhone, you can also use iTunes on your computer to install and delete apps. When you use iTunes, you'll have to sync your iPhone with your computer for the new software changes to appear on your iPhone (see Project 12).

Installing Software in iTunes

Using iTunes to find iPhone apps can be convenient, since you can read an entire screen of information about a particular app rather than trying to read information on the screen of the iPhone.

To install a program through iTunes, do this:

1. Open iTunes on your computer.
2. Click **iTunes Store** under the STORE category in the left pane. The iTunes screen appears, as shown in Figure 11-11.

FIGURE 11-11: You can find new software in the iTunes Store.

3.   Click **App Store** in the iTunes STORE pane. A list of categories appears, as shown in Figure 11-12.

FIGURE 11-12: Choose an option from the list of App Store Categories.

4. Click a category, such as **Books**, **Photography**, or **Travel**. A list of apps appears.

5. Click an app to read information about it, as shown in Figure 11-13.

FIGURE 11-13: *Information about an app appears in iTunes.*

✳ *NOTE:* If an app costs money, be sure you're willing to pay for it before you click the GET APP button.

6. Click the **GET APP** button to download the app into iTunes. After downloading a program into iTunes, you'll need to synchronize your iPhone with your computer to transfer the app to your iPhone (see Project 12).

Deleting Software in iTunes

You can also delete apps from within iTunes by following these steps:

1. Open iTunes on your computer.

2. Plug your iPhone into your computer using the iPhone USB cable.

3. Click **Applications** under the LIBRARY category in the left pane of the iTunes window. A list of applications that you've downloaded appears.

4. Right-click the app you want to delete from your iPhone. A pop-up menu appears, as shown in Figure 11-14.

FIGURE 11-14: *Right-click the app you want to delete.*

5. Click **Delete**. A dialog appears, asking if you really want to delete the chosen app.
6. Click **Remove**. Another dialog appears, asking if you want to keep the files or move them to the Trash.
7. Click **Move to Trash** (or click **Keep Files** if you think you might want to rein-stall that app again in the future). The next time you synchronize your iPhone, iTunes will update your iPhone with the newly added or deleted apps.

Additional Ideas for Installing and Uninstalling Applications

The more programs you install on your iPhone, the harder it will be to find the one you want. You should feel free to install as many programs as you want, but the moment you don't need an app any more, don't be afraid to get rid of it.

With so many free programs available, it's tempting to download and install as many as possible. Resist that urge and install only the programs you really need. Then you can keep your iPhone lean and uncluttered so you can actu-ally get important work done and have fun at the same time, which you'd be hard pressed to do with many other mobile phones on the market.

Lose Weight with Your iPhone

Uninstalling unwanted apps can lighten the load on your iPhone and give you more storage space to install other apps. If you're interested in losing weight yourself, one free app you might want to consider is Lose It!. The next time you're in a restaurant, run this app and find out how many calories a turkey sandwich or cup of yogurt contains. By watching what you eat, you can lose weight or learn to eat healthier so you can live longer.

Lose It!   *http://www.loseit.com/*

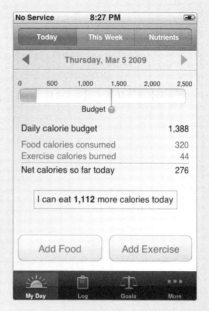

The Lose It! app can help you watch what you eat.

12

Synchronizing Data Between Your Computer and Your iPhone

Chances are you have data stored on your computer that you want to store on your iPhone. For example, you might have a huge music library that you want to transfer to your iPhone so you can listen to your favorite songs while you're away from your computer.

If you have crucial names, addresses, or appointments stored on your computer, you'll probably want that information stored on your iPhone as well. You could retype all this information into your iPhone, but a better solution is to *synchronize* data to transfer it between your computer and iPhone automatically.

To synchronize your data, you need to use the USB cable that came with your iPhone and the iTunes program. Every Macintosh comes with iTunes, but if you have a Windows PC, you'll need to download and install iTunes directly from the Apple website (*http://www.apple.com/itunes/download*). After you have installed iTunes, you'll be ready to synchronize your data.

Project goal: Learn how to synchronize data between your computer and your iPhone.

What You'll Be Using

To synchronize data, you need to use the following:

 iTunes (on your Mac or PC)

 The iPhone USB cable

* **NOTE:** **The iPhone can transfer data to or from a Macintosh or a Windows PC, but if you have data trapped on another mobile phone, such as a Black-Berry or Palm Treo, visit Mark/Space (*http://www.markspace.com/*) and buy a copy of the Missing Sync for iPhone program. This program can transfer data from other mobile phones and store it on your iPhone. Then you can toss your other mobile phone in the trash (or recycle it!) and happily use your iPhone instead.**

Synchronizing Data

You can synchronize data between your iPhone and only one computer. If you have a laptop and a desktop computer, and each computer contains different music files and contact information, your iPhone can synchronize data with only one of them. If you try to synchronize with more than one computer, you'll risk losing all your iPhone data.

You can synchronize the following types of data:

▸ Contacts and appointments

▸ Email

▸ Safari browser bookmarks

▸ Ringtones

▸ Music

▸ Digital photographs

▸ Podcasts

▸ Video

▸ iPhone applications

When synchronizing data, select the type of data you want to synchronize (such as email), and then choose the specific data you want to transfer (such as email from a particular account). After you select everything you want to transfer, you can synchronize the data with a click of the mouse.

Defining Synchronization Options

When you plug your iPhone into a computer with the iPhone USB cable, you have three choices for synchronizing your data:

▶   Automatically synchronize all your selected data

▶   Automatically synchronize only audio and video files

▶   Manually synchronize audio and video files

If you select the third option, you'll have to synchronize all of your data *manually*. To do this, just select the content you want to put on your iPhone in the right pane of iTunes library window, then drag it over to the icon for your iPhone in the Devices list in left pane of the iTunes window. Managing your data manually can be particularly convenient if the data on your computer is too large to fit on your iPhone; you can just pick and choose your favorites. (If your music library is too large to fit on your iPhone, you can create a playlist in iTunes with the content you want to transfer to your iPhone, and just sync this playlist.)

To select synchronization options, follow these steps:

1. Connect your iPhone to your computer using the iPhone USB cable.
2. Open iTunes on your computer.
3. Click the name of your iPhone under the DEVICES category in the left pane of the iTunes window. The Summary tab should appear automatically, but if it doesn't, just click the **Summary** tab to view the options for synchronizing your iPhone, as shown in Figure 12-1.

FIGURE 12-1: *Your iPhone appears in the iTunes window under the DEVICES category in the left pane.*

4. Click one or more of the checkboxes under the Options category.
5. (Optional) Click **Apply** to start synchronizing, or click another tab to define additional synchronization options, as described later in this project.

Syncing Contacts, Appointments, Email, and Bookmarks

If you've stored contact information in Address Book (on Mac OS X), in your Yahoo! Address Book Contacts, or in Google Contacts, you can synchronize this data and store it on your iPhone. The main reason you'd do this is to make sure you have the same data stored in multiple locations.

You can also synchronize appointments, email, and even bookmarks stored in Safari. Doing this essentially duplicates your computer data in your iPhone so you'll never risk missing an appointment or an email message.

＊ **NOTE:** If you use a Mac browser other than Safari, you can import bookmarks from your other browser into Safari, and then synchronize your bookmarks to your iPhone. If you have a PC, you can import bookmarks from either Safari or Internet Explorer.

To synchronize contacts, appointments, email, and Safari bookmarks to your iPhone, follow these steps:

1. Connect your iPhone to your computer and open iTunes.
2. Click the **Info** tab. Contacts and Calendars options appear, as shown in Figure 12-2.

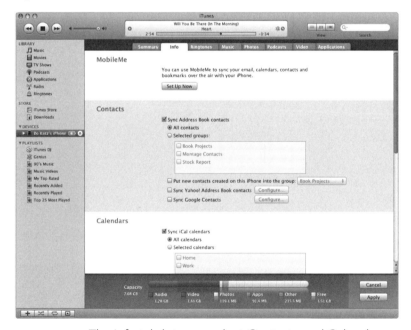

FIGURE 12-2: The Info tab lets you select Contacts and Calendars options to synchronize.

3. Click the checkboxes for the data you want to synchronize. If you want to synchronize Google Contacts or Yahoo! Address Book contacts, you'll be prompted to type your ID and password.

4. (Optional) If you have a MobileMe account, click the **Set Up Now** button to synchronize your iPhone with your MobileMe data. (You can find out more about this service at *http://www.apple.com/mobileme/*.)

5. Scroll down to view the Web Browser, Mail Accounts, and Advanced options, as shown in Figure 12-3. (If you have multiple email accounts, you can select which ones you want to sync with your iPhone.)

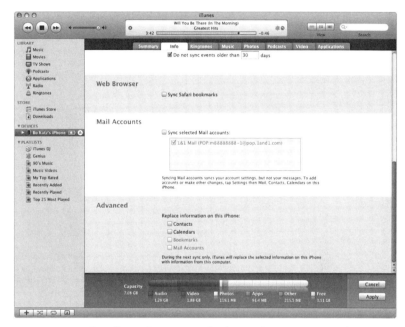

FIGURE 12-3: *Scrolling down reveals the Web Browser, Mail Accounts, and Advanced options on the Info tab.*

6. (Optional) Click **Apply** to start synchronizing, or click another tab to define additional synchronization options.

Syncing Ringtones and Music

To synchronize ringtones and music, follow these steps:

1. Connect your iPhone to your computer and open iTunes.

2. Click the **Ringtones** tab. A list of available ringtones appears, as well as the option to sync these ringtones, as shown in Figure 12-4.

FIGURE 12-4: *The Ringtones tab lets you select ringtones to synchronize.*

3. Click the **Music** tab. Audio file options appear, as shown in Figure 12-5.

FIGURE 12-5: *The Music tab lets you choose audio files to synchronize.*

4. (Optional) Click **Apply** to start synchronizing, or click another tab to define additional synchronization options.

Syncing Photographs

You can also synchronize photographs stored in iPhoto or in any folder you choose. To synchronize photographs, follow these steps:

1. Connect your iPhone to your computer and open iTunes.
2. Click the **Photos** tab. Photos options appear, as shown in Figure 12-6.

FIGURE 12-6: *The Photos tab lets you choose digital photographs to synchronize.*

3. Click the appropriate options. If you want to synchronize photos from iPhoto, you can select specific albums. You can also select images stored in your Pictures or Documents folder.
4. (Optional) Click **Apply** to start synchronizing, or click another tab to define additional synchronization options.

Syncing Podcasts

When synchronizing podcasts, you must choose not only which podcasts to sync, but which episodes of that podcast to sync. You can select episodes based on a time duration, such as the most recently played episodes, unplayed episodes, or least recent (that is, older) episodes, as shown in Figure 12-7.

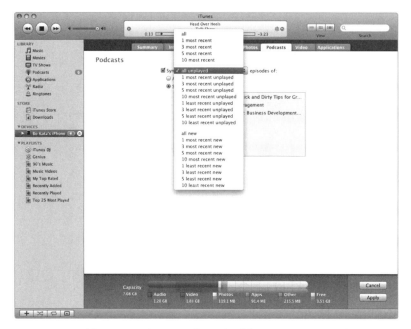

FIGURE 12-7: *You can select unplayed, older, or newer podcasts to synchronize.*

∗ **NOTE:** Before you can see any podcasts in the Podcasts tab, you'll first have to find and select one or more podcasts to which you want to subscribe (subscriptions are usually free) from the iTunes store (see Project 25).

To synchronize podcasts, select the podcasts and episodes you want by following these steps:

1. Connect your iPhone to your computer and open iTunes.
2. Click the **Podcasts** tab. Podcasts options appear, as shown in Figure 12-8.
3. Click the **Sync** drop-down menu and choose an option, such as **5 most recent new** (see Figure 12-7).
4. Click the checkboxes to select the podcasts you want to synchronize.
5. (Optional) Click **Apply** to start synchronizing, or click another tab to define additional synchronization options.

Syncing Videos

The Videos category represents TV show episodes and movies you've downloaded through iTunes. To synchronize videos, follow these steps:

1. Connect your iPhone to your computer and open iTunes.
2. Click the **Video** tab. TV Shows and Movies options appear, as shown in Figure 12-9.

FIGURE 12-8: The Podcasts tab lets you choose which podcasts to synchronize.

FIGURE 12-9: The Video tab lets you choose TV shows and movie files to synchronize.

3. Click the TV shows and movies you want to synchronize. If you select any TV shows, you can click the Sync drop-down menu to choose the episodes you want to select, such as all unplayed episodes of a particular show.

4. (Optional) Click **Apply** to start synchronizing, or click another tab to define additional synchronization options.

Syncing Applications

You can download iPhone applications directly to your iPhone or to iTunes on your computer. In either case, you can synchronize applications to store them on both your computer and your iPhone by following these steps:

1. Connect your iPhone to your computer and open iTunes.

2. Click the **Applications** tab. A list of Applications options appear, as shown in Figure 12-10.

FIGURE 12-10: The Applications tab lets you choose programs to synchronize.

3. Click an option. If you click the Selected applications radio button, you'll be able to choose which applications to synchronize by clicking the appropriate checkboxes.

4. (Optional) Click **Apply** to start synchronizing, or click another tab to define additional synchronization options.

Additional Ideas for Synchronizing Data

Keeping your music and data synchronized is crucial, so make sure you regularly synchronize your iPhone to your computer. If you plug your iPhone into your computer using the iPhone USB cable, you can recharge your iPhone and keep your data synchronized at the same time.

Ultimately, your iPhone will only be as useful as your synchronization habits. If you fail to synchronize your data and your iPhone gets stolen or your computer suffers a hard disk crash, all your precious songs and contact information could be wiped out forever.

Make it a habit to synchronize regularly. That way, if you lose your computer or your iPhone, you'll be able to restore your data. Remember that the most important part of your iPhone is its data. You can always buy another iPhone, but you can never easily replace your data once it's gone.

Automatically Sync Your iPhone's Contact Information

If you have contact information trapped in Gmail, Yahoo!, or Windows Live Hotmail, you can synchronize your information using the free TrueSwitch Mobile Sync app. Although this app only synchronizes contact information (if you want to learn how to sync your calendar, see "Syncing Contacts, Appointments, Email, and Bookmarks" on page 92), this Rolodex information is usually the most important part of everyone's data.

To make sure everything remains updated, you can schedule this app to synchronize data for you automatically. Now when you look up someone's contact information, you can be assured that it's accurate.

TrueSwitch Mobile Sync   *http://mobi.trueswitch.com/*

The TrueSwitch Mobile Sync app can keep your contact information organized and updated.

PART 3

Making
Phone Calls

13 Making Calls

Although the iPhone is an all-in-one personal digital assistant (PDA), digital music player, and handheld computer, it's also a full-featured mobile phone. Like other mobile phones, the iPhone lets you make calls, but you can do a whole lot more with your calls. As you'll see in this project, making calls with your iPhone can be as simple or as sophisticated as you want. Talking to people is the main reason to use your iPhone, so learning how to make calls is important.

Project goal: Learn how to make phone calls with your iPhone.

What You'll Be Using

To learn how to make calls with your iPhone, you need to use the following:

 The Settings application

 The Phone application

Dialing a Phone Number

Your iPhone gives you four ways to dial a phone number and make a call:

▶ **Keypad**   Lets you dial a number directly

▶ **Contacts**   Lets you search for a name stored in the Contacts program so you can dial the saved phone number for that person

▶ **Recents**   Tracks the phone numbers of people who have called you so you can return their calls

▶ **Favorites**   Lets you select names of people you call frequently from the Contacts program

Dialing a Number with the Keypad

The most straightforward way to dial a number is to use the keypad to type the phone number one digit at a time. To dial a number with the keypad, do this:

1. From the Home screen, tap **Phone**. The Phone screen appears.
2. Tap **Keypad** at the bottom of the screen. The numeric keypad appears, as shown in Figure 13-1.
3. Type the phone number with the numeric keypad. If you tap the wrong number by mistake, tap the Backspace key (the button directly to the right of Call) to correct it.
4. Tap **Call** to make your phone call.

Using the Keypad to Store a Number in the Contacts Program

If you dial a phone number and decide you want to save it for future use, you can store it in the Contacts program. That way, you'll always be able to find it again and can just tap the phone number to call rather than typing the whole number.

FIGURE 13-1: *The Phone screen with the numeric keypad*

To store a phone number in the Contacts program, do this:

1. From the Home screen, tap **Phone**. The Phone screen appears.
2. Tap **Keypad**. The numeric keypad appears (see Figure 13-1).
3. Tap the phone number on the numeric keypad.
4. Tap the Add Contact icon, which appears directly under the asterisk key. (It looks like a silhouette of a man with a plus sign next to it.) Create New Contact and Add to Existing Contact buttons appear, as shown in Figure 13-2.
5. Tap **Create New Contact**, and a New Contact screen appears, where you can type the person's name and other data, such as a street address or email address.
6. Tap **Add to Existing Contact**, and the Contacts screen appears, where you can tap an existing name to store the currently displayed phone number.
7. Tap **Save** to save your phone number in the Contacts program. The numeric keypad appears again.
8. Tap **Call** to dial the currently displayed phone number, or press the Home button to return to the Home screen.

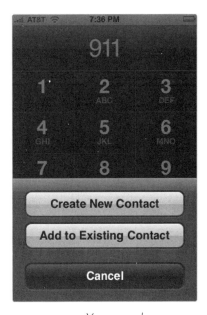

FIGURE 13-2: *You can choose where you want to store a phone number.*

Dialing a Number from the Contacts Program

If you've already saved a contact number in the Contacts program, you can easily dial that number by doing this:

1. From the Home screen, tap **Phone**. The Phone screen appears.
2. Tap **Contacts**. The Contacts screen appears, listing all your stored names.
3. Tap the name of the person you want to call. An Info screen appears, listing that person's phone number.
4. Tap the phone number. Your iPhone automatically dials the number and lets you know what it's doing, as shown in Figure 13-3.

∗ NOTE: While you're on the phone, you can use the keypad to navigate voice-mail and automated customer service systems. Just move your phone away from your head and tap *Keypad*.

Dialing a Number from the Recents List

If you have called someone or somebody has called you (whether you answered the call or not), your iPhone will store that phone number in the Recents list. This gives you a chance to return a call without having to write down the caller's phone number. To dial a number stored on the Recents list, do this:

1. From the Home screen, tap **Phone**. The Phone screen appears (see Figure 13-1).
2. Tap **Recents** near the bottom of the screen. The Recents list appears, as shown in Figure 13-4.

∗ NOTE: If a name appears instead of a phone number, that means that person's name and phone number are already stored in the Contacts program.

3. (Optional) Tap the **All** tab to view a list of phone numbers you have called and phone numbers that have called you. Tap the **Missed** tab to view only a list of calls you received but did not answer.
4. Tap the name of the person or phone number that you want to call. An Info screen appears, show-ing the person's phone number. Your iPhone automatically dials the number you choose (see Figure 13-3).

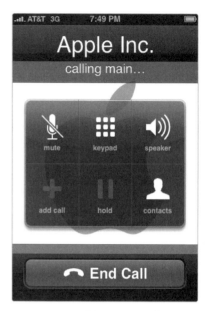

FIGURE 13-3: *Tapping a phone number stored in the Contacts program automatically dials that number.*

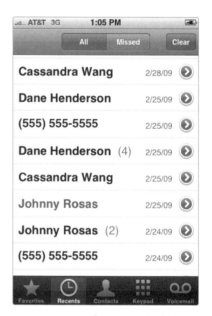

FIGURE 13-4: *The Recents list tracks who you called and who has called you.*

Storing a Number from the Recents List

If someone recently called you, his or her phone number appears on the Recents list. If you want to store that phone number in the Contacts program, you could type that phone number with the keypad (and risk making a mistake), or you could let your iPhone store that number for you so you can access it with a simple tap.

To store a number from the Recents list in your Contacts, do this:

1. From the Home screen, tap **Phone**. The Phone screen appears.
2. Tap **Recents**. The Recents list appears (see Figure 13-4).
3. (Optional) Tap the **All** or **Missed** tab.
4. Tap the blue-and-white arrow to the far right of the phone number that you want to save. An Incoming, Outgoing, or Missed Call screen appears, as shown in Figure 13-5.

✳ **NOTE:** An *Incoming Call* is a phone number that called you, which you answered. An *Outgoing Call* is a phone number that you called. A *Missed Call* is a phone number that called you, but you did not answer.

5. Tap **Create New Contact** or **Add to Existing Contact**. (Adding a phone number to an existing contact can be handy if you've stored someone's home number and recently received his or her mobile phone number, or vice versa.)

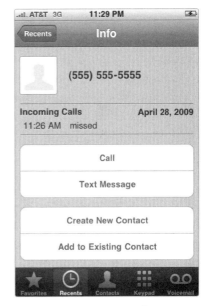

FIGURE 13-5: You can choose how you want to store a recent incoming or outgoing phone number.

Storing a Number in the Favorites List

The Contacts program can store hundreds of names and phone numbers. Chances are good that out of all the names and phone numbers stored in the Contacts program, you'll need quick access only to a handful of those numbers. Rather than wade through the Contacts program to find a phone number, you can store that phone number in your Favorites list. That way, you'll be able to access the phone number quickly and easily.

To store a number in the Favorites list, do this:

1. From the Home screen, tap **Phone**. The Phone screen appears.
2. Tap **Favorites**. A Favorites list appears, as shown in Figure 13-6.

3. Tap the plus sign in the upper-right corner of the screen. The Contacts screen appears.
4. Tap the name of the person whose phone number you want to store on your Favorites list. The selected name appears on the Favorites list.
5. (Optional) To remove a name from the Favorites list, tap **Edit** in the upper-left corner of the screen. Tap the red circle with a minus sign that appears next to the name you want to remove, and then tap **Remove**.

* **NOTE:** Removing a name from the Favorites list does not delete that name and phone number from the Contacts program.

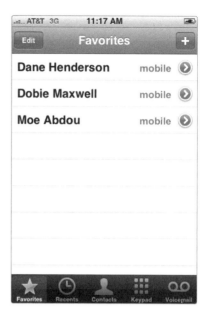

FIGURE 13-6: *The Favorites list can store your most frequently called numbers from the Contacts program.*

Dialing a Number from the Favorites List

After you've stored one or more names and phone numbers in your Favorites list, you can dial those numbers quickly by doing this:

1. From the Home screen, tap **Phone**. The Phone screen appears.
2. Tap **Favorites**. The Favorites list appears (see Figure 13-6).
3. Tap the name of the person you want to call. Your iPhone automatically dials the number (see Figure 13-3).

* **NOTE:** Try pressing the Home button twice in quick succession. By default, this will take you to the Favorites list. See Project 3 to learn how to change what happens when you press the Home button twice.

Hiding Your Caller ID

When you call somebody, that person may be able to see your caller ID. If you want to turn this feature off (or on again), do this:

1. From the Home screen, tap **Settings**. The Settings screen appears.
2. Scroll down and tap **Phone**. The Phone screen appears, as shown in Figure 13-7.
3. Tap **Show My Caller ID**. The Show My Caller ID screen appears, as shown in Figure 13-8.

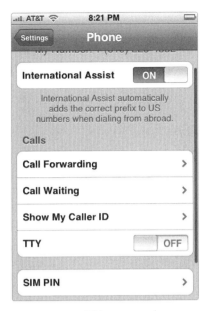

FIGURE 13-7: *This screen lets you modify your calling options.*

FIGURE 13-8: *The Show My Caller ID screen lets you turn caller ID on or off.*

4. Tap the **ON/OFF** button next to Show My Caller ID to turn it on or off.
5. Press the Home button to return to the Home screen.

Additional Ideas for Making Calls from Your iPhone

If you're terrified of technology, you can still make calls from the iPhone by using the familiar numeric keypad, which turns your expensive iPhone into a simple telephone. If you often need to make calls to the same people, you can store your most frequently called numbers in the Contacts program and in your Favorites list.

Add the names and phone numbers of your immediate family members to your Favorites list (unless you don't want to talk to them). Add your friends' names and numbers to the Favorites list, too. You can also store emergency numbers, such as your automotive club phone number, in the Contacts program. That way, if you're driving and get stuck on the road, you can dial for help without having to search for the right number to call.

Making calls from your iPhone is easy, simple, and fun—which is how all our technological appliances should work. The first time you get an iPhone, practice calling different people using all the methods described in this chapter. You can brag to your friends and family about your new iPhone while learning all the different ways to dial a phone number and make a call.

14 Answering Calls

Answering a phone call might seem like a trivial task, but your iPhone offers a variety of options for responding to a call. If you can't answer your iPhone when it rings, you can set up voicemail or forward your calls to another phone number. While you're talking to someone, you can answer another call by using call waiting. With so many different ways to answer an iPhone, it's possible to receive calls at your convenience, whatever that may be at the time.

Project goal: Learn how to answer phone calls and use voicemail and other options on your iPhone.

What You'll Be Using

To learn how to answer and manage calls with your iPhone, you need to use the following:

 The Settings application

 The Phone application

 The Contacts application

Answering and Ending a Call

If you receive a call on your iPhone while your iPhone is in sleep mode, the screen displays the phone number of the caller and gives you the option of answering the call by sliding the arrow across the bottom of the screen.

If you are using your iPhone when you receive a call, the caller's phone number appears on the screen along with a red Decline button and a green Answer button, as shown in Figure 14-1.

FIGURE 14-1: *Decline and Answer buttons appear when you receive a phone call.*

* **NOTE:** **If you want your iPhone to display the caller's name on the screen instead of his or her telephone number, you'll need to store that person's name and phone number in the Contacts program (see Project 13).**

If you want to take the call, tap Answer. If you don't want to answer the call, tap Decline. (You can also ignore the call completely, but then your iPhone will continue vibrating or ringing, which you may find annoying.)

If you're wearing your iPhone headset and receive a call, you can answer it by pressing the mic button attached to the cord, as shown in Figure 14-2.

Mic button

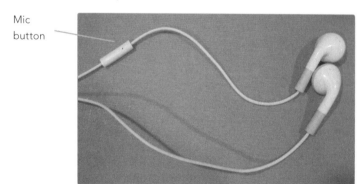

FIGURE 14-2: *The mic button lets you answer a call while wearing the headset.*

When you're ready to end your call, move the iPhone away from your ear; the iPhone automatically displays a red End Call button at the bottom of the screen, as shown in Figure 14-3. To end your call, tap **End Call**.

Using Ringtones

Storing a person's name and phone number in the Contacts program can help identify that person by name whenever he or she calls you. To help you identify who is calling, you can also set up different ringtones for each caller.

Normally, when you receive a call, your iPhone plays the same sound, whether the person calling is your best friend or a bill collector. Ringtones give you the option of assigning each caller a particular ringtone. The ringtone your iPhone makes when you get a call can help you decide whether or not you want to answer that call.

To define a ringtone for a name already stored in the Contacts program, do this:

1. From the Home screen, tap **Contacts**. (You may need to slide the Home screen to the side to see the second screen where the Contacts icon appears.) The Contacts screen appears.
2. Tap a name that you want to identify with a unique ringtone. The Info screen appears, showing the stored information about that person, as shown in Figure 14-4.

FIGURE 14-3: *The End Call button appears when you move the iPhone away from your ear.*

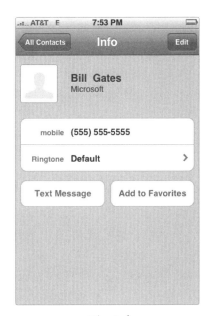

FIGURE 14-4: *The Info screen lets you choose a ringtone for a caller.*

3. Tap **Ringtone**. A Ringtones screen appears, as shown in Figure 14-5.
4. Tap a ringtone name and press the Home button. The next time this person calls, his or her name will appear, and you'll hear a unique ringtone play.

Using Voicemail

Since you can't always answer every call, you can do the next best thing (besides ignoring people) and set up your voicemail account. Now if people call and you don't answer, they'll get routed to your voicemail, where they can hear a brief message and then leave a message of their own.

Setting Up Voicemail

When you first get an iPhone, you'll need to set up a password and record a greeting by doing this:

1. From the Home screen, tap **Phone**. The Phone screen appears.
2. Tap **Voicemail** in the lower-right corner of the screen. A Setup screen appears.

* **NOTE:** If you have already set up your voicemail, you can modify your outgoing message by tapping Greeting in the upper-left corner of the screen. Skip to step 6.

3. Tap **Set Up Now**. A Password screen appears, asking you to type a four-digit voicemail password, as shown in Figure 14-6.

* **NOTE:** Rather than try to memorize a numeric password, think of a short, memorable word that you'll never forget and type that word as your password, using the letters on the numeric keys as a guide.

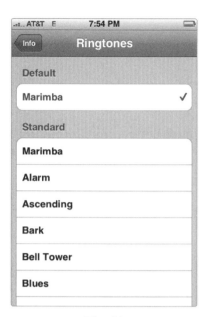

FIGURE 14-5: The Ringtones screen lists all the different ringtones available.

FIGURE 14-6: The Password screen lets you define a voicemail password.

4. Type a password and tap **Save** in the upper-right corner of the screen. The Password screen appears again, asking that you re-enter your password.

5. Type your password again and tap **Save**. The Greeting screen appears, as shown in Figure 14-7.

6. Tap **Default** or **Custom**. (If you tap Default, callers will hear a generic voicemail greeting. If you tap Custom, you can record your own greeting.)

7. Tap **Save**. The Voicemail screen appears. Since you just set up your voicemail, you won't see any messages saved there yet.

8. Press the Home button to return to the Home screen.

Listening to Voicemail

If you miss a call or have voicemail waiting for you, your iPhone screen displays an alert so you can take action (or just ignore that call altogether). To listen to your voicemail messages, do this:

1. From the Home screen, tap **Phone**. The Phone screen appears. A number in a red circle appears in the upper-right corner of the Voicemail icon to let you know how many voicemail messages you haven't heard yet, as shown in Figure 14-8.

2. Tap **Voicemail** at the lower-right corner. The Voicemail screen appears and displays a blue dot next to all new messages.

3. Tap a message that you want to hear. The message starts playing, as shown in Figure 14-9.

4. (Optional) Drag the horizontal slider left or right to hear all or parts of the message again.

FIGURE 14-7: The Greeting screen lets you choose a voicemail greeting for people to hear.

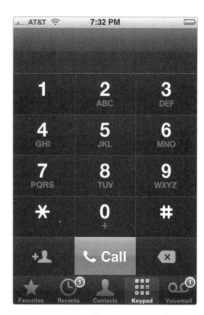

FIGURE 14-8: The Voicemail icon identifies how many new messages you've received.

✳ **NOTE:** If you have stored the caller's name and phone number in the Contacts program, you can tap the arrow that appears to the right of the caller's name to view contact information for that person.

5. Tap **Call Back** to call that person back, or tap **Delete** to erase the message. (If you tap Delete, your iPhone stores the deleted message in a special Deleted Messages area. If you tap the Voicemail icon and then tap Deleted Messages, you'll see a Deleted screen, where you can undelete a message or clear it and wipe it out for good, as shown in Figure 14-10.)
6. Press the Home button to return to the Home screen.

FIGURE 14-9: *The Voicemail screen displays and lets you listen to stored messages.*

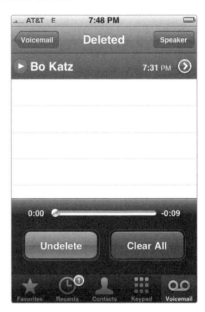

FIGURE 14-10: *The Deleted screen lets you undelete messages or delete them permanently.*

Setting Up Call Forwarding and Call Waiting

If you don't want to miss a phone call, the iPhone gives you the option of setting up call forwarding. If someone calls you on your iPhone, you can automatically route the call to another phone and answer it there. This feature lets callers call your iPhone number so you don't have to give out new phone numbers whenever you happen to be somewhere else, such as a place that doesn't have cell phone service.

Another way to answer calls is through call waiting. This feature lets you put your current caller on hold so you can answer a new incoming call.

To set up call forwarding and call waiting, follow these steps:

1. From the Home screen, tap **Settings**. The Settings screen appears.
2. Scroll down and tap **Phone**. The Phone screen appears, as shown in Figure 14-11.
3. Tap **Call Forwarding**. The Call Forwarding screen appears, as shown in Figure 14-12.
4. Tap the **ON/OFF** button next to Call Forwarding to turn this option on. The Forwarding To screen appears, as shown in Figure 14-13.
5. Type a phone number and then tap **Call Forwarding** in the upper-left corner of the screen.
6. Tap **Phone** in the upper-left corner of the screen. The Phone screen appears again.

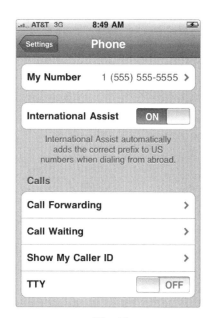

FIGURE 14-11: *The Phone screen displays the Call Forwarding button.*

FIGURE 14-12: *The Call Forwarding screen lets you turn on call forwarding and specify another phone number.*

FIGURE 14-13: *The Forwarding To screen lets you type the phone number at which you would like to receive calls.*

7. Tap **Call Waiting**. A Call Waiting screen appears.
8. Tap the **ON/OFF** button next to Call Waiting to turn this option on.
9. Press the Home button to return to the Home screen.

Additional Ideas for Answering Calls

To help screen your calls, you can store the names and phone numbers of people you know in the Contacts program. That way, every time you receive a call, you'll see a real name on the screen instead of a meaningless phone number. Once you see a name that you recognize, you'll know whether the caller is someone you want to talk to or avoid.

To help you identify a caller from a ringtone, you can choose distinctive ringtones for each caller. Play a happy sound for someone you like and a mournful sound for someone you want to avoid.

By using voicemail, you can effectively turn your iPhone into an answering machine, so you'll never have to take another phone call again. Get creative with answering your iPhone. Remember that just because someone calls you, it doesn't mean you're obligated to talk to that person. The less time you let others interrupt you with phone calls, the more time you'll have to pursue and achieve the goals most important to you.

15

Making Conference Calls and Other Stuff to Do While Talking on Your iPhone

You can do more than just talk on your iPhone. If you need to speak to someone standing next to you while you're using your iPhone, you can mute the iPhone so you can chat in private. Or, if you want everyone around you to hear your caller's comments and make comments of their own, you can turn on the iPhone's built-in speakerphone and let everyone participate.

If you're talking on your iPhone and you need to look up somebody's phone number in the Contacts program, you can do that quickly without having to end your call. If you find yourself talking to someone important, you can make a conference call so multiple people can join in the conversation. With so many options available, you can make talking on the iPhone both convenient and productive.

Project goal: Learn the different options for talking on your iPhone.

What You'll Be Using

To learn to use the various talk options on your iPhone, you need to use the following:

 The Phone application

Displaying Options

When you're talking on your iPhone, you can't see the screen since it's pressed against your ear. The moment you move your iPhone away from your ear, it senses the movement and displays a screen with seven different options, as shown in Figure 15-1:

▶ Mute

▶ Keypad

▶ Speaker

▶ Add Call

▶ Hold

▶ Contacts

▶ End Call

To choose an option, just tap it.

FIGURE 15-1: *Seven different options are available during a phone call.*

Muting the Speaker

If you're talking on your iPhone and need to speak to someone standing next to you, you can cover the iPhone's speaker so that the caller can't hear your side conversation, or you can mute the speaker.

To mute the speaker during a call, do this:

1. Move the iPhone away from your face so you can see its screen.
2. Tap **Mute**. The Mute icon appears highlighted, and you can say anything you want without the caller hearing what you say (unless you accidentally tap Mute again).

Using Keys on the Keypad

If you call many businesses, you may often wind up listening to a computer telling you to choose different options by pressing a number. To tap numeric keys on the iPhone, do this:

1. Move the iPhone away from your face so you can see its screen.
2. Tap **Keypad**. The Keypad screen appears, as shown in Figure 15-2. Tap any numeric keys you need to indicate your choices.
3. Tap **Hide Keypad** to hide the Keypad screen.

Turning on the Speakerphone

Talking on the phone is usually a private affair, but if you're in a crowded room with other people, you may want your cohorts to hear what the caller has to say. Rather than force everyone to crowd around your iPhone, you can turn on your iPhone's speakerphone so that everyone nearby can hear the conversation.

To turn on the iPhone's speakerphone, do this:

1. Move the iPhone away from your face so you can see its screen.
2. Tap **Speaker**. The Speaker icon appears highlighted, as shown in Figure 15-3. Now your iPhone will broadcast the conversation through the speakerphone.
3. Tap **Speaker** again to remove the highlight and turn off the feature.

FIGURE 15-2: *The Keypad screen lets you tap a key to choose a number.*

FIGURE 15-3: *A highlighted icon means that the feature is turned on.*

Using Conference Calls

A conference call lets you connect with up to five people simultaneously. This can be handy for speaking to multiple people at once without the nuisance of calling each person individually. To set up a conference call, you first call one person and then add other people to that call. Repeat the process to add additional callers.

Initiating a Conference Call

You can start a conference call at any time while chatting on your iPhone with another person. To start a conference call, do this:

1. Call someone on your iPhone, either by tapping the number on the keypad or selecting a stored number in your Contacts program.
2. Move the iPhone away from your face so you can see its screen.
3. Tap **Add Call**. The Contacts screen appears, where you can select a stored number to dial.
4. (Optional) Tap **Keypad** and dial a phone number of the person you want to add to your conference call.

✴ **NOTE:** While you're dialing another number to add to your conference call, you automatically put your other callers on hold. When you put a caller on hold, that caller can still chat with others in the same conference call.

FIGURE 15-4: *The Merge Calls and Swap icons appear when you initiate a conference call.*

5. Move the iPhone away from your face so you can see its screen after you've connected to another caller. Notice that Merge Calls and Swap icons now appear on the screen, as shown in Figure 15-4.
6. (Optional) Tap **Swap** to put your current caller on hold and talk to the other person currently on hold.
7. Tap **Merge Calls** to merge all calls so everyone can chat with each other.

Dropping a Caller and Chatting Privately on a Conference Call

If you're in the midst of a conference call and want to hang up on one of your conference callers or chat with someone privately, do this:

1. Move the iPhone away from your face so you can see its screen. Notice that the top of the screen displays the word *Conference* to let you know you're currently in a conference call, as shown in Figure 15-5.
2. Tap the arrow to the right of the word *Conference* at the top of the screen. The Conference screen appears, as shown in Figure 15-6.

FIGURE 15-5: *Identifying a conference call while chatting on the iPhone*

FIGURE 15-6: *The Conference screen lets you see all the people currently in on your conference call.*

3. (Optional) To end a conversation and hang up, tap the red phone button that appears to the left of a name, and then tap **End Call** when it pops up.
4. (Optional) Tap **PRIVATE**, which appears to the right of a name, to have a private conversation with that person. Others involved in the conference call will not be able to hear you speak in this private conversation.
5. When you want to rejoin the conference call, move the iPhone away from your face and tap **Merge Calls**.
6. (Optional) Tap **Swap** to put the current caller on hold and chat with someone else waiting on hold.

Putting a Caller on Hold

If you're in the middle of a call and suddenly need to temporarily halt your conversation, you can put the caller on hold by doing this:

1. Move the iPhone away from your face so you can see its screen.
2. Tap **Hold**. The Hold icon appears highlighted.
3. Tap **Hold** again to return to your initial conversation.

Taking Another Call While Talking to Someone Else

If you're in the middle of a call and someone else calls, you have three choices. First, you can ignore the incoming call. Second, you can put your current call on hold and then answer the incoming call. Third, you can end your current call and answer the incoming call.

To choose one of these options, do the following while you're on a call:

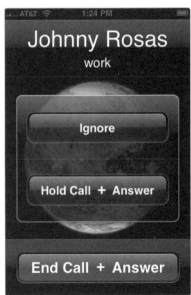

1. When an incoming call comes in, move the iPhone away from your face so you can see its screen. The phone number or person's name (if you've stored it in the Contacts program) of the incoming call appears, along with a menu of three buttons, as shown in Figure 15-7.
2. Tap **Ignore** to send the incoming call directly to your voicemail.
3. Tap **Hold Call + Answer** to switch calls and talk exclusively to the incoming caller. After you answer a call, you can swap callers (put the new caller on hold and go back to your first caller) or merge the new caller into a conference call.
4. Tap **End Call + Answer** to hang up on the current caller and talk to the incoming caller.

FIGURE 15-7: *When an incoming call interrupts your current conversation, you'll have three options for handling that new call.*

Viewing Your Contacts

In the middle of a conversation, someone may ask you for another person's email address or phone number. If you've stored this information in the Contacts program, you can view this information without having to end your call. To view the Contacts screen during a phone call, do this:

1. Move the iPhone away from your face so you can see its screen.
2. Tap **Contacts**. The Contacts screen appears.
3. Tap the person's name to view his or her information.

Additional Ideas for Talking on Your iPhone

Using the speakerphone can be particularly handy when you're driving and you don't want to hold your iPhone against your ear, so you can keep both hands on the steering wheel. The Mute feature is also useful for times when you want to say something that you don't really want the caller to hear. You can pretend to make a call to your boss and launch into a tirade of insults (with the Mute feature turned on, of course) so that your co-workers will think you're brave (or just extremely foolhardy).

16 Sending and Receiving Text Messages

To contact someone immediately, you'll usually make a phone call. However, sometimes you or the other person can't speak on the phone (maybe the person is in a library, a classroom, or a business meeting). In that case, you can still contact that person by sending him or her a text message.

A *text message* (also called an *SMS*, for *short message service*) is a short message that you type and send directly to another person's mobile phone number. (Sending a text message to a non–mobile phone number won't work and will return an error message.) You can also send audio (using the Voice Memos app explained in Project 36) and pictures (captured through the built-in camera) via text messages. Sending audio and picture files is known as *MMS*, for multimedia messaging service. Just remember that not all mobile phones support MMS, so your message may not be delivered.

Students and bored co-workers often text message each other so they don't bother anyone around them. Other people text message rather than make an actual phone call because they enjoy the whole text messaging process. (Then again, some people have been known to walk into walls or oncoming traffic because they're too busy text messaging to pay attention to their surroundings—so be careful when you decide to read or write text messages.)

Project goal: Learn how to write, send, and read text messages with your iPhone.

What You'll Be Using

To learn how to text message with your iPhone, you need to use the following:

 The Messages application

 The Contacts application

Sending Text Messages

The two parts of any text message are the message itself and the mobile phone number to which you want to send that message. You can type a phone number or tap a phone number saved in your Contacts program. Each time you send or receive a text message from the same person (identified by his or her mobile phone number), your iPhone stores that message in a list.

To write and send a text message, do this:

1. From the Home screen, tap **Messages**. The Messages screen appears, listing all your text messaging conversations, as shown in Figure 16-1. (The number of unread text messages appears in parentheses next to the *Messages* heading.)
2. Tap the New Message icon (the square with the pen) in the upper-right corner of the screen. A New Message screen appears, as shown in Figure 16-2.
3. Type a phone number in the To text box, or tap the plus sign that appears in the blue circle to the right of the To text box to display the Contacts screen, where you can tap the name of the person you want to receive your text message.
4. Tap the message text box and type a message.

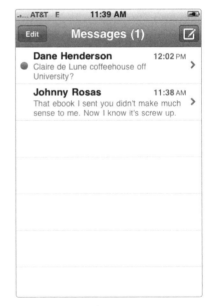

FIGURE 16-1: *The Messages screen displays all your current text message conversations.*

5.   Tap **Send** to send your text
      message.

Replying to a Text Message

If you receive a text message from someone, you can reply to that message without bothering to type a phone number or
selecting a name. To reply to a text message, do this:

1.   From the Home screen, tap
      Messages. The Messages screen
      appears (see Figure 16-1), dis-
      playing all your text message
      conversations.
2.   Find and tap the message to which
      you'd like to reply. You will see your
      previous messages to and from this
      person, as shown in Figure 16-3.
3.   Tap the text box at the very bottom
      of the screen. The virtual keyboard
      appears.
4.   Type a message and tap **Send**.
      Your iPhone sends the text
      message.

Sending a Text Message from the Contacts Program

You can also send a text message
through the Contacts program. Suppose
you've just looked up information about
someone stored in your Contacts program, and you want to send that person a
text message. Rather than exit the Contacts program and load the Messages
application, do this:

1.   From the Home screen, tap
      Contacts. The Contacts screen
      appears.
2.   Tap the name of the person to
      which you want to send a text
      message. An Info screen appears,
      listing the person's information. If
      you have stored a mobile phone

FIGURE 16-2: *The New Message screen appears with the virtual keyboard.*

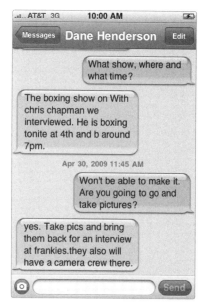

FIGURE 16-3: *Previous text messages appear in dialogue balloons.*

number for that person, a Message button will appear, as shown in Figure 16-4.

3. Tap **Message**. A New Message screen appears with a phone number already included for you.

4. Type a message in the text box and tap **Send** to send your text message.

Sending a Picture

Through the magic of MMS, you can now send a picture with the Messages app. This picture can be something you've already stored on your iPhone, or it can be a new picture that you've captured through the built-in camera.

To send a picture as a message, do this:

1. From the New Message screen, tap the Camera icon that appears to the left of the text box for typing a message, as shown in Figure 16-5. Take Photo, Choose Existing, and Cancel buttons appear at the bottom of the screen, as shown in Figure 16-6.

2. (Optional) Tap **Take Photo** to take a picture using the built-in camera.

3. (Optional) Tap **Choose Existing** to display the Photo Albums where you can scroll and tap a picture you want to use.

4. Type any text message you want to send with your picture, which appears in a message balloon like the one shown in Figure 16-7. If you're creating a new message, you may need to specify the phone number of the recipient. When you're done, tap **Send**.

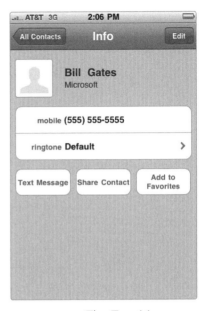

FIGURE 16-4: *The Text Message button lets you send a text message from the Contacts application.*

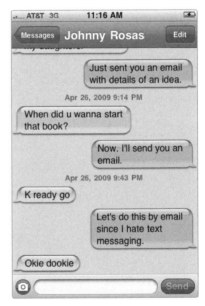

FIGURE 16-5: *The Camera icon lets you select a picture to send as a message.*

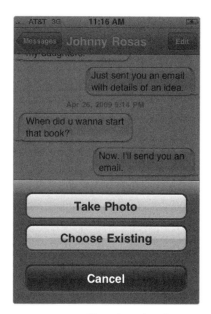

FIGURE 16-6: Tapping the Camera icon displays options for capturing a new picture or using an existing one.

FIGURE 16-7: A thumbnail view of your chosen picture appears in a message balloon.

Sending an Audio File

If you recorded something through the Voice Memos app, you can send that audio file as a message. Since speaking is easier than typing for most people, this can be a fast way to communicate without bothering someone with a disruptive phone call. To send an audio file, do this:

1. From the Home screen, tap **Voice Memos**. The Voice Memos screen appears.
2. Tap the button in the lower-right corner of the screen that displays three horizontal lines. The Voice Memos screen appears, listing all your recorded audio files.
3. Tap **Share**. Email Voice Memo and MMS buttons appear at the bottom of the screen, as shown in Figure 16-8.

FIGURE 16-8: You can send an audio file through the Voice Memos app.

4. Tap **MMS**. A New MMS screen appears, as shown in Figure 16-9.
5. Tap in the **To** text box at the top of the screen and type the phone number of the recipient of your message. (You can also tap the plus sign to select a number stored in the Contacts app.)
6. Tap **Send**.

Viewing Text Messages

Every time you send or receive text messages, your iPhone saves those messages so you can review them later. If your text message exchanges are lengthy, you may need to scroll up and down the screen to read your entire dialogue.

While reading a text message list, you have three options:

▶ Telephone that person and talk using your actual voice.

▶ Store that person's phone number in the Contacts program.

▶ View that person's information if you have already stored his or her phone number in the Contacts program.

Calling Someone from a Text Message

When viewing past text messages, you may decide that you want to talk to the person. To call a person you've been text messaging, do this:

1. From the Home screen, tap **Messages**. The Messages screen appears, listing all your text messaging conversations (see Figure 16-1).
2. Tap the text message conversation that you want to view. The list appears, as shown in Figure 16-10.

FIGURE 16-9: *An audio file appears as a Quicktime file icon in a message balloon.*

FIGURE 16-10: *The Call button appears at the top of every text message list.*

3. Tap **Call** at the top of the screen. (You may need to scroll up to see the Call button if a large number of text messages appear.) Your iPhone dials the phone number from which you received the text messages.

Saving a Name and Number from a Text Message

If somebody sends you a text message and the person is not in your Contacts program, you can still receive and reply to those text messages. However, if this person is important, you may want to store his or her contact information in the Contacts program.

To store information about someone who has sent you a text message, do this:

1. From the Home screen, tap **Messages**. The Messages screen appears, listing all your text messaging conversations (see Figure 16-1).
2. Tap the text message conversation that you want to view. The text message list appears on the screen (see Figure 16-10).
3. Tap **Add to Contacts** at the top of the screen. (You may need to scroll up to find the Add to Contacts button if you have a large number of text messages. If you see a Contact Info button, you've already stored this mobile phone number in the Contacts program.) Create New Contact and Add to Existing Contact buttons appear, as shown in Figure 16-11.

FIGURE 16-11: *Two options appear for storing a phone number in the Contacts program.*

4. Tap **Create New Contact**. The New Contact screen appears, where you can type the person's name and other information.
5. (Optional) Tap **Add to Existing Contact**. The Contacts screen appears, where you can tap an existing name to store his or her phone number.

Viewing Contact Information

After you have stored one or more names and phone numbers in the Contacts program, you can view a person's information while reading his or her text messages by doing this:

1. From the Home screen, tap **Messages**. The Messages screen appears, listing all your text messaging conversations (see Figure 16-1).

2. Tap the text message conversation that you want to view. The text message list appears on the screen (see Figure 16-10).
3. Tap **Contact Info** at the top of the screen. (If you see an Add to Contacts button, that means you have not yet stored this mobile phone number in the Contacts program.) An Info screen appears, listing additional information you may have stored about that person.
4. Tap the back button in the upper-left corner of the screen to return to the Messages screen.

Clearing and Deleting Text Messages

When you start receiving text messages, your iPhone sorts them by phone number so that you can read all text messages received from each cell phone number. However, the more text messages you receive, the more cluttered your collection of text messages will get. To reduce the number of text messages stored on your iPhone, you can clear all text messages sent from a phone number or delete an entire collection of text messages from a phone number.

Clearing Text Messages

Once you start sending messages, you'll wind up with long lists of old messages from specific people. You can choose to clear out all your stored messages or just select the messages that you want to delete.

To clear one or more messages from a particular mobile phone number, do this:

1. From the Home screen, tap **Messages**. The Messages screen appears, listing all your text messaging conversations (see Figure 16-1). (If you just see messages from a specific conversation, tap the Messages button in the upper-left corner of the screen to view the entire list of conversations stored on your iPhone.)
2. Tap a conversation that contains the messages you want to clear. The screen displays all messages for that phone number.
3. Tap **Edit**. Radio buttons appear to the left of each message, as shown in Figure 16-12.

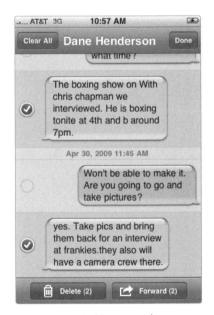

FIGURE 16-12: *You can choose which messages to delete.*

4. (Optional) Tap **Clear All**. A red Clear Conversation button appears. Tap **Clear Conversation** to delete all messages.
5. Tap the radio button that appears to the left of each message that you want to delete. Checkmarks appear next to each selected message.
6. Tap **Delete** at the bottom of the screen. Your selected messages disappear for good.

✳ *NOTE:* **If you tap the Forward button in step 6, you can forward a message to another mobile phone number.**

Deleting a Text Message List

If you want to wipe out both your text messages and the mobile phone number from which you've been receiving those text messages, you can delete an entire text message list. This can come in handy if you no longer need to store someone's mobile phone number (because you no longer need to talk to that person or because that number has been changed).

To delete an entire text message list, do this:

1. From the Home screen, tap **Messages**. The Messages screen appears, listing text messaging conversations (see Figure 16-1).
2. Tap **Edit** in the upper-left corner of the screen. A white minus sign inside a red circle appears to the left of each text message conversation.
3. Tap the red circle next to the text message conversation that you want to delete. A red Delete button appears, as shown in Figure 16-13.
4. Tap **Delete**. Your iPhone deletes the chosen text message list and the associated mobile phone number. (If you suddenly change your mind and don't want to delete a message, just tap the white minus sign in the red circle again.)
5. Tap **Done** in the upper-left corner of the screen.

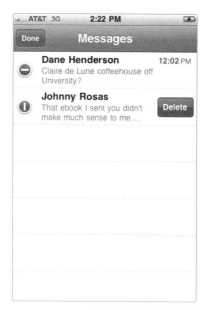

FIGURE 16-13: *Tapping the red circle displays a Delete button.*

Additional Ideas for Using Text Messages

Messaging can be a less intrusive and more reliable way to communicate with someone. Rather than leave a voicemail that someone might not understand or listen to, you can type a message, send a picture, or send an audio file so he or she can read, see, or hear your message right away.

Messages are perfect for communicating with someone without the hassle of making an actual phone call. For example, you might want to message someone to send a note of encouragement right before he goes to an important business meeting or takes a crucial exam. That way, you can send your message without interrupting his concentration.

Sending messages is also handy for communicating short bits of information that would seem trivial to ask via a phone call, such as reminding your spouse to pick up eggs and milk when he's on his way to the supermarket or letting someone know that you're running late to an appointment.

If you're on vacation, send pictures of yourself relaxing on the beach or visiting an exotic location. Use messages wisely, and you can increase your communication with others at your convenience.

17

Reviewing Your Bill and Other Information

After using your iPhone, you might be curious to know how much storage space is available, how many songs or pictures you've saved, how many minutes you've used to make calls, or even what your phone number is. Fortunately, your iPhone saves this information and much more, so you can review the technical details of your iPhone at any time.

Project goal: Learn how to view information about your iPhone and iPhone account.

What You'll Be Using

To browse information about your iPhone, you need to use the following:

 The Settings application

Finding Your Phone Number

Every iPhone has its own telephone number, but this number is easy to forget since most people rarely call themselves. To find out your iPhone's number right away so you can give it to someone else, do this:

1. From the Home screen, tap **Settings**. The Settings screen appears.
2. Scroll down and tap **Phone**. The Phone screen appears with your number displayed at the top, as shown in Figure 17-1.

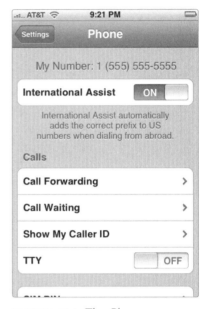

FIGURE 17-1: *The Phone screen displays your phone number.*

Viewing Your Account Information

You most likely have a subscription plan with a cellular telephone company that provides service for your iPhone. Since you may have a limited number of minutes available each month, you might be curious to know how many minutes you've used up and how many are remaining.

To find this information, you can access your account by doing this:

1. From the Home screen, tap **Settings**. The Settings screen appears.
2. Tap **Phone**. The Phone screen appears.
3. Scroll down to the last button on the Phone screen, which will display your cellular network's name, such as AT&T Services. Tap this button, and the Services screen appears, as shown in Figure 17-2.

4. Tap the **View My Minutes** button to receive a text message showing how many available minutes you have on your account.

5. Tap **MyAccount**. This loads a web page where you can view your account information such as your current rate plan and details of your previous bills. (If you have not yet set up an account with a cellular network provider, you must create one before you can view your account information.)

Checking Your iPhone's Usage

By viewing your iPhone usage periodically, you can determine how much battery life you have left before you need to recharge. You can also see how much time you've spent recently talking on the phone and sending and receiving data. This could be useful if you lent your iPhone to your child to do research for school and you want to see if he spent an hour talking on the phone instead.

To view your iPhone usage at a glance, do this:

1. From the Home screen, tap **Settings**. The Settings screen appears.

2. Tap **General**. The General screen appears.

3. Tap **Usage**. The Usage screen appears, as shown in Figure 17-3.

4. (Optional) Scroll down and tap **Reset Statistics** to clear all the information from the Usage screen.

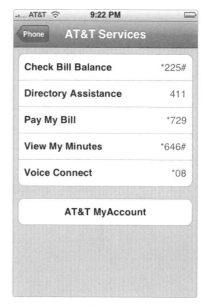

FIGURE 17-2: The Services screen displays options for learning more about your account.

FIGURE 17-3: The Usage screen tracks your iPhone use.

Three categories of information are displayed on the Usage screen:

- **Time since last full charge** This field tells you how much time you've spent on your iPhone since you last charged it. Viewing this information periodically can show you how long your battery lasts between rechargings.

- **Call Time** This field lists the time you've spent talking since the last recharge and since you first started using the iPhone.

- **Cellular Network Data** This field displays how much data you've sent and received on your iPhone.

Viewing the Technical Details of Your iPhone

Some of the technical details you can review about your iPhone include the name of your cellular network provider (such as AT&T), the total storage and available storage capacity of your iPhone, and the model and serial number of your iPhone.

To view the technical details of your iPhone, do this:

1. From the Home screen, tap **Settings**. The Settings screen appears.
2. Tap **General**. The General screen appears.
3. Tap **About**. The About screen appears, as shown in Figure 17-4.

To view all the information on your About screen, you may need to scroll up and down. (See Project 3 for more information about controlling the iPhone's user interface.) The About screen displays the following information:

FIGURE 17-4: *The About screen displays technical details of your iPhone.*

- **Network** The name of your cellular telephone company
- **Songs** The number of audio files stored on your iPhone

- ▶ **Videos**   The number of video files stored on your iPhone
- ▶ **Photos**   The number of digital pictures stored on your iPhone
- ▶ **Capacity**   The total storage capacity of your iPhone
- ▶ **Available**   The free storage space available
- ▶ **Version**   The version number of your iPhone software
- ▶ **Carrier**   The name of your phone carrier (usually identical to the Network name) along with the version number of its system
- ▶ **Serial Number**   The unique serial number of your iPhone
- ▶ **Model**   The model number that identifies the type of iPhone you have
- ▶ **Wi-Fi Address**   The Wi-Fi address your iPhone uses to connect to a Wi-Fi hotspot
- ▶ **Bluetooth**   The Bluetooth address your iPhone uses to connect to other Bluetooth devices
- ▶ **IMEI**   The International Mobile Equipment Identity number of your iPhone—if you lose your iPhone, you can contact your cellular network provider and have it block this IMEI number from making any calls. That way, you can keep someone from finding your lost iPhone and ringing up charges.
- ▶ **ICCID**   The Integrated Circuit Card ID of your SIM (Subscriber Identity Module) card, which allows you access to your cellular telephone network
- ▶ **Modem Firmware**   The version number of your iPhone's firmware—this can be important to determine whether your firmware needs updating

Additional Ideas for Reviewing Your iPhone Information

The technical details of your iPhone (such as the model number or version number) might seem irrelevant, but you should take the time to jot down this information and store it in a safe place. That way, if you lose your iPhone, you'll be able to provide technical identification numbers to the authorities in case they find it so they can give your iPhone back to you.

If you keep storing songs, videos, and pictures on your iPhone, review your storage capacity periodically so you won't run out of room. You don't want to try to capture a picture of a UFO or the Loch Ness monster that could be worth a million bucks, only to find out your iPhone can't save the picture since it ran out of free space three days ago.

18

Creating Ringtones

A *ringtone* is a unique sound, typically a fragment of a popular song, that you can set as your default ringtone to notify you of a call or that you can associate with a specific person in your Contacts program. When ordinary people call, you'll hear a default audio ring, but if you've set a ringtone for a person in your Contacts program, you'll hear that particular ringtone only when that person calls. You can use unique ringtones to identify certain types of people (such as customers or family members) or to identify a specific person such as your boss, stockbroker, or significant other.

The most common way to get a ringtone is to buy it through the iTunes Store, usually for 99 cents. However, there are ways to create ringtones that won't cost you anything, and you'll learn about them in this chapter.

Project goal: Learn how to create ringtones from music already stored on your computer.

What You'll Be Using

To create ringtones for your iPhone, you need to use the following:

 iTunes (on your Mac or PC)   The Contacts application

 Garageband '09 (on your Mac)

Creating Ringtones in iTunes

After you buy a favorite song, you can turn it into a ringtone.

✳ **NOTE: You can convert only purchased songs into ringtones. If you burn songs from an audio CD and store them in iTunes, you won't be able to convert those songs into ringtones.**

To turn a purchased song in iTunes into a ringtone, do this from your computer:

1. Open iTunes on your computer.
2. Click **Music** under the LIBRARY category in the left pane. A list of all your stored songs appears in the main iTunes window.
3. Right-click a purchased song that you want to turn into a ringtone. A pop-up menu appears, as shown in Figure 18-1.

FIGURE 18-1: *Right-clicking a song displays a pop-up menu with the Create Ringtone command.*

4. Choose **Create Ringtone**. The bottom of the iTunes window displays your selected song along with a highlighted 15 second segment, as shown in Figure 18-2.

FIGURE 18-2: *Your ringtone appears at the bottom of the iTunes window.*

5. (Optional) Drag this highlighted segment left or right to select the part of the song you want to use.
6. (Optional) Drag the left or right edges of this highlighted segment to define the length of time you want your ringtone to play.
7. Click the **Preview** button to hear your ringtone.
8. Click the **Buy** button when you're ready to buy your ringtone for 99 cents.

Creating Ringtones in GarageBand '09

The problem with creating ringtones in iTunes is that you can convert only songs you purchased through iTunes into ringtones. If you just imported a song from an audio CD, and you try to use it as a ringtone, iTunes will display an error message saying that it can convert only purchased songs, indirectly scolding you for not doing your part to spend money at the iTunes Store.

If you use a Macintosh, however, you can create free ringtones with the GarageBand program. Use GarageBand to convert your song into a ringtone by doing this:

1. Open GarageBand on your computer. The GarageBand opening screen appears, as shown in Figure 18-3.

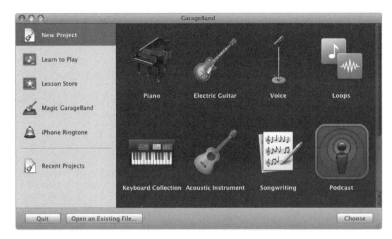

FIGURE 18-3: *The GarageBand opening screen offers lots of options.*

2. Click **Podcast**. A dialog appears, asking you to name your file.
3. Type a descriptive name (such as the song title that you want to convert into a ringtone) and click **Create**. A new GarageBand window appears, as shown in Figure 18-4.

FIGURE 18-4: *The GarageBand window*

4.   Open iTunes on your computer.

5.   Drag a song from iTunes to the Podcast Track in the upper-left corner of the GarageBand window. GarageBand displays your song in a separate track.

6.   Click the Cycle Region button (which looks like two arrows curved in a circle) that appears at the bottom of the screen to the right of the fast-forward button (see Figure 18-5). The highlighted cycle region appears (in yellow) at the top of the tracks in the GarageBand window. Typically the cycle region defines the first 8 seconds of a song.

FIGURE 18-5: *The Cycle Region button defines a cycle region area of a song.*

7.   Drag the cycle region area to define a shorter or longer period of time, such as 10 or 15 seconds.

8.   Choose **Share ▸ Send Ringtone to iTunes**. Your ringtone appears in the iTunes window under the Ringtones category.

9.   Choose **GarageBand ▸ Quit GarageBand**, and then click **Don't Save** to exit the GarageBand program.

✳ **NOTE:** You can create ringtones with earlier versions of GarageBand as well. These instructions are specific to GarageBand '09.

Additional Ideas for Using Ringtones

After you create a ringtone on your computer, you'll have to sync your iPhone to your computer to transfer it (see Project 12). You can then assign a ringtone to a contact (see Project 14).

While most people use song fragments for their ringtones, you can use any audio recording as a ringtone, so get a copy of various sound effects and let your imagination go wild. Grab a sound effect of a man snoring, and use that as a ringtone to identify your boss. (Don't worry. If your boss is within earshot, he'll never be calling you, so he will never hear the snoring ringtone.)

Rather than use sound effects, you can also use parts of recorded speeches as ringtones. Assign part of Martin Luther King, Jr.'s "I have a dream" speech as a ringtone to identify when a prominent business leader or politician calls you. Use your favorite movie quotes as a ringtone, such as Clint Eastwood saying, "You've got to ask yourself one question, 'Do I feel lucky?' Well, do ya, punk?" Between your favorite songs, sound effects, and speeches, you're sure to find the perfect ringtone for everyone who calls you most often.

PART 4

Enjoying Music, Pictures, and Movies

19 Listening to Music

Your iPhone comes with external speakers, so you can listen to your favorite songs by holding your iPhone up to your ear (so you can pretend that you're actually making a call). Or you can listen through ear buds or headphones that you plug into the audio output jack at the top.

As soon as you store your favorite songs on your iPhone, you'll probably want to start listening to them, so this chapter will show you how to do that right away.

Project goal: Learn how to play audio files on your iPhone.

What You'll Be Using

To learn how to listen to music with your iPhone, you need to use the following:

 The iPod application

Playing Your Songs

After you've stored songs on your iPhone, you can listen to the songs stored in your music library in two ways:

▶ In alphabetical order by song title

▶ In random order

✳ **NOTE:** You'll learn how to play groups of songs in Project 20.

Playing Songs in Alphabetical Order

Your iPhone stores songs in alphabetical order, which is handy when you're trying to find a particular song by name. If you want to play every song in your music library, tap the first song in the alphabetical list and your iPhone will play that song, and then all the songs that follow it in the list. If you select a song from the middle of the list, such as the first song whose title begins with the letter *E*, your iPhone will play all songs whose titles start with the letters *E* through *Z* and then cycle back to the beginning with all song titles starting with the letter *A*.

To play music in alphabetical order, do this:

1. From the Home screen, tap **iPod**. The iPod screen appears.

2. Tap **Songs**. The Songs screen appears, listing songs in alphabetical order, with the entire alphabet displayed vertically on the right side of the screen, as shown in Figure 19-1.

3. Scroll down to a song you want to hear, or tap a letter on the alphabetical list on the right side of the screen to see song titles that begin with that letter.

4. Tap the song title that you want to hear first. Your iPhone plays the chosen song, and will then play the rest of the songs on the list in alphabetical order. When it reaches the end of the list, it starts all over again from the top, starting with the letter *A*.

FIGURE 19-1: *The Songs screen lists all your songs in alphabetical order.*

Playing Songs in Random Order

If you don't want to hear songs in alphabetical order, you can listen to songs in random order by doing this:

1. From the Home screen, tap **iPod**. The iPod screen appears.
2. Tap **Songs**. The Songs screen appears (see Figure 19-1).
3. Tap **Shuffle** at the top of the screen. Your iPhone starts playing the songs in your music library in random order.

Choosing the First Song to Start Playing in Random Order

If you open the Songs screen and tap **Shuffle**, your iPhone will randomly pick a song to start playing first. If you want to choose the first song to hear before letting your iPhone play the rest of your music in random order, do this:

1. From the Home screen, tap **iPod**. The iPod screen appears.
2. Tap **Songs**. The Songs screen appears (see Figure 19-1).
3. Scroll down until you reach the song you want to hear, or tap a letter in the alphabetical list on the right side of the screen.
4. Tap the song you want to hear first. Your chosen song appears in the Now Playing screen, which displays its album artwork.
5. Tap the screen to display the position slider at the top, along with a shuffle icon, as shown in Figure 19-2. (If you tap the screen again, the position slider and shuffle icon disappear from view.)
6. Tap the shuffle icon. Your iPhone plays the currently displayed song and then randomly chooses the next song to play from your music library.

FIGURE 19-2: *Tapping the Now Playing screen displays a position slider and shuffle icon at the top of the screen.*

Controlling Your Music

When your iPhone plays a song, you have several options for controlling the song or viewing information about it. If you want, you can ignore all these options and just listen to music, but by learning what you can do while listening to a song, you can better control your listening experience.

Adjusting the Volume and Pausing

The most obvious way to adjust a song is by changing the volume. The Volume Up and Volume Down buttons on the side of the iPhone let you adjust the volume, but while each song is playing, you'll see a horizontal volume slider at the bottom of the Now Playing screen that you can slide to the left or right with your fingertip, as shown in Figure 19-3.

* **NOTE:** If you press the Volume Up and Volume Down buttons on the side of the iPhone, you'll see the volume slider move left and right.

Previous / Pause / Next / Volume slider

FIGURE 19-3: A volume control appears at the bottom of the Now Playing screen.

If you need to pause a song, tap the pause button, which then changes to a play button. When you're ready to hear your song again, tap the play button.

Skipping Songs

Sometimes you may hear a song and decide that you want to skip over it. To skip a song, do one of the following:

▶ Tap the next button.

▶ Press the mic button on the iPhone headset twice.

Playing the Previous Song

Rather than skip a song, you might want to play the previous song again. If you tap the previous button twice in rapid succession, you can play the song that you heard prior to the current song.

Suppose, for example, you listened a song by Jessica Simpson and are now listening to a song by the Rolling Stones. Tapping the previous button twice will jump back to play the Jessica Simpson song from the beginning.

Choosing Which Part of a Song to Play

Your iPhone always plays a song starting from the beginning, but you can start listening to a song at a different position, such as in the middle of the song.

To choose a position to start playing a song, do this:

1. Follow the steps in "Playing Your Songs" on page 152 to listen to a song.
2. (Optional) Tap the previous button to start playing a song from the beginning after it has already started playing.
3. Tap the screen to display the position slider at the top of the screen (see Figure 19-2).
4. Drag the position slider left or right to listen to a different part of the song.

Repeating Songs

When you tap the screen while a song is playing, the position slider appears near the top of the screen. In the lower-left corner of the position slider is the repeat icon (see Figure 19-2).

This repeat icon can appear in one of three ways, as shown in Figure 19-4:

▶ **Off**   The repeat icon is not highlighted and all songs play only once.

▶ **On**   The repeat icon is highlighted in blue and keeps playing all the songs in your library or playlist indefinitely.

▶ **Single**   The number 1 appears on the blue highlighted repeat icon, which causes the currently playing song to keep playing over and over again.

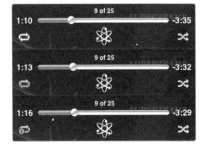

FIGURE 19-4: *The repeat icon lets you choose to repeat a song or a playlist.*

Each time you tap the repeat icon, it changes; keep tapping it until it displays the repeat cycle that you want for your song or playlist.

Navigating Between Screens While Playing Music

When you play a song, you can continue doing other things on your iPhone, such as playing games, looking up names in your Contacts, or browsing the Internet. (Your iPhone temporarily shuts off your music when you're making an actual phone call.) While you're listening to a song, you can either switch to another program altogether or view other screens in the music program.

Running Another App

To run another app while continuing to play music, do this:

1. Follow the steps in "Playing Your Songs" on page 152 to start listening to a song.
2. Press the Home button. The Home screen appears. From here, you can tap the icon for any app to start using that app while listening to music.
3. To view your currently playing song again, press the Home button to return to the Home screen, and then tap **iPod**.

Viewing Another Part of the iPod Screen

To navigate your way around the various music screens in the iPod application while continuing to play music, do this:

1. Follow the steps in "Playing Your Songs" on page 152 to start listening to a song.
2. Tap the back arrow button that appears in the upper-left corner of the screen (see Figure 19-3). The Songs screen appears with a Now Playing button in the upper-right corner. At this point, you can tap any of the icons at the bottom of the screen to view other screens, such as your list of videos.
3. Tap **Now Playing** in the upper-right corner of any iPod screen (see Figure 19-1) to see the Now Playing screen for the currently playing song.

Additional Ideas for Listening to Music

Listening to music can turn your iPhone into a portable jukebox so you can hear your favorite songs any time no matter where you go. Of course, you don't have to limit yourself to music. You can listen to inspirational or motivational speeches and turn your iPhone into a private and portable audio-educational center. Add recordings of foreign-language tutorials and learn to speak another language. The more audio files you store on your iPhone, the larger your audio collection will get and the more likely you'll be able to listen to everything in your music library without hearing the same thing twice.

Turn Your iPhone into a Musical Instrument

Almost everybody loves music of one kind or another (although nearly everyone can get just as passionate about the types of music they don't like). While listening to music can be fun, you might want to go one step further and learn how to make your own music.

Rather than buy or rent an expensive instrument, download one of many apps that can turn your iPhone into everything from a piano or drum kit to a kazoo or a flute. While these apps aren't a substitute for a real instrument, they can help you make simple music while also learning the basics of different types of instruments.

The next time you get tired of listening to recorded music, start making your own. Who knows? You just might find yourself playing music more than just listening to it.

Mini Piano *http://jyproduct.webhop.net/jyblog/index.php/minipiano/*

Kalimba *http://discovolos.com/Discovolos/Discovolos.html*

You can turn your iPhone into a keyboard or other musical instrument.

20

Listening to Groups of Songs

If you have a large music library on your iPhone, listening to every song could take hours or even days. Rather than listen to all your songs, you may want to listen to a handful of songs, such as songs by a particular recording artist or perhaps a collection of songs that you like best for driving, meditating, or exercising.

Project goal: Learn how to create playlists and play a selected part of your audio file collection stored on your iPhone.

What You'll Be Using

To learn how to create playlists and listen to particular music on your iPhone, you need to use the following:

 The iPod application

 iTunes (on your Mac or PC)

 The iPhone USB cable

Creating a Playlist

A *playlist* is a collection of songs that you've grouped together for any reason, such as a list of your favorite heavy metal songs, the best songs to hear while you're meditating, or some old favorite songs from a specific year.

You can create a playlist in three ways:

▶ Create an on-the-go playlist on your iPhone.

▶ Create a Genius playlist on your iPhone.

▶ Create a playlist on your computer using iTunes.

Creating an On-the-Go Playlist

Making a playlist on your iPhone is handy when you're in the mood for listening to certain songs and don't have time to create a playlist through iTunes on your computer. You can create only one *on-the-go* playlist. After you create an on-the-go playlist, you can later edit or clear songs on the list.

To create an on-the-go playlist, do this:

1. From the Home screen, tap **iPod**. The iPod screen appears.
2. Tap **Playlists** at the bottom of the screen. The Playlists screen appears. If you've created other playlists and synchronized them through iTunes, you'll see those playlists displayed as well, as shown in Figure 20-1.
3. Tap **On-The-Go**. The Songs screen appears, where you can choose the songs you want to add to the on-the-go playlist, as shown in Figure 20-2.

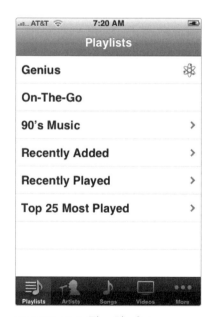

FIGURE 20-1: *The Playlists screen lists all available playlists.*

4.	Tap the plus sign to the right of each song you want to add to your on-the-go playlist. (You may need to scroll down to see all your songs.) Each song title you choose appears dimmed to let you know that you've chosen it for your playlist.

5.	When you're done adding songs to your on-the-go playlist, tap **Done** in the upper-right corner of the screen. The On-The-Go screen appears with a list of all your songs, as shown in Figure 20-3.

6.	At this point, you can tap **Shuffle** to play your entire on-the-go playlist randomly, or you can tap a song name to play it first and then let your iPhone play the songs in alphabetical order.

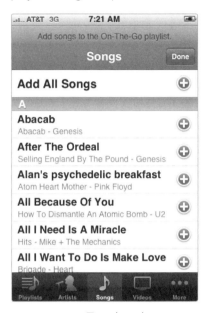

FIGURE 20-2: Tap the plus sign next to all the songs you want to include in your on-the-go playlist.

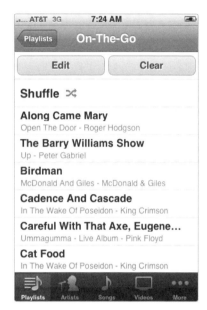

FIGURE 20-3: The On-The-Go screen lists all songs in your playlist.

Deleting an On-the-Go Playlist

You can have only one on-the-go playlist at a time on your iPhone, so if you want to change it, you can either edit individual songs on the playlist or clear the whole thing out and start over again. To clear out your entire on-the-go playlist, do this:

1.	From the Home screen, tap **iPod**. The iPod screen appears.

2.	Tap **Playlists**. The Playlists screen appears (see Figure 20-1).

3.	Tap **On-The-Go**. The On-The-Go screen appears.

4.	Tap **Clear** at the top of the screen, and then tap **Clear Playlist** at the bottom of the screen to clear out your entire on-the-go playlist.

Editing an On-the-Go Playlist

If you want to delete or add some songs to your on-the-go playlist, you don't have to clear the whole thing out and start from scratch. It's much easier to delete and add songs individually. To edit your on-the-go playlist, do this:

1. From the Home screen, tap **iPod**. The iPod screen appears.
2. Tap **Playlists**. The Playlists screen appears (see Figure 20-1).
3. Tap **On-The-Go**. The On-The-Go screen appears.
4. Tap **Edit**. Red circles with white minus signs appear to the left of each song title, and three horizontal bars appear to the right of each song title.
5. (Optional) Slide the three horizontal bars to the right of a song up or down to rearrange the order of your songs.
6. Tap the white minus sign in the red circle next to a song you want to remove from the list. A red Delete button appears to the right of the song, as shown in Figure 20-4.
7. Tap **Delete** to remove the song from the on-the-go playlist (or tap the minus sign again to keep the song in your playlist).

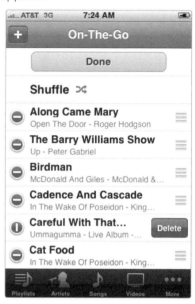

FIGURE 20-4: *Editing the On-The-Go playlist*

* **NOTE:** Deleting a song from the playlist does not delete the song from your iPhone.

8. Tap the plus sign in the upper-left corner of the screen. The Songs screen appears.
9. Tap the plus sign to the right of each song you want to add to your on-the-go playlist. Repeat for each song you want to add.
10. Tap **Done** in the upper-right corner of the Songs screen. The On-The-Go screen appears again.
11. Tap **Done** at the top of the On-The-Go screen.

Creating a Genius Playlist

If you like a particular song, you may also like similar songs recorded by other artists. To help you find similar songs stored on your iPhone, you can create a *Genius playlist*. A Genius playlist lets you choose a song and then tries to identify similar songs. So if you picked a hip-hop song, the Genius playlist would look for similar songs and likely ignore love ballads or country music.

✳ *NOTE:* Before you can create a Genius playlist on your iPhone, you must turn on the Genius feature in iTunes on your computer, which you can do by choosing Store ▸Turn On Genius.

To create a Genius playlist, do this:

1. Play a song that you like and want to use as the basis for your Genius playlist.
2. Tap the screen to display the position slider and Genius icon (the little atomic symbol), as shown in Figure 20-5.
3. (Optional) You can also create a Genius playlist by tapping the Playlists icon at the bottom of the iPod screen. When a Playlists screen appears, tap the Genius icon.
4. Tap the Genius icon. The Genius screen appears, listing up to 25 songs on your iPhone that go with the song that's currently playing, as shown in Figure 20-6.

Genius icon

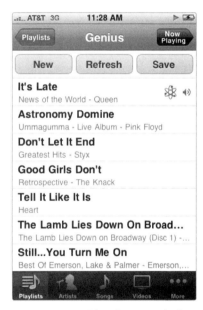

FIGURE 20-5: The Genius icon appears under the position slider after you tap the screen.

FIGURE 20-6: The Genius playlist chooses several songs that are similar to the song you chose (this song appears at the top of the list, highlighted by the Genius icon).

5. (Optional) Tap **Refresh** to change the songs on your Genius playlist.

✳ *NOTE:* If you tap New, you can choose a new song on which to base a new Genius playlist.

6. Tap **Save** to save your Genius playlist. The Genius playlist screen displays Refresh and Delete buttons, as shown in Figure 20-7.

Editing a Genius Playlist

After you've created one or more Genius playlists, you can edit a playlist by doing this:

1. From the Home screen, tap **iPod**. The iPod screen appears.
2. Tap **Playlists** at the bottom of the screen. The Playlists screen appears. The song you used to create the Genius playlist appears as the name of your Genius playlist. A Genius icon appears to the right of each Genius playlist name, as shown in Figure 20-8.

✳ **NOTE:** If you tap the Genius icon at the top of the screen, you can create another Genius playlist.

3. Tap the Genius playlist that you want to edit.
4. (Optional) Tap **Refresh** to change the songs on the Genius playlist.
5. (Optional) Tap **Delete** to delete the Genius playlist.

Creating a Playlist with iTunes

When you create a playlist with iTunes on your computer, you'll have to synchronize it with your iPhone, as explained in Project 12. For a fast way to create a playlist with iTunes, do this:

1. Open iTunes on your computer.
2. Click **Music** under the Library category in the left pane of the iTunes window. The right pane displays all the songs currently stored in your iTunes library.

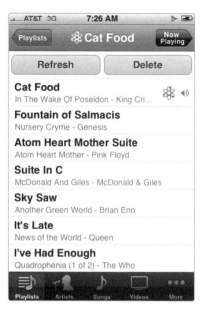

FIGURE 20-7: *The Refresh and Delete buttons appear after you create a Genius playlist.*

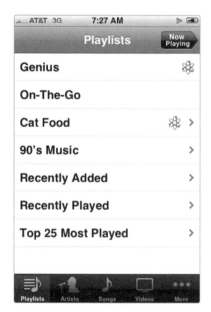

FIGURE 20-8: *You can identify a Genius playlist by the Genius icon that appears to the right of the playlist name.*

3. Hold down ⌘ (Mac) or CTRL (Windows) as you click each song that you want to add to your playlist.

4. Choose **File ▸ New Playlist From Selection**. A new playlist appears under the Playlists category in the left pane.

5. Type a descriptive name for your playlist. Your playlist is now ready to be synchronized with your iPhone.

Playing Songs in a Playlist

When you want to hear songs stored in a specific playlist, do this:

1. From the Home screen, tap **iPod**. The iPod screen appears.
2. Tap **Playlists**. The Playlists screen appears (see Figure 20-1).
3. Tap the playlist that contains the songs you want to hear. Your chosen playlist appears.
4. Tap **Shuffle** or tap the title of the first song you want to hear.

Listening to Songs by Album

In addition to listening to songs that you've added to playlists, you can listen only to songs from the same album. You can find an album in your music collection in two ways: You can browse for the name of the album listed alphabetically, or you can browse albums organized alphabetically by artist.

Searching by Album Name

If you know the name of the album that contains the songs you want to hear, do this:

1. From the Home screen, tap **iPod**. The iPod screen appears.
2. Tap **More** at the bottom of the screen. The More screen appears, as shown in Figure 20-9.
3. Tap **Albums**. The Albums screen appears, as shown in Figure 20-10.
4. Tap the name of an album that you want to hear. A list of one or more songs appears.

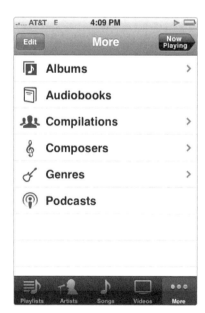

FIGURE 20-9: *The More screen lists different options for choosing the music you want to hear.*

5. Tap **Shuffle** to play the album in a random order, or tap the name of the song you want to hear first.

＊ *NOTE:* **Instead of tapping Albums from the More screen (see Figure 20-9), you can tap Compilations, Composers, or Genres to hear music organized into different compilations, written by different composers, or that fall within a specific genre such as pop or country music.**

Browsing for Albums by Recording Artist

If you want to hear music from a specific recording artist, you can search through all your albums by artist names by following these steps:

1. From the Home screen, tap **iPod**. The iPod screen appears.
2. Rotate your iPhone sideways. All your album covers appear in Cover Flow, as shown in Figure 20-11.

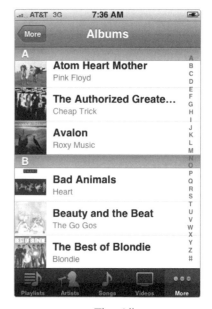

FIGURE 20-10: The Albums screen displays all the albums included in your music library.

FIGURE 20-11: Cover Flow lets you flip through different album covers.

3. Slide your finger right or left across the screen to scroll through your albums. Notice that Cover Flow displays all of a particular artist's album covers sequentially to help you find all songs by that particular artist.

4.   Tap the album cover that contains the songs you want to hear. The album cover flips around to show you the list of songs from that particular album, as shown in Figure 20-12.

FIGURE 20-12: *You can view a list of songs from a particular album.*

5.   Tap the name of the song you want to hear. Your iPhone starts playing the chosen song.

✳ **NOTE:** **To get album artwork, choose Advanced ▸ Get Album Artwork in iTunes. Then transfer the album artwork to your iPhone the next time you sync with iTunes.**

Listening to Other Songs from the Album of the Currently Playing Song

If you're listening to a song and want to hear other songs (stored on your iPhone, of course) from the same album, you can do this:

1.   Play a song. The song plays and displays its album artwork in the Now Playing screen.

2.   Tap the screen, and the playlist icon appears in the upper-right corner, as shown in Figure 20-13.

Playlist icon

FIGURE 20-13: *The playlist icon appears when you tap the Now Playing screen.*

3.   Tap the playlist icon. It spins around and displays the album cover, and a list of all the songs from the same album you have stored on your iPhone appears, as shown in Figure 20-14. Your iPhone now plays all songs starting from the current song all the way to the bottom of the album song list.

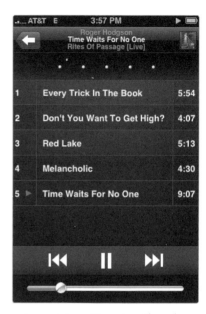

Additional Ideas for Listening to Playlists

Playlists give you a convenient way to group related songs together, even if they have no apparent connection to anyone but you. You might think a tender ballad by Frank Sinatra fits in perfectly with a heavy metal song by Metallica, so why not add these two songs to the same playlist? In addition to creating your

FIGURE 20-14: *Tapping the playlist icon displays all songs from that album.*

own playlists and listening to tunes from it, you can listen to songs from the same album. That way, you can hear the best songs from a particular album without wasting time listening to the boring stuff on the same album.

Remember that songs can appear in more than one playlist. You can add the same song to one playlist of love songs and another playlist of songs you enjoy hearing while gardening. If you run out of ideas for how to group your songs together, let the Genius feature create playlists for you.

As a general rule, the larger your music collection gets, the more helpful you'll find playlists for keeping everything organized. Everyone's audio tastes can range dramatically, and it's unlikely that you'll want to listen to all your music all the time, so you can create playlists to accommodate your every mood.

Identify Music with Your iPhone

If you like a song you hear on the radio or over a speaker in a restaurant or store, you might want to buy that song to store on your iPhone. Unfortunately, if you don't hear the name of a song or recording artist, you may never know how to find that song again.

Unless, of course, you get the Shazam app. The next time you hear a song you like, just place your iPhone next to the audio source and run Shazam. This app listens to the song and tries to identify the title and recording artist so you can buy that song from iTunes. In addition, the app also lists the recording artist's discography so you can find other songs from that same artist.

Shazam can listen to a song and identify its title and recording artist.

If you love music and are constantly hearing new songs that you like, let Shazam help you track down that song so you'll always keep your music library fresh with new music.

Shazam   *http://www.shazam.com/music/web/pages/iphone.html*

21 Customizing Your iPod Settings

To get the most out of your listening enjoyment, you can take a few moments to customize the way your iPhone's audio settings work. By modifying your audio settings along with the icons that appear at the bottom of the iPod screen, you can truly make your iPhone work just the way you like it when playing your favorite music.

Project goal: Learn how to customize the audio settings of your iPhone.

What You'll Be Using

To learn how to customize the iPod settings of your iPhone, you need to use the following:

   The Settings application

   The iPod application

Modifying Audio Output

Most people are happy with the ability to play music on their iPhone without dealing with bothersome obstacles or problems. However, some people are pure audio fanatics who appreciate the ways they can modify how their iPhone plays audio files:

▸ **Shake to Shuffle** Lets you choose the shuffle command just by shaking your iPhone

▸ **Sound Check** Lets you play songs recorded at different volume levels at nearly identical volume

▸ **EQ** Lets you define equalizer settings to adjust the different sounds in an audio file

▸ **Volume Limit** Lets you define a maximum volume limit for playing any audio files, keeping you or someone else from playing songs too loud and risking hearing loss

To modify one or more of these audio settings, do this:

1. From the Home screen, tap **Settings**. The Settings screen appears.
2. Scroll down and tap **iPod**. The iPod screen appears, as shown in Figure 21-1.
3. Tap the **ON/OFF** button next to Sound Check to adjust the levels of songs you play on your iPhone.
4. Tap the **ON/OFF** button next to Shake to Shuffle to turn this option on.
5. Tap **EQ**. The EQ screen appears, listing the available equalizer settings, as shown in Figure 21-2. The equalizer provides predefined settings for playing specific types of music, such as Classical or Rock,

FIGURE 21-1: *The iPod screen displays audio settings you can modify.*

but you can choose any setting that you think makes your music sound best.

6.   Tap an option such as **Classical** or **Dance**, and then tap **iPod** in the upper-left corner to return to the iPod screen.

✳ *NOTE:* **Turning on the equalizer can drain your iPhone's battery, so if you value longer battery life over high-quality sound, keep the equalizer turned off.**

7.   Tap **Volume Limit**. The Volume Limit screen appears, as shown in Figure 21-3.

8.   (Optional) Tap **Lock Volume Limit**. A Set Code screen appears, as shown in Figure 21-4, where you can type a four-digit passcode to lock the volume control so nobody else (including you, if you forget

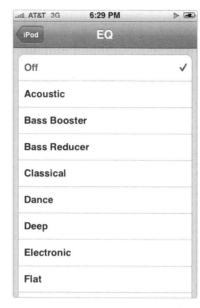

FIGURE 21-2: *The EQ screen displays various equalizer settings.*

FIGURE 21-3: *The Volume Limit screen lets you adjust the maximum volume to play and lock it in.*

FIGURE 21-4: *The Set Code screen lets you type a four-digit number to lock the volume settings.*

this four-digit passcode) can modify the volume settings. This passcode is completely different from any other passcodes you may be using to lock your iPhone and prevent others from using it without your permission. You'll need to type this passcode twice to verify that you typed it correctly.

Modifying the iPod Icons

The bottom of the iPod screen displays icons you can tap to access your playlists or video files. By default, you'll see five icons:

▶ Playlists

▶ Artists

▶ Songs

▶ Videos

▶ More

If you don't use an icon very often, you can remove it and replace it with an icon that you use more often. Up to four icons can appear at the bottom of the screen at a time. (The More icon always remains on the screen.)

To modify an iPod screen icon, do this:

1. From the Home screen, tap **iPod**. The iPod screen appears.
2. Tap **More**. The More screen appears.
3. Tap **Edit** in the upper-left corner of the screen. The Configure screen appears, as shown in Figure 21-5.
4. Slide your finger over an icon in the middle of the screen and drag it over an icon that you want to replace at the bottom of the screen. The new icon appears at the bottom of the screen.
5. Tap **Done** in the upper-right corner of the screen.

FIGURE 21-5: The Configure screen lets you choose which icons will appear at the bottom of the iPod screen.

Additional Ideas for Customizing Your iPod Settings

If you want to make sure you or anyone else who uses your iPhone doesn't suffer from hearing loss by playing music too loud, you can set the volume limit and lock it with a four-digit passcode. Of course, you could always help someone prevent hearing loss by taking away his or her iPhone altogether, but that's probably not practical.

Although the audio quality of the iPhone is perfectly fine for most people, you can experiment with the equalizer settings to make your iPhone sound even better. If you regularly plug your iPhone into a separate stereo or car radio adapter, you may need to experiment with different settings to get the best sound out of your iPhone in these listening environments.

Your iPhone may be a great music player, but with a little bit of tweaking on your part, it can be an even better music player that's customized just for you.

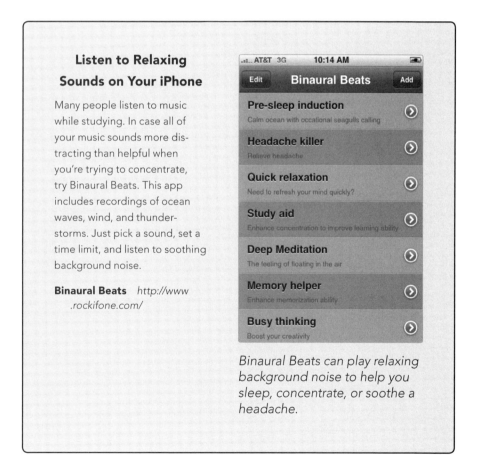

Listen to Relaxing Sounds on Your iPhone

Many people listen to music while studying. In case all of your music sounds more distracting than helpful when you're trying to concentrate, try Binaural Beats. This app includes recordings of ocean waves, wind, and thunderstorms. Just pick a sound, set a time limit, and listen to soothing background noise.

Binaural Beats   *http://www .rockifone.com/*

Binaural Beats can play relaxing background noise to help you sleep, concentrate, or soothe a headache.

22 Turning Your iPhone into a Radio

No matter how much storage space is available on your iPhone, it's probably not enough to store every possible song you might ever want to hear. Rather than switch to another iPhone with more storage capacity, you can download and install free apps on your iPhone that let the iPhone act like a radio, which means you can listen to a lot more music and other audio.

   Although these apps won't let you access all your local radio stations on your iPhone, as a real radio would, they will let your iPhone access *streaming audio* broadcasts over the Internet, essentially giving you free music or information from around the world. The only costs you incur are any Wi-Fi Internet and cellular telephone network connection fees. (Unfortunately, if you cannot connect to your cellular telephone company's network or a Wi-Fi connection, you can't listen to streaming audio.)

Project goal: Learn how to listen to radio stations through your iPhone.

What You'll Be Using

To turn your iPhone into a radio, you need to use the following:

 The App Store application   The AOL Radio application

 The Pandora Radio application   The Stitcher Radio application

Finding Radio Applications in the App Store

Your iPhone can't play streaming audio from radio stations until you download and install special radio apps from the App Store. Some of these apps cost money, but many are free, and these free programs are the focus of this chapter.

Three popular and interesting free radio applications are:

▶ **AOL Radio**   Offers more than 200 radio stations, covering a wide variety of categories including comedy, classical, blues, rock, jazz, sports, pop, and talk radio

▶ **Pandora Radio**   Allows you to enter a song or artist, then automatically plays music similar in style to your selection

▶ **Stitcher Radio**   Lets you put together (*stitch*) your own radio channel from different stations offering news and talk radio content

✳ *NOTE:* **AOL, Pandora, and Stitcher are not the only free radio apps you can load on your iPhone; more free (and fee-based) radio apps are becoming available all the time.**

To download and install a radio app on your iPhone, do this:

1.   From the Home screen, tap **App Store**.
2.   Tap **Search** at the bottom of the screen.
3.   Tap in the search text box at the top of the screen. The virtual keyboard appears at the bottom of the screen.
4.   Type **radio** in the search text box and tap **Search** at the bottom of the screen.

5. The Info screen showing the radio apps appears, as shown in Figure 22-1, along with price information to the right of each app name. Tap the radio app you want to download and install. The Price button turns green and displays INSTALL.

6. Tap **INSTALL**. Your chosen app is installed on your iPhone.

Listening to AOL Radio

AOL Radio organizes its available stations into categories such as Blues, Country, and Oldies. Not only does AOL Radio offer access to established stations all over the world, but it offers access to many popular Internet-only stations. After installing AOL Radio on your iPhone, you can listen to a radio station by doing this:

1. From the Home screen, tap **AOL Radio**. The AOL Radio Stations screen appears, displaying various options, as shown in Figure 22-2.

2. Tap a genre category, such as **Rock** or **Metal**. A list of available stations appears, as shown in Figure 22-3.

3. (Optional) Tap **Favorites** at the bottom of the screen to view all stations you've identified as favorites. Tap **Recents** to see the last stations you listened to. Tap **Locals** to listen to local radio stations that are broadcasting over the Internet.

4. Tap the name of a station you want to hear. The station screen appears, displaying an image from the currently playing artist's album, a volume slider, and a row of icons at the bottom of the screen, as shown in Figure 22-4.

FIGURE 22-1: *The Info screen displays Price buttons for each app; in this case, all apps are free.*

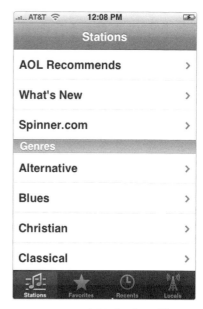

FIGURE 22-2: *AOL Radio offers several options for finding a radio station.*

FIGURE 22-3: *Each AOL Radio category contains multiple stations.*

FIGURE 22-4: *The station screen shows information about the music currently playing.*

5. (Optional) Slide your fingertip left or right on the volume slider to increase or decrease the volume.

6. (Optional) Tap **Favorites** to store the station in your list of favorites.

7. Press the Home button when you want to stop listening to AOL Radio, or tap the back button in the upper-left corner of the screen to view other stations.

✳ **NOTE:** AOL Radio continues playing even when your iPhone drifts into sleep mode.

Listening to Pandora Radio

Pandora Radio creates a custom radio station that plays music just for you, based on songs or artists that you choose. You simply type the name of an artist, band, or song that you like into a Create a New Station field, and Pandora Radio plays music that is similar in style and sound. Type **Beatles**, and Pandora Radio will not only play various Beatles songs, but music from other artists that are similar to the Beatles.

Before you can use Pandora Radio, you need to set up a free account either through the Pandora Radio website (*http://www.pandora.com/*) or through your iPhone. After you've created an account and installed the application on your iPhone, you can listen to Pandora Radio by doing this:

1. From the Home screen, tap **Pandora Radio**. The Welcome to Pandora screen asks if you already have a Pandora account, as shown in Figure 22-5.

2. (Optional) If you haven't created a Pandora account, you'll need to tap the **I am new to Pandora** button and then activate your account with the code that appears on the screen.

3. Tap **I have a Pandora account**. A Sign In screen appears, as shown in Figure 22-6.

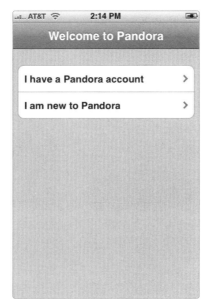

FIGURE 22-5: *The Welcome to Pandora screen asks if you already have a Pandora account.*

FIGURE 22-6: *Access to Pandora Radio requires a valid email account and password.*

4. Type your email address in the Email text box.

5. Type your password in the Password text box, and then tap the blue **Go** button.

6. Pandora displays the Stations screen. If you haven't created any stations yet, this screen will be blank. If you have created stations already, this screen shows all your Pandora stations, as shown in Figure 22-7.

7. (Optional) Tap the **New Station** icon at the bottom of the screen to create a new station. You'll need to choose a recording artist or song name to define the type of music this station will play for you.

8. Tap a station that you want to hear. Pandora displays a screen that shows the currently playing song along with a volume control slider. Pandora also displays thumbs up and thumbs down icons so you can approve or disapprove of the currently playing song, as shown in Figure 22-8. Tap the thumbs up icon to approve a song and keep it in your playlist; tap the thumbs down icon to disapprove a song and prevent that song from playing again. Each time you approve or disapprove of a song, Pandora remembers your preferences and gradually only plays those songs that you like best.

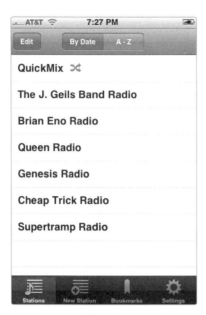

FIGURE 22-7: *The Stations screen lists all the Pandora stations you've created.*

FIGURE 22-8: *Pandora displays the currently playing song along with thumbs up and down icons that let you approve or disapprove the song.*

9.   Press the Home button when you want to stop listening to Pandora Radio, or tap the back button in the upper-left corner of the screen to go back and view other stations.

* **NOTE:** Pandora Radio continues playing even when your iPhone drifts into sleep mode.

Listening to Stitcher Radio

While Pandora Radio tries to play music that is similar to tunes or artists you like, Stitcher Radio tries to find news and talk radio show content that you might like.

Stitcher Radio divides its stations into Topics and Sources. Topics list different types of information such as Health & Fitness, Sports, and Business & Finance. Sources lists specific content providers such as Associated Press, CNN, Fox, and Reuters.

After installing Stitcher Radio on your iPhone, you can listen to it by doing this:

1.   From the Home screen, tap **Stitcher Radio**. The Stitcher Radio screen appears.

2. Tap **Topics** or **Sources** at the bottom of the screen to view a list of available topics or sources, as shown in Figure 22-9.

FIGURE 22-9: *Tap Topics to see the Topics screen on the left; tap Sources to see the list of sources on the right.*

3. Tap a topic (such as **American News & Politics**) or a content source (such as **Bloomberg**). Your chosen station appears, displaying thumbs up and thumbs down icons, as shown in Figure 22-10. By tapping the thumbs up or down icons, you can customize Stitcher to play the talk stations you like best.

4. Press the Home button when you want to stop listening to Stitcher Radio, or tap the **Back** button in the upper-left corner of the screen to go back and view other stations.

✳ **NOTE:** Stitcher Radio continues playing even when your iPhone drifts into sleep mode.

FIGURE 22-10: *When listening to a station, you can give it a thumbs up or down to accept or reject it.*

Additional Ideas for Listening to the Radio on Your iPhone

AOL Radio is most useful when you want to browse different stations and listen to both music and news. One unique feature of AOL Radio is that it offers access to international music, so if you ever want to listen to your favorite Brazilian, African, or Japanese pop songs, turn on AOL Radio and satisfy your audio cravings.

If you live in a major city that Stitcher Radio supports, such as Boston, Chicago, Los Angeles, New York, Philadelphia, or San Francisco, Stitcher Radio can give you access to radio stations in those cities so that you can catch the latest traffic news.

By letting you listen to radio stations all over the world, your iPhone can be your constant companion at work and at home. Plug your iPhone into a power source, put on headphones or ear buds, and listen to the radio at your convenience. With a good pair of noise-canceling headphones, you can listen to the radio on your iPhone at work and never hear your boss screaming at you for not getting anything done.

Find Your Favorite NPR Station

If you're a fan of National Public Radio (NPR), grab a copy of the NPR Mobile app, and you'll be able to find your local NPR station no matter what part of the country you may be in. Besides helping you track down a local NPR station, this app also lets you retrieve podcasts of past shows so you can hear your favorite NPR show at your convenience.

NPR Mobile *http://www .passtimesoftware.com/*

NPR Mobile lets you stay tuned to your local National Public Radio station.

23

Watching YouTube Videos

One way to keep yourself amused with your iPhone is by watching short video clips on YouTube. Since watching YouTube videos is such a popular pastime, Apple added a special YouTube app to the iPhone so you can access videos right away without having to load Safari and type the YouTube web address.

YouTube can be handy for watching old music videos, interesting news clips of planes or cars crashing, or homemade videos of people doing strange things or animals acting in bizarre ways. The video quality on YouTube may not always be the best, but the sheer quantity of material available gives you a variety of ways to entertain yourself.

Project goal: Learn how to view YouTube videos on your iPhone.

What You'll Be Using

To watch YouTube videos on your iPhone, you need to use the following:

 The YouTube application

Browsing YouTube's Video Library

YouTube offers thousands of videos. The biggest problem is finding a particular video to watch. Your iPhone uses multiple categories that can help you browse and find a video in YouTube's massive video library:

▶ **Featured**   Displays videos currently promoted by YouTube

▶ **Most Viewed**   Displays the most watched videos on YouTube

▶ **Top Rated**   Displays the highest rated videos on YouTube

▶ **Most Recent**   Displays the latest videos available

▶ **History**   Displays a list of videos you viewed previously

▶ **Favorites**   Displays a list of videos you bookmarked to view again

To see some common ways you can browse YouTube's video library, do this:

1. From the Home screen, tap **YouTube**. The YouTube screen appears.
2. Tap **Featured** at the bottom of the screen. YouTube displays a list of the latest featured videos, as shown in Figure 23-1.
3. Tap **Most Viewed**. YouTube displays a list of the most viewed videos, as shown in Figure 23-2.
4. Tap **Today**, **This Week**, or **All** at the top of the screen.
5. Tap **More** at the bottom of the screen. The More screen appears, as shown in Figure 23-3.
6. Tap **Most Recent**. The Most Recent screen appears, listing the newest YouTube videos.
7. Tap **More**, and then tap **Top Rated**. The Top Rated screen appears, listing the highest rated YouTube videos.

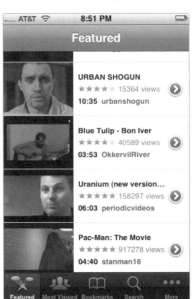

FIGURE 23-1: *The Featured screen shows you a list of the latest featured videos.*

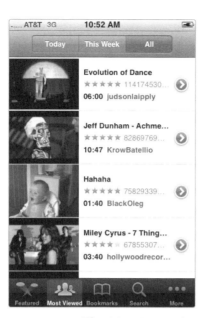

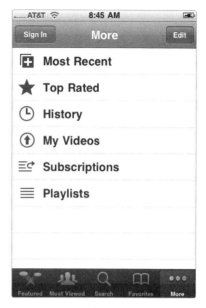

FIGURE 23-2: *The Most Viewed list shows you the most popular YouTube videos available.*

FIGURE 23-3: *The More screen displays additional options for selecting a YouTube video.*

8. Tap **More**, and then tap **History**. A list of your latest viewed YouTube videos appears. (If you haven't viewed any YouTube videos, this screen won't show any videos.)
9. Scroll through the list of available videos and tap the name of the YouTube video you want to watch.
10. If you have a YouTube account, you can tap My Videos, Subscriptions, or Playlists to view your own posted videos, additional videos you've subscribed to, or videos you've stored in a playlist.

✳ **NOTE:** Tap the red Clear button in the upper-right corner of the History screen to clear your history list so other people can't see which YouTube videos you've been watching.

Searching for a YouTube Video

Browsing YouTube's video library can help you find videos that are new to you, but sometimes you may want to find a particular video, such as a music video of your favorite song. To search for a video in YouTube, do this:

1. From the Home screen, tap **YouTube**. The YouTube screen appears.
2. Tap **Search**. A search text box appears at the top of the screen.

3. Type a word or descriptive phrase and then tap **Search**. A list of YouTube videos matching your search criteria appears.
4. Scroll through the list of available videos and tap the name of the video you want to watch.

Watching a YouTube Video

When you watch a YouTube video, your iPhone displays it horizontally, which means you'll need to rotate your iPhone on its side to watch the video. After rotating your iPhone horizontally, you'll see a variety of controls on the iPhone screen. The main controls are shown in Figure 23-4.

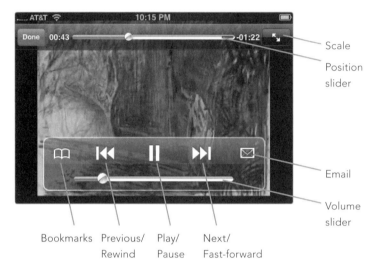

FIGURE 23-4: *The YouTube video controls appear when you rotate the iPhone.*

▶ **Done**   Tap to stop playing the video and return to the YouTube screen.

▶ **Scale**   Tap the icon in the upper-right corner to expand or shrink the video on screen.

▶ **Position slider**   Slide left or right to move backward or forward in the video.

▶ **Bookmarks**   Tap the book icon to bookmark a video.

▶ **Previous/Rewind**   Tap the double-left pointing arrows to play the video from the beginning. (If you hold down your finger on this button, you'll rewind the video.)

▶ **Play/Pause**   Tap to play or pause the current video.

▶ **Next/Fast-forward**   Tap the double-right pointing arrows to skip the currently playing video and play the next video on the list. (If you hold down your finger on this button, you'll fast-forward the video.)

▸ **Email** Tap to email someone a link to the video. (If you haven't set up an email account to work with your iPhone, you won't be able to email a YouTube link. See Project 32 to learn how to set up an email account on your iPhone.)

▸ **Volume slider** Slide left and right to adjust the volume.

These controls appear when a video first starts playing, but they soon disappear so you can see the video. If you want to see these controls again, tap the screen once. To make these controls disappear, tap the screen again or wait a few seconds.

Viewing Bookmarked YouTube Videos

While you're watching a YouTube video, you can tap the Bookmarks icon to bookmark that video. After you've bookmarked a YouTube video, you can view it again or delete it from your bookmark list.

Playing a Bookmarked YouTube Video

After you've bookmarked a video, you can play it again by doing this:

1. From the Home screen, tap **YouTube**. The YouTube screen appears.
2. Tap **Favorites**. The Favorites screen appears, listing all the YouTube videos you've bookmarked.
3. Scroll through the list of available bookmarked videos and tap the name of the video you want to watch.

Deleting a Bookmarked YouTube Video

After you've bookmarked a YouTube video, you can delete it from your bookmarks list by doing this:

1. From the Home screen, tap **YouTube**. The YouTube screen appears.
2. Tap **Favorites**. The Favorites screen appears, listing all the YouTube videos you've bookmarked.
3. Tap **Edit**. A white minus sign inside a red circle appears to the left of each YouTube video.
4. Tap the red circle next to the video that you want to delete from your bookmarks list. A red Delete button appears, as shown in Figure 23-5.

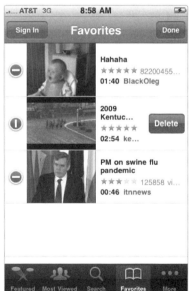

FIGURE 23-5: Tap Delete to remove a bookmarked video from your list.

5. Tap **Delete** to remove the video from your bookmarks (or tap the red circle again if you've changed your mind).
6. Tap **Done**.

Additional Ideas for Watching YouTube Videos

YouTube offers plenty of old music videos, both the official versions issued by the recording artists and tribute videos that individuals have created for their favorite songs. If you're stuck somewhere and want to hear your favorite music, you can browse YouTube and watch music videos or clips from concerts.

YouTube is also a great place to watch trailers for movies about to be released as well as old favorites. If you're thinking about renting a video, check out its trailer first, and if the trailer interests you, the movie might be worth watching. Or you might save yourself a few hours and a couple bucks if the trailer looks like a dud.

YouTube also offers clips of popular comedians, skits from amateur film-makers, and videos of unusual events such as hurricanes ripping roofs off buildings, monkeys riding bicycles, or cars crashing into each other.

People have also posted hundreds of educational and instructional videos, so if your idea of entertainment isn't watching some guy get hit in the crotch, you can view yoga, martial arts, or how-to videos so you can learn something new.

Think of YouTube as a chaotic television channel that offers a wealth of video content if you have the time to dig and find it all. The next time you have a free moment waiting for an airplane or sitting in a doctor's office, browse through YouTube and see what it offers. With YouTube and your iPhone, there's no reason to be bored again—unless your iPhone's battery runs out of power.

24 Watching TV Shows and Movies

If you missed a movie or TV show episode in the old days, you'd be out of luck. If you took the time to record it (assuming you could figure out how to work your VCR or DVR), you could watch your favorite missed TV show or movie at your convenience.

Now there's another way to watch TV shows and movies: You can buy them from the iTunes Store and then download them to your iPhone. Now you can turn your iPhone into a portable TV screen and watch your favorite TV programs or the latest Hollywood blockbusters wherever you take your iPhone—whether on a long airplane ride or while waiting in line at a government office to fill out paperwork.

Project goal: Learn how to watch TV shows and movies on your iPhone.

What You'll Be Using

To watch TV shows and movies on your iPhone, you need to use the following:

 iTunes (on your Mac or PC)　　 The Settings application

 The iPhone USB cable　　 The iPod application

Downloading TV Shows and Movies

The fastest and most convenient way to download TV shows and movies is through a fast Internet connection using iTunes on your computer. Since TV shows and movies are stored in large files (such as 60 megabytes or more for TV shows and 1 gigabyte or more for movies), downloading TV shows and movies directly to your iPhone is much slower, even when using a Wi-Fi connection.

To search for and download TV shows, movies, or music videos, do this:

1. Open iTunes on your computer.
2. Click **iTunes Store** under the Store category in the left pane of the iTunes window, as shown in Figure 24-1.

FIGURE 24-1: The iTunes Store displays categories of products along with ads for the latest songs or videos.

3.   Click the **Movies**, **TV Shows**, or **Music Videos** category under the iTunes Store category, or click the **Genres** drop-down menu and choose a category. You can select a file to download by clicking its image or by clicking its name in the category list.

4.   Click the **Buy** button that appears to the right of the TV show or movie name to purchase it and download it to your computer.

∗ *NOTE:* After you've downloaded a video file to your computer, you'll need to transfer it to your iPhone, as explained in Project 12.

Viewing a Video

After you've downloaded a show or movie to your iPhone, you'll probably want to watch it eventually. To watch a show or movie, do this:

1.   From the Home screen, tap **iPod**. The iPod screen appears.

2.   Tap **Videos** at the bottom of the screen. The Videos screen appears, as shown in Figure 24-2.

3.   Tap a TV show or movie that you want to view. Your chosen TV show or movie appears sideways on your iPhone screen. You'll need to rotate the iPhone to view it properly.

4.   Tap the screen to display the video controls, as shown in Figure 24-3, and tap the play button to start playing the video.

Long videos, such as movies, are often divided into chapters. Chapters simply make it easier to jump to a different part of the video without tediously rewinding or fast-forwarding through the entire video.

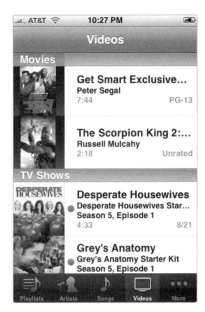

FIGURE 24-2: The Videos screen displays all the TV shows and movies you've downloaded to your iPhone.

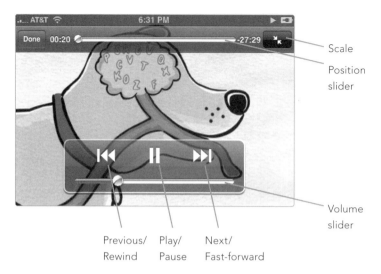

FIGURE 24-3: *The video controls let you control how the video plays.*

Seven video controls are available:

▶ **Previous/Rewind**   Tap once to move to the previous chapter of your video (or back to the beginning if your video doesn't contain chapters). Hold down to rewind.

▶ **Next/Fast-forward**   Tap once to move to a new chapter of your video. Hold down to fast-forward.

▶ **Play/Pause**   Tap to play or pause the current video.

▶ **Volume slider**   Slide left or right to adjust the volume.

▶ **Position slider**   Slide left or right to play different parts of your video.

▶ **Done**   Tap to stop playing the video and return to the Videos screen.

▶ **Scale**   Tap to change the aspect ratio of the movie.

Customizing Video Playback

If you need to stop watching a movie or TV show part of the way through, tap Done in the upper-left corner of the screen. When you return to viewing the movie or show, you can set your iPhone to start playing where you left off, or you can start playing the video from the beginning.

To determine how to play a partially viewed movie or TV show, do this:

1. From the Home screen, tap **Settings**. The Settings screen appears.
2. Scroll down and tap **iPod**. The iPod screen appears, as shown in Figure 24-4.
3. Tap **Start Playing** in the Video group. A Start Playing screen appears, as shown in Figure 24-5.

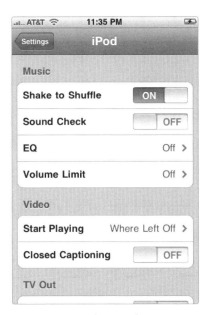

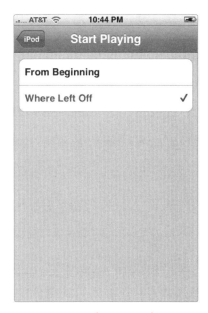

FIGURE 24-4: *The iPod screen lets you customize how your iPhone plays video.*

FIGURE 24-5: *The Start Playing screen displays two options for playing a movie or TV show.*

4. Tap **From Beginning** to start the video from the beginning or **Where Left Off** to start playing it where you left off when you last watched it.
5. Press the Home button to return to the Home screen.

Putting Home Movies on Your iPhone

Grabbing TV shows and movies from iTunes is one way to load videos on to your iPhone, but buying new videos can get expensive. As an alternative, you can load your own video files into iTunes and transfer them to your iPhone. Then you can watch and enjoy movies of your child's first steps whenever you want on your iPhone.

You can play the following types of video files on an iPhone:

▶ H.264

▶ MPEG-4 (.*mp4* and .*m4v*)

▶ QuickTime (.*mov*)

✳ **NOTE:** **If you have video trapped in a different file format, such as AVI or WMA, you'll need to convert it into one of the supported file formats before you can play it on your iPhone. For a free video converter program that works on Windows, Linux, and Mac OS X, grab a copy of Handbrake (***http:// handbrake.fr/***).**

Once you have a video file stored in a compatible file format, you can download it into iTunes by doing this:

1. Open iTunes on your computer.
2. Choose **File ▸ Add to Library**. An Add to Library dialog appears, displaying folders and files.
3. Click the file you want to add to iTunes. (You may need to dig through different folders to find the file you want.) After the file is loaded into iTunes, you can synchronize and transfer this video file to your iPhone by following the synchronization steps described in Project 12.

Additional Ideas for Watching TV Shows and Movies

You can buy movies for $9.99 and up (more for the latest releases) and TV show episodes for $1.99 and up. If you find a TV show that you really like, you can subscribe to a whole season for a much lower cost than purchasing individual episodes. However, many networks release a single episode of popular or new TV shows for free. The hope is that people will watch the shows on their iPhone, get hooked, and either watch the shows on TV when they're officially broadcast or buy more episodes through the iTunes Store. Movie studios also release free trailers of the latest movies so you can watch them and decide whether you want to see the whole movie.

If you have a Macintosh, you can use the iMovie video editing program to create your own movies that you can store on your iPhone. Instead of storing still images of your loved ones, store videos so you can relive special moments in your life that no Hollywood production could possibly capture.

With the ability to download and view classic TV show episodes and movies or store and play your home movies, you can turn your iPhone into an entertainment time machine that lets you relive the past through the wonders of old video, TV shows, and movies. Laugh at the strange clothes, poke fun at the dated hairdos, and then congratulate yourself for living in modern times, where everyone looks and acts cool—until you look back one day at these TV shows and movies to realize how silly we all really look in hindsight.

Watch Your Favorite TV Shows and Movie Trailers on Your iPhone

If you've missed your favorite CBS show, you can still catch up on the latest episodes by downloading the TV.com app. Developed by CBS, this app only lets you view select CBS shows and television schedules.

For those more interested in movies, download Flixster and check out the latest DVD releases, currently playing movies, and upcoming movies. While you can't watch entire movies through Flixster, you can peek at trailers and track the movies you want to see next (or avoid altogether).

TV.com *http://www.tv.com/*

Flixster *http://www.flixster.com/*

TV.com and Flixster can help satisfy your TV- and movie-watching desires.

25 Listening to Audiobooks and Podcasts

Although nearly everyone enjoys listening to music on their iPhone, some people prefer using the iPhone's audio-playing capabilities to expand their minds by listening to audiobooks and podcasts.

An *audiobook* is a recording of someone reading a book. A *podcast* is often an audio recording of a radio show, TV show, or another spoken presentation that focuses on a particular topic, such as managing your money or stopping smoking. The next time you get tired of listening to music and want some audio variety, try listening to an audiobook or a podcast.

Project goal: Learn how to listen to audiobooks and podcasts on your iPhone.

What You'll Be Using

To listen to audiobooks and podcasts on your iPhone, you need to use the following:

 iTunes (on your Mac or PC)   The iPod application

 The iPhone USB cable   The iTunes application

Downloading Audiobooks and Podcasts

Audiobooks tend to be large files that can contain up to several hours' worth of audio, so you can only download them to your iPhone from iTunes. Podcasts are usually much smaller, so you can download them directly to your iPhone or through iTunes. Some podcasts are strictly audio files, while others contain video as well.

Audiobooks almost always cost money to download. Depending on the book and the length of the audio file, an audiobook can cost as little as $1 or as much as $20 or more. Podcasts, on the other hand, are usually free to download, although you can purchase subscriptions to some podcasts for a minimal cost that's usually much lower than the price of an audiobook.

Downloading in iTunes

To download an audiobook or podcast in iTunes, do this:

1. Open iTunes on your computer.
2. Click **iTunes Store** under the Store category in the left pane of the iTunes window, as shown in Figure 25-1.
3. Click the **Audiobooks** or **Podcasts** category under the iTunes Store category on the main screen.
4. Click **Genres** and choose a genre from the pop-up window, click a category under the Categories section, or select an audiobook or podcast to download by clicking its image in the middle pane.
5. After you've made a selection, a new screen appears with more information about the particular audiobook or podcast you selected. Click **Buy Book** to purchase the audiobook and download it to your computer. Click **Subscribe** to subscribe to a podcast and download episodes to your computer.

✳ *NOTE:* **After you've downloaded an audiobook or podcast to your computer, you'll need to transfer it to your iPhone, which is explained in Project 12.**

You can find and download audiobooks in other places, such as Audible (*http://www.audible.com/*), AudioBooks (*http://www.audiobooks.com/*), Amazon.com (*http://www.amazon.com/*), and LibriVox (*http://librivox.org/*). LibriVox is particularly attractive, since this site focuses exclusively on free audiobooks.

FIGURE 25-1: *The iTunes Store*

Downloading Podcasts to Your iPhone

Most podcasts are part of a larger collection of related podcasts, so when you download a podcast, you're actually downloading a single episode of an ongoing show. For example, if you download a podcast from ESPN, you'll have a choice of downloading one of many podcasts all recorded by ESPN.

To download a podcast directly on to your iPhone, do this:

1. From the Home screen, tap **iTunes**. The iTunes Store screen appears.
2. Tap **Podcasts** at the bottom of the screen. The Podcasts screen appears.
3. Tap **New Releases** or **What's Hot** at the top of the screen. A list of the latest or hottest podcasts appears, as shown in Figure 25-2.

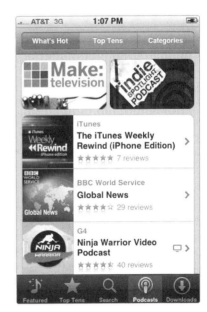

FIGURE 25-2: *The What's Hot category lets you see the latest podcasts available.*

4. Tap **Top Tens** or **Categories**. These lists can help you search for a particular type of podcast, such as one related to comedy or sports, as shown in Figure 25-3.
5. Tap a podcast that you want to download. A list of available podcasts appears.
6. Tap the Price button (many podcasts display a FREE button). The Price button turns into a green DOWNLOAD button, as shown in Figure 25-4.

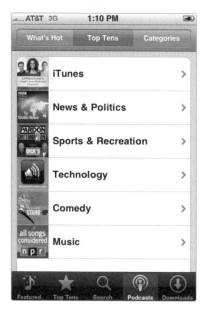

FIGURE 25-3: *Tap Top Tens to see the most popular podcasts in various categories.*

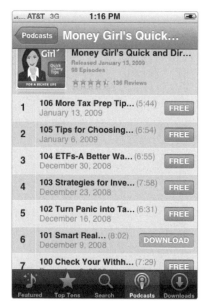

FIGURE 25-4: *Tapping the DOWNLOAD button starts transferring your podcast to your iPhone.*

7. Tap **DOWNLOAD** to download the podcast.
8. When you're done, press the Home button to return to the Home screen.

Listening to Audiobooks

After you've transferred an audiobook to your iPhone, you can listen to it by doing this:

1. From the Home screen, tap **iPod**. The iPod screen appears.
2. Tap **More** at the bottom of the screen. The More screen appears, as shown in Figure 25-5.
3. Tap **Audiobooks**. The Audiobooks screen appears, as shown in Figure 25-6.

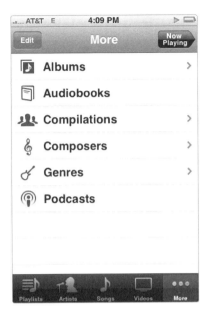

FIGURE 25-5: *The More screen displays audiobook and podcast categories.*

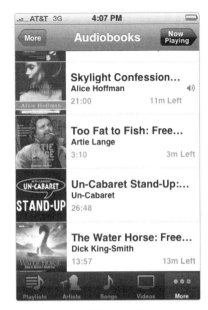

FIGURE 25-6: *The Audiobooks screen lists all the audiobooks you've downloaded.*

4. The Audiobooks screen lists all the audiobooks you've downloaded. Tap the audiobook that you want to hear. (You'll need to tap the screen to display the position slider, repeat, and shuffle icons at the top of the screen, as shown in Figure 25-7.)

5. Tap the play/pause button to pause or play the audiobook.

6. When you're done listening to the audiobook, press the Home button.

✳ **NOTE:** Your audiobook continues playing even if you switch to another application.

FIGURE 25-7: *Tap the screen to display the controls for playing an audiobook.*

Listening to Podcasts

After you've stored a podcast on your iPhone, you can listen to it by doing this:

1. Press the Home button. The Home screen appears.
2. Tap **iPod**. The iPod screen appears.
3. Tap **More** at the bottom of the screen. The More screen appears (see Figure 25-5).
4. Tap **Podcasts**. The Podcasts screen appears, as shown in Figure 25-8.
5. Tap a podcast. A list of episodes for that podcast appears, as shown in Figure 25-9.

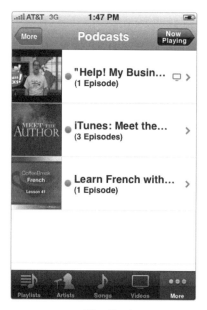

FIGURE 25-8: *The Podcasts screen lists all available podcasts on your iPhone.*

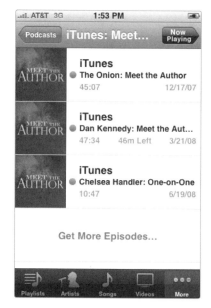

FIGURE 25-9: *A podcast often has several episodes.*

6. Tap the podcast episode you want to hear. Your iPhone starts playing the audio. You'll see controls for playing the audio file, but if you tap the screen, you'll see additional controls at the top of the screen (see Figure 25-7).

✳ **NOTE:** Your podcast continues playing even if you switch to another application.

Additional Ideas for Listening to Audiobooks and Podcasts

If you want to listen to audio files other than music, you can start with podcasts, since most of them are free. Many radio and TV shows offer podcasts that let you enjoy the show even if you missed it when it first aired. Once you get used to listening to podcasts, you may want to graduate to audiobooks and listen to the latest best-sellers. Just remember that audiobooks usually cost money, while most podcasts are free.

Audiobooks and podcasts can both entertain and educate you. Listen to the latest best-sellers, business or health tips, or amusing commentary from people all over the planet. With the right audiobook or podcast, you can either stimulate your brain or numb it through mindless entertainment.

Listen to an App Podcast on Your iPhone

One problem with the App Store is that there are so many apps available that you may not have time to dig through all the selections to find an app that you might need. To help you sift through the App Store, Jerad Hill offers an App Podcast that highlights a different app so you can learn what it does before wasting time downloading, installing, and trying it yourself.

To find Jerad Hill's App Podcast, tap **iTunes** from the Home screen, then tap the Search icon at the bottom of the screen. Type `Jerad Hill` and you'll see a list of App Podcast episodes ready for you to download.

The App Podcast *http:// theapppodcast.com/*

Jerad Hill's App Podcast can help you learn what iPhone apps do before you download them yourself.

26 Browsing the iTunes Store

The *iTunes Store* is an online music store where you can search for your favorite recording artists and songs and download music directly to your iPhone. When downloading videos, you'll need to use a Wi-Fi connection for maximum speed, since downloading videos through a cellular phone network will be very slow. Ideally, you should download videos through your computer and then copy these videos to your iPhone. That way you'll spend less time downloading video files and more time actually enjoying them.

Project goal: Learn how to browse and shop for songs through the iTunes Store on your iPhone.

What You'll Be Using

To browse and download audio content from the iTunes Store, you need to use the following:

 The iTunes application

Browsing Through iTunes

The iTunes Store sells all types and genres of audio content, including rock, classical, jazz, country, hip-hop, spoken word, and comedy. When you find a song or audio clip that you want to download, you can buy it and download it directly to your iPhone.

To help you navigate your way through this massive online library of songs, your iPhone provides several categories that can help narrow your search in finding music you enjoy:

▶ **Featured**   Displays currently promoted songs, organized in three categories: New Releases, What's Hot, and Genres

▶ **Top Tens**   Offers the top ten songs in every genre, such as Pop and Alternative

▶ **Search**   Lets you search for a song or recording artist by name

Viewing the Featured Category

The Featured category typically displays the latest or most popular songs. Most people find popular songs worth a listen, so by browsing the Featured category, you can find out what other people think are the best songs available at the moment.

To browse through the Featured category, do this:

1. From the Home screen, tap **iTunes**. The iTunes Store screen appears.
2. Tap **Featured** at the bottom of the screen. The Featured list of songs appears, as shown in Figure 26-1.
3. Tap **New Releases** at the top of the screen to view the newest songs.
4. Tap **What's Hot** to view the most popular songs, regardless of how new (or old) they may be.

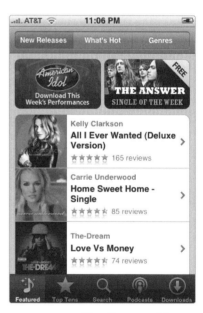

FIGURE 26-1: *The Featured list shows currently promoted songs.*

5.   Tap **Genres**. A list of different music genres appears, as shown in Figure 26-2.
6.   Tap a genre category, such as **Rock**. A list of albums appear.
7.   Tap an album to view its song list and album cover art, as shown in Figure 26-3.

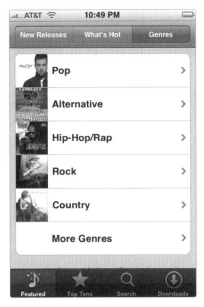

FIGURE 26-2: *A list of genres available on iTunes*

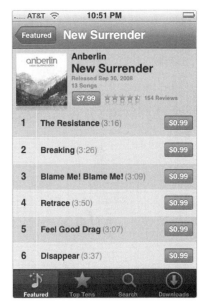

FIGURE 26-3: *Tapping an album reveals its song list and artwork.*

8.   Tap a song. A short audio preview of the selected song plays.
9.   (Optional) Tap the Price button that appears to the right of a song name. The Price button changes into a green BUY NOW button. Tap **BUY NOW** to purchase and download this song.
10. Press the Home button to return to the Home page.

✳ *NOTE:* **If you buy a song or album, you can monitor the download progress by tapping Downloads in the lower-right corner of the screen.**

Viewing the Top Tens Category

The Top Tens category lets you view the ten most popular songs in any genre. To view the Top Tens category, do this:

1.   From the Home screen, tap **iTunes**. The iTunes Store screen appears.
2.   Tap **Top Tens** at the bottom of the screen. The Top Tens screen appears, listing different genres.

3. Tap a genre name. A screen appears with two buttons at the top, Top Songs and Top Albums, as shown in Figure 26-4.

4. Tap **Top Songs** or **Top Albums** to view the most popular individual songs or the most popular albums.

5. Tap a song or album. If you tap an album, you'll see a list of songs that you can tap to select. Tapping a song plays a preview of that song.

6. (Optional) Tap the Price button that appears to the right of a song name. The Price button changes into a green BUY NOW button. Tap **BUY NOW** to purchase and download this song.

Searching for a Song or Artist

Rather than browse the latest or most popular songs or albums, you can find a particular song by its title or by the name of the recording artist. To search for a specific song or artist, do this:

1. From the Home screen, tap **iTunes**. The iTunes Store screen appears.

2. Tap **Search** at the bottom of the screen. A Search screen appears.

3. Tap in the search text box at the top of the screen. A virtual keyboard appears at the bottom of the screen.

4. Type the song title or artist name. As you type, the screen displays a list of songs or artists that match what you've typed so far, as shown in Figure 26-5.

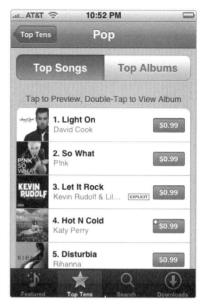

FIGURE 26-4: *You can choose to view the Top Tens list of songs or albums within a genre.*

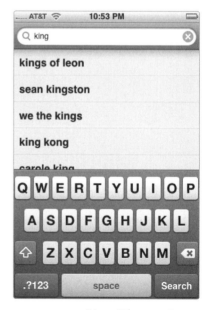

FIGURE 26-5: *Your iPhone tries to guess the song or artist you want to find.*

5. Tap a song or artist name. The screen displays a list of albums and songs that match your search, as shown in Figure 26-6.

6. (Optional) Tap the Price button that appears to the right of a song name. The Price button changes into a green BUY NOW button. Tap **BUY NOW** to purchase and download this song.

Additional Ideas for Browsing the iTunes Store

If you are squeamish about buying music from the iTunes Store, you can start by downloading free songs. Every Tuesday, Apple releases one to three songs for free as a way to entice people to start downloading songs and listening to different recording artists. When the next Tuesday rolls around, Apple releases a new batch of free songs, and the week's previously free songs will then cost money to download.

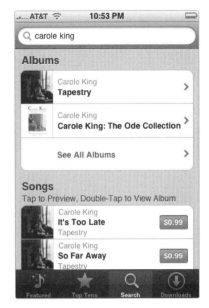

FIGURE 26-6: *When you search for a song title or artist, you can view a list of matching items in the iTunes Store.*

To find a list of the currently free iTunes songs, use any search engine (such as Google) to search for *free iTunes songs*. Various websites keep track of the latest free songs. Browse through this list, search for the free songs in the iTunes Store, and start building up your music collection for free while learning how to browse and download songs to your iPhone at the same time.

After you've downloaded audio files to your iPhone, you can synchronize your files to copy them on to your computer (see Project 12). As another alternative, you may find it convenient to browse and download audio files using iTunes on your computer and then synchronize your iPhone with your computer to transfer newly downloaded audio files to your iPhone. As long as you synchronize your iPhone regularly with your computer, you can be sure that your music collection will always remain current, whether you're at your computer or traveling with your iPhone.

Use Your iPhone to Learn About New Apps

Everyday, a flood of new iPhone apps appears in the App Store. To help you sort through the latest releases, grab a copy of AppVee, which shows you the newest apps along with the latest apps in specific categories, such as Music or Productivity. By using this app, you can snap up the most promising apps without wasting your time fiddling with apps you may not care about.

AppVee *http://www.appvee .com/*

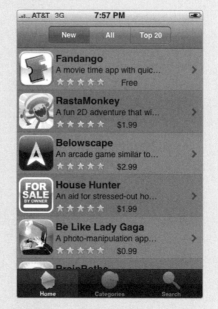

AppVee tracks the latest iPhone apps.

PART 5

Browsing the Internet

27 Viewing Web Pages

Browsing the Internet is easy on a desktop or laptop computer, but on most mobile phones, finding and viewing different websites can be an exercise in frustration. Many mobile phones can't display actual web pages; instead, they display simplified pages designed for small mobile phone screens.

Fortunately, the iPhone is different. Not only can you view web pages exactly as they appear on a regular computer, but you can easily select links simply by tapping them with your fingertip. On your iPhone, you'll find that web browsing can be just as easy and fun as it is on a full-size computer.

✳ *NOTE:* The version of Safari on your iPhone can't display Flash animations on websites. If you visit a website that uses Flash, you'll see a blank space where a Flash animation should be playing.

Project goal: Learn how to view web pages on your iPhone.

What You'll Be Using

To browse the Internet with your iPhone, you need to use the following:

 The Safari application

Connecting to the Internet

Your iPhone can connect to the Internet through a Wi-Fi network or through your cellular company's network (see Project 31 for more on connecting to Wi-Fi). Connecting through a Wi-Fi network is much faster than connecting through your cell phone service. The one significant drawback to Wi-Fi is that you must be within range of a Wi-Fi network to use it, and you may need to enter a password to access that network. If the Wi-Fi network to which you're trying to connect isn't yours and it's protected by a password you don't know, you won't be able to connect.

When you attempt to connect to the Internet, your iPhone always tries to connect to a Wi-Fi network first. If your iPhone can't connect through a Wi-Fi network, it can still connect through your cellular telephone network. The advantage of connecting with your cell service is that you'll be able to access the Internet while riding in your car or walking down the street, as long as you can get cell coverage. The drawback is that surfing the Internet through the cellular network can be painfully slow.

To connect to a Wi-Fi network, do this:

1. From the Home screen, tap **Safari**. The Safari screen appears. If you're within range of multiple Wi-Fi networks, a dialog appears, listing all available Wi-Fi networks, as shown in Figure 27-1.
2. A lock icon next to a Wi-Fi name means you need to enter a password to access that network. If a lock icon does not appear, you can access that network without typing a password. The signal strength is represented by the radio signal

FIGURE 27-1: *You can access a Wi-Fi network by tapping its name.*

icon. The stronger the signal, the more shaded bars will appear. Generally, the closer you are to a Wi-Fi router, the stronger the signal. A weak Wi-Fi signal can be unpredictable and may cut you off suddenly.

3. Tap the Wi-Fi network you want to access. If you need a password, a dialog will appear, asking you to enter the password.

Viewing a Website

You can visit a website in two ways. You can enter its address (such as *http://www .nostarch.com/*) and go directly to the site, but this method can be clumsy, especially if the address is long. Alternatively, you can enter a word or phrase in the search field, and when a list of websites appears on the search engine page, you can tap the site you want to visit. This method is handier when you want to visit a website but don't know its actual address (or *URL*, which stands for *Uniform Resource Locator*). Most likely, you'll wind up using both methods to find websites.

Entering a Website Address

If you know the exact URL of a website that you want to visit, you can use the virtual keyboard to enter its address by doing this:

1. From the Home screen, tap **Safari**. The Safari screen appears, as shown in Figure 27-2.
2. Tap the address text box on the left side of the title bar. A virtual keyboard appears, as shown in Figure 27-3.

FIGURE 27-2: *The Safari screen lets you access websites.*

FIGURE 27-3: *The address text box and virtual keyboard*

3. (Optional) Tap the clear button (the X in a gray circle) to the right of the address field to clear any text displayed there.

4. Type an address in the address text box.

✳ **NOTE:** You can save time by skipping the *http://www* part of the address and starting with the actual website name itself—such as *nostarch.com*.

5. Tap **Go**. Safari displays the website.

✳ **NOTE:** If you hold your finger on the .com button, the virtual keyboard displays a list of other common URL domains, such as *.org* and *.net*, as shown in Figure 27-4.

Using a Search Engine

If you don't know the exact address for a website, you can often find it through a search engine. To use a search engine, follow these steps:

1. From the Home screen, tap **Safari**. The Safari screen appears.

2. Tap the search text box (to the right of the address text box). A virtual keyboard appears (see Figure 27-3).

3. (Optional) Tap the clear button (the X in a gray circle) to the right of the search text box to clear any previous search.

4. Type a word or phrase in the search text box. As you type, your iPhone displays previous search terms you have typed, as shown in Figure 27-5. You can tap a displayed search term or finish typing in a different word or phrase.

5. Tap **Google**. Safari displays your search results.

6. Tap the link for the website you want to visit.

FIGURE 27-4: Holding down the .com button displays other common URL domains.

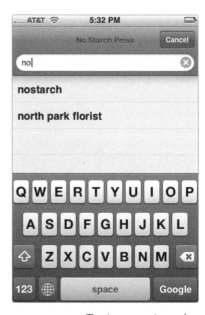

FIGURE 27-5: Typing text into the search text box displays previous search terms you've typed.

Changing How Your iPhone Displays Web Pages

No matter how you view a web page, you may still find the iPhone's tiny screen too small to read comfortably. To solve this problem, the iPhone offers two solutions that you can use alone or together:

► Rotate your iPhone sideways, and the currently displayed web page rotates to show more of it, as shown in Figure 27-6.

FIGURE 27-6: *Rotating the iPhone displays a web page in landscape or portrait mode.*

► Pinch two fingers on the screen and then spread them apart to zoom in. Close the two fingers on the screen to zoom out.

Opening and Switching Between Multiple Websites

On a regular computer, you can use a browser such as Safari to open multiple websites and quickly switch between them. You can do the same on your iPhone, but the process is slightly different. Instead of displaying multiple web pages as tabs, your iPhone displays multiple web pages as *thumbnail images*. You tap a thumbnail image to switch between sites.

To open and view multiple web pages, do this:

1. From the Home screen, tap **Safari**. The Safari screen appears.
2. Tap the New Page icon (the two little screens) in the lower-right corner of the Safari screen, as shown in Figure 27-7.

FIGURE 27-7: *The New Page icon*

3. Safari shows a thumbnail image of the current web page, as shown in Figure 27-8.
4. Tap **New Page**. A blank Safari screen appears.
5. Tap the address field and type a URL (such as *nostarch.com*), or tap the search text box and type a word or phrase to search.
6. Tap **Go**. Notice that the New Page icon in the lower-right corner of the screen displays a number that tells you how many web pages are currently open, as shown in Figure 27-9. You can have up to eight pages open at one time.
7. Tap the New Page icon. Safari displays thumbnail images of each web page, as shown in Figure 27-10.

FIGURE 27-8: *The thumbnail image appears on the screen.*

FIGURE 27-9: *The New Page icon displays the number of open web pages.*

FIGURE 27-10: *A red close circle appears in the upper-left corner of each thumbnail image of an open web page.*

8. Slide your finger left or right across the screen to view another open web page.

9. (Optional) Tap the red close circle in the upper-left corner of a thumbnail image to close the web page.

10. Tap **Done**—or simply tap the page itself—to view the currently displayed web page.

Additional Ideas for Browsing the Internet on Your iPhone

You can think of the iPhone as a miniature computer in your pocket (or purse) that can connect to the Internet from almost anywhere. If you're inside your favorite electronics store, pull out your iPhone, browse the Internet, and check the store's prices compared to prices for the same items online. If you're stuck in line somewhere, pull out your iPhone and browse through your favorite news websites to catch up on the latest headlines and pass the time.

With few exceptions, browsing the Internet on the iPhone is nearly identical to browsing the Internet on a normal computer. With the Internet available from your iPhone, you can view the world's information at your fingertips. It's up to you to decide what you need and what you're going to do once you have the information you want.

Use Your iPhone to Search Google with Voice Commands

Browsing the Internet on the iPhone is no different than browsing the Internet on a normal computer. To take full advantage of the iPhone, Google offers its Google Mobile App, which lets you search using your voice. Just load the app, say a word or phrase, and this app searches for your spoken phrase through Google. Now you can search the Internet without typing anything at all.

Google Mobile App *http://www.google.com/mobile/apple/app.html*

Voice Search lets you search Google just by speaking into your iPhone.

28

Bookmarking Your Favorite Websites

Almost everyone has a list of favorite websites to visit. While you could memorize and type the web address of each website whenever you want to see it, it's much simpler to save your favorite web addresses as *bookmarks*.

When you bookmark a site, you can quickly jump to that site just by tapping its bookmark. To help you get started, your iPhone comes with a bookmark list of popular websites such as Yahoo! and Apple. You can add your own favorites to this list to create your own custom bookmarks.

Project goal: Learn how to bookmark websites on your iPhone.

✳ **NOTE:** If you already have a set of bookmarks on your home computer, you can easily sync them to your iPhone instead of tediously re-entering each one. See Project 12 for instructions on how to sync your bookmarks between the iPhone and Internet Explorer or Safari.

What You'll Be Using

To bookmark websites on your iPhone, you need to use the following:

 The Safari application

Viewing a Bookmarked Website

For your convenience, your iPhone includes a list of popular websites that have already been bookmarked for you (you can modify this list if you want). To view a bookmarked site, do this:

1. From the Home screen, tap **Safari**. The Safari screen appears.
2. Tap the Bookmarks icon (the open book symbol) at the bottom of the screen. The Bookmarks screen appears, as shown in Figure 28-1.
3. Tap a bookmark, such as **Yahoo!** or **Apple**. Its website appears on the screen.

✳ **NOTE:** A bookmark folder appears in the Bookmarks screen with a right-pointing arrow next to it. Tapping a bookmark folder displays a submenu of bookmarked websites.

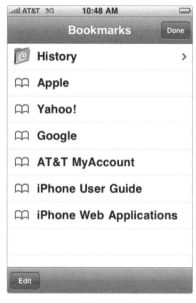

FIGURE 28-1: *The Bookmarks screen lists current bookmarks.*

Saving a Bookmark

When you run across a particularly interesting website that you think you will want to revisit, you can save it as a bookmark and store it in your bookmark list or as an icon on the Home screen.

Adding a Bookmark to the Bookmark List

The bookmark list is usually the easiest place to store a link to a favorite website. To add a bookmark to the list, do this:

1. From the Home screen, tap **Safari**. The Safari screen appears.

2. Open a website by typing its address or searching for it in the search text box.
3. Tap the plus sign at the bottom of the screen. Four options appear, as shown in Figure 28-2.
4. Tap **Add Bookmark**. An Add Bookmark screen appears, as shown in Figure 28-3, where you can enter a descriptive name for your bookmark and choose a place to store it.

FIGURE 28-2: *You can choose where you want to store a bookmark.*

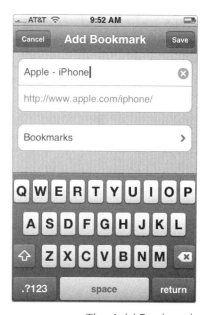

FIGURE 28-3: *The Add Bookmark screen lets you type a name and choose a location for your bookmark.*

5. Type a descriptive name for your bookmark.
6. Tap **Bookmarks**. A screen appears, displaying several folders where you can store your bookmark.
7. Tap the folder where you want to store your bookmark. The Add Bookmark screen appears again (see Figure 28-3).
8. Tap **Save**. Now you can visit this website again by tapping the Bookmarks icon at the bottom of the screen and then tapping the site's bookmark.

Adding a Bookmark to the Home Screen

Saving a website as a bookmark can help you quickly find that site whenever you want to revisit it. But if you visit a site often (such as Amazon.com or eBay, for example), you might want to save a link to that website as an icon directly on your Home screen. Adding a bookmark to the Home screen gives you immediate access to a website just by tapping its icon; no need to open Safari first.

To create an icon for a website on your Home screen, do this:

1. From the Home screen, tap **Safari**. The Safari screen appears.
2. Type the address of a website or search for it using the search text box.
3. Tap the plus sign at the bottom of the screen. Four options appear (see Figure 28-2).
4. Tap **Add to Home Screen**. The Add to Home screen appears, where you can type a descriptive name for your bookmark icon, as shown in Figure 28-4.
5. Type a descriptive name for your bookmark (*Apple - iPhone* in this example).
6. Tap **Add** in the upper-right corner of the screen. Your iPhone will display a bookmark icon on the Home screen titled *Apple - iPhone*.

FIGURE 28-4: *The Add to Home screen lets you type a name for your bookmark.*

∗ **NOTE:** To remove a bookmark icon from the Home screen, hold your finger on the icon until a close button appears in the upper-left corner. This causes all icons on your Home screen to jiggle. Tap the close button, and when the Delete Icon dialog appears asking if you want to delete this icon, tap Delete, and then press the Home button to stop all your icons from jiggling.

Emailing a Website Link

You can share a website with a friend by emailing your friend a link to that site.

∗ **NOTE:** To email a website link, you'll first need to set up an email account, as explained in Project 32.

To email a website link, do this:

1. From the Home screen, tap **Safari**. The Safari screen appears.
2. Tap the plus sign at the bottom of the screen.
3. Tap **Mail Link to this Page**. A message screen appears, where you can type an email address and modify the subject of your message, as shown in Figure 28-5.
4. Enter an email address in the To text box and type a brief description of your message in the Subject text box.

* **NOTE:** If you tap the plus sign to the far right of the To text box, you can open the Contacts program and retrieve a stored email address.

5. Tap **Send**.

* **NOTE:** Sending a website link by email does not save that link on your iPhone. If you want to save a website address, you'll have to bookmark it.

Organizing Bookmarks

After a while, you may save so many bookmarks that it becomes difficult to find the one you want. To solve this bookmark clutter problem, you can delete bookmarks you no longer need or reorganize related bookmarks into folders.

Deleting Bookmarks

The simplest way to organize your bookmarks is to delete those you no longer need. To delete a bookmark, do this:

1. From the Home screen, tap **Safari**. The Safari screen appears.
2. Tap the Bookmarks icon. The Bookmarks screen appears (see Figure 28-1).
3. Tap **Edit** in the lower-left corner of the screen. Red circles with white dashes appear to the left of all your bookmarks.
4. Tap the red circle next to a bookmark you want to delete. A red Delete button appears to the right of the bookmark, as shown in Figure 28-6.

FIGURE 28-5: *You can email a website link to share a website with others.*

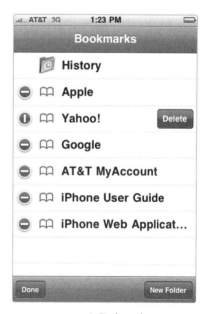

FIGURE 28-6: *A Delete button appears next to a bookmark that you select to delete.*

5. Tap **Delete**. The selected bookmark disappears.
6. Tap **Done** in the lower-left corner of the screen.
7. Tap **Done** in the upper-right corner of the screen to display the Safari screen again.

Creating Bookmark Folders

You can organize bookmarks by grouping related websites into folders. For example, you might create a folder that contains bookmarks to news sites and another with bookmarks to your favorite funny cat or skiing sites.

Before you can store bookmarks in folders, you'll first need to create a folder. To create a folder, do this:

1. From the Home screen, tap **Safari**. The Safari screen appears.
2. Tap the Bookmarks icon. The Bookmarks screen appears (see Figure 28-1).
3. Tap **Edit** in the lower-left corner of the screen. A New Folder button appears in the lower-right corner of the screen.
4. Tap **New Folder**. The Edit Folder screen appears, as shown in Figure 28-7.
5. Type a descriptive name for your folder in the Title field.
6. Tap **Bookmarks**. The Bookmarks screen appears.
7. Tap the location where you want to store your folder.
8. Tap **Bookmarks** in the upper-left corner of the screen. The Bookmarks screen displays your newly created folder.
9. Tap **Done** in the lower-left corner of the screen.
10. Tap **Done** in the upper-right corner of the screen. The Safari screen appears again.

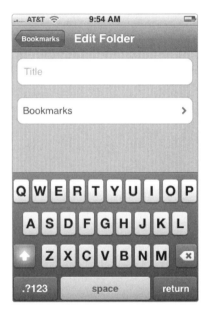

FIGURE 28-7: *The Edit Folder screen lets you add a descriptive name and location for your folder.*

Rearranging Bookmarks and Moving Bookmarks to Another Folder

After you have stored a bookmark in a folder, you can rearrange it or move it to another folder later. (However, you cannot rearrange or move bookmarks that are not inside a folder.) To move a folder, do this:

1. From the Home screen, tap **Safari**. The Safari screen appears.
2. Tap the Bookmarks icon. The Bookmarks screen appears (see Figure 28-1).
3. Tap a folder that contains the bookmark you want to rearrange or move. The screen lists all the bookmarks in the selected folder.
4. Tap **Edit** in the lower-left corner of the screen. A minus sign in a red circle appears to the left of each bookmark, and three horizontal bars appear to the right of each bookmark, as shown in Figure 28-8.
5. (Optional) Place your fingertip on the three horizontal bars to the right of a bookmark, and then slide your finger up or down to change the location of the bookmark in the list. Lift your finger to drop the bookmark at its new location.
6. Tap a bookmark. The Edit Bookmark screen appears, as shown in Figure 28-9.
7. Tap the name of the folder that appears directly above the virtual keyboard (in Figure 28-9, this is the Bookmarks Menu folder). The Bookmarks screen appears, listing

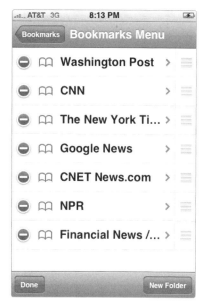

FIGURE 28-8: *A minus sign in a red circle lets you delete a bookmark; three horizontal bars let you rearrange bookmarks.*

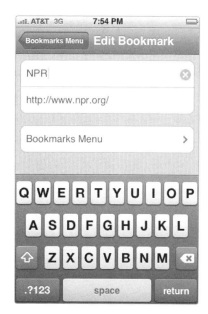

FIGURE 28-9: *The Edit Bookmark screen lets you edit the bookmark name, address, or folder.*

all your current bookmark folders, as shown in Figure 28-10.

8. Tap a folder where you want to place the bookmark. The Edit Bookmark screen appears again (see Figure 28-9).

9. Tap **Bookmarks Menu** in the upper-left corner of the screen to see how your list of bookmarks has changed.

10. Tap **Done** in the lower-left corner of the screen.

11. Press the Home button to return to the Home screen.

✻ *NOTE:* **If you've synchronized your bookmarks from your computer to your iPhone, you may see two folders: Bookmarks Menu and Bookmarks Bar. These simply refer to the folder names of the bookmarks stored on your computer. Your iPhone will not display bookmarks in drop-down menus or as toolbar icons as a browser does on a standard computer.**

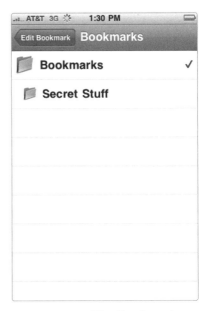

FIGURE 28-10: *The Bookmarks screen displays all available bookmark folders.*

Revisiting Previously Viewed Websites

Have you ever wanted to revisit a website, but you didn't bother to bookmark it? To help you find previously visited websites, Safari automatically tracks your visited websites in a special History list. This essentially bookmarks every website you've visited recently. To access this list and revisit your favorite websites, do this:

1. From the Home screen, tap **Safari**. The Safari screen appears.

2. Tap the Bookmarks icon. The Bookmarks screen appears (see Figure 28-1).

3. Tap **History** at the top of the screen. The History screen appears, as shown in Figure 28-11.
4. Tap a bookmark. Safari reloads that website. (You may need to tap a folder to open a list of sites that you visited on a particular date.)

Additional Ideas for Saving Bookmarks

Unless you have a photographic memory and don't mind doing a lot of extra typing, you should take some time to bookmark your favorite sites. Turn your favorite bookmarks into icons on the Home screen, and you'll always have fast, one-tap access to the sites you visit most often. Store links to less frequently visited sites as ordinary bookmarks so you won't forget them.

For fun, create a folder to store the silliest websites you can find. Then when you need a laugh with your friends, let them browse through these silly sites. How about starting with these?

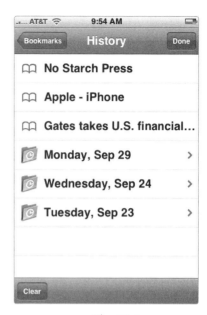

FIGURE 28-11: *The History screen lets you see all previously visited websites.*

▶ Read parodies of the latest news headlines   *http://www.theonion.com/*

▶ See photographs of cats in amusing poses   *http://www.funnycatsite.com/*

▶ Read the latest weird news from around the world   *http://www.fark.com/*

Bookmarks can be time savers (or time wasters, depending on which sites you bookmark), so go ahead and browse the Internet, save your favorite sites, and visit them often so that you won't have to do any actual work during the day.

Use Your iPhone to Save Web Clips

Ordinary bookmarks are nice for storing addresses to entire web pages, but if you only want to save part of a web page, such as images or text, you should use the Evernote app. To use this app, you'll need to set up an account, but then you'll be able to clip text and pictures from web pages or anything else on your screen that you want to save.

More remarkable is that Evernote can actually identify text stored in images, so, for example, you can take pictures of signs and search for the text captured in the image. Evernote also offers free desktop versions of the program for PC and Macintosh, so you'll be able to synchronize your iPhone notes with notes on your computer and vice versa.

Evernote lets you clip and store text or graphic images.

If you find bookmarks too limiting, try Evernote and start clipping and saving only the information you really want to save. If you save part of a web page, Evernote is even smart enough to store the web page's address so you can find and view that information again.

Evernote   *http://evernote.com/*

29

Personalizing the Safari Browser

Many people are happy to use Safari just the way it comes on their iPhone. However, not everyone will want to accept these default settings. Fortunately, you can customize Safari to make it work exactly the way you want.

You might want to customize Safari for personal reasons. Perhaps you prefer using a search engine other than Google. You might also want to customize Safari for added security. If you don't like the idea of websites tracking your activity through cookies, you might want to turn this feature off.

Whatever your reasons for customizing Safari, you'll be happy to know you have plenty of settings you can change to make it work exactly the way you want.

Project goal: Learn how to modify the Safari web browser.

What You'll Be Using

To customize Safari, you need to use the following:

 The Settings application

 The Safari application

Switching Search Engines

By default, Safari uses the Google search engine, but if you don't like Google you can switch to Yahoo! (only these two options are available). To change search engines, do this:

1. From the Home screen, tap **Settings**. The Settings screen appears.
2. Tap **Safari**. (You may need to scroll down the Settings screen to find it.) The Safari screen appears, as shown in Figure 29-1.
3. Tap **Search Engine**. The Search Engine screen appears, as shown in Figure 29-2.

FIGURE 29-1: The Safari screen

FIGURE 29-2: The Search Engine screen

4. Tap **Google** or **Yahoo!**, and Safari will use your chosen search engine.
5. Press the Home button.

Turning AutoFill On and Off

Many websites require you to log in with your name or email address and a password. Since typing this information repeatedly using the virtual keyboard can get tiresome and clumsy, Safari offers an AutoFill feature, which can store and enter this information for you. To turn the AutoFill feature on or off, do this:

1. From the Home screen, tap **Settings**. The Settings screen appears.
2. Tap **Safari**. The Safari screen appears.
3. Tap **AutoFill**. The AutoFill screen appears, as shown in Figure 29-3.
4. (Optional) Tap the **ON/OFF** button next to Use Contact Info. When this switch is ON, tap **My Info** to display your Contacts program. From there, you can tap your own name to access your information.
5. (Optional) Tap the **ON/OFF** button next to Names & Passwords. When this switch is ON, Safari will remember the data you type into login forms and re-enter it on subsequent web page visits.
6. (Optional) Tap the **Clear All** button to clear all stored names and passwords.

FIGURE 29-3: *The AutoFill screen lets you choose the data you want Safari to automatically enter.*

Securing Safari

Although your iPhone is currently safe from most online security risks, that probably won't be true forever, as some hackers like to play with and distribute malicious code. To protect your iPhone from websites that contain malicious code that can be downloaded on your iPhone, you can turn off various features; unfortunately, doing so will probably make browsing less enjoyable. Some of the features you can turn on and off include the following:

▶ **Fraud Warning**   Lets Safari warn you when you might visit malicious sites attempting to masquerade as legitimate ones

▶ **JavaScript**   Used to create interactive web pages

▶ **Plug-ins**   Used to play video and audio

- ▶ **Pop-ups** Used to display pop-up ads or additional website content
- ▶ **Cookies** Used to store information that identifies you to a particular website

Fraud Warning can detect sites that may be trying to trick you into typing in your password by mimicking a bank or other trusted website. Hackers set up these fraudulent websites and then send an email to millions of people, telling them that their account has been compromised and they need to type their password into a new security site. This "security site" then captures people's passwords or credit card information.

JavaScript is a simple programming language used on websites to offer interactive games or menus. Turning off JavaScript on your iPhone can make Safari run faster, but at the expense of some websites' features, because they will not be able to display some interactive options. Try turning off JavaScript and see how it affects the websites you visit the most. If you don't notice any difference, you can leave JavaScript turned off for good.

Plug-ins are programs that add features to Safari, such as the ability to play audio or video files stored on a website. Disabling this feature can speed up your web browsing, but it prevents you from seeing all the content on some websites.

Blocking pop-ups can keep websites from opening additional web pages that show ads, which can slow down your web-browsing experience. Unless you like being bombarded with ads, you'll probably want to keep the *Block pop-up* feature turned on.

There are three options for allowing *cookies*: Never, From visited, and Always. If you choose the Never option, websites won't be able to identify you or track your browsing history. This might prevent you from shopping online (but is that a bad thing?), and it will likely prevent sites such as Amazon.com from displaying a list of recommended books for you. I'll leave it up to you to decide whether this is a good or a bad thing.

If you choose the From visited option, Safari will store cookies only from sites that you visit. If you choose the Always option, Safari can store cookies from sites you haven't even visited. (In general, there are very few reasons to choose the Always option.)

To turn these features on or off, do this:

1. From the Home screen, tap **Settings**. The Settings screen appears.
2. Tap **Safari**. The Safari screen appears (see Figure 29-1).
3. Tap the **ON/OFF** button next to Fraud Warning, JavaScript, Plug-Ins, or Block Pop-ups.

4. Tap **Accept Cookies**. The Accept Cookies screen appears, as shown in Figure 29-4.
5. Tap **Never**, **From visited**, or **Always**.
6. Press the Home button.

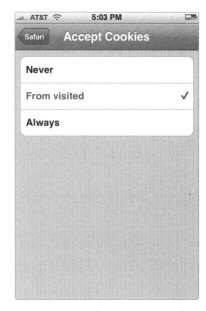

FIGURE 29-4: *The Accept Cookies screen*

Clearing Your Tracks

Every time you browse the Internet, you leave behind traces of where you've been in your web history; these are called *cookies*, and they are saved in a *cache*. (This is not unique to the iPhone; it's the case with most web browsers.)

The iPhone's history list stores a list of all the websites you've visited. The cookies list stores cookies on your iPhone left by sites you've visited. (You might think of these as breadcrumbs that you've left behind, except that each one has identifying information on it. Sites such as Amazon.com store cookies so they can recognize you when you revisit the site.) The cache stores bits and pieces of visited websites, so the next time you visit that site, your iPhone can retrieve part of the web page from its cache, which can make the web page load faster.

The problem with storing this sort of history information on your iPhone is that anyone who has access to your iPhone can examine your browsing habits. If this bothers you, take some time to wipe out your browsing records by doing the following:

1. From the Home screen, tap **Settings**. The Settings screen appears.
2. Tap **Safari**. The Safari screen appears (see Figure 29-1).
3. Tap one or more of the following buttons: **Clear History**, **Clear Cookies**, or **Clear Cache**. A dialog pops up, asking if you really want to clear the chosen option.
4. Tap your choice (such as **Clear Cookies**), or tap **Cancel** if you change your mind.
5. Press the Home button.

Additional Ideas for Modifying Safari

For most people, Safari's default settings work perfectly fine. Still, if you just don't like the way Safari works, or if you like digging into the guts of a program to find ways to tweak it, feel free to dig into these customization settings.

While changing the default search engine to Google or Yahoo! may be a matter of personal preference, changing the other settings in Safari can speed up your web browsing and protect your privacy. If someone manages to peek at your iPhone without your permission, he or she could open Safari and see all the websites you've visited.

If you give your iPhone away, make sure you clear out your history and cache settings. Otherwise, someone else can visit the websites you've browsed and use the cookies stored on your iPhone to impersonate you on a website such as Amazon.com. (Of course, this works the other way around, too, so if you can grab your boss's iPhone, you can blackmail him based on websites that he's been visiting.)

Whatever your reasons for customizing Safari, you can modify a lot of settings, a few, or none at all. Safari works perfectly fine on its own, but with a little customization, you can make it work exactly the way you want it to.

Browse the Internet Privately on Your iPhone

The Safari browser works fine for surfing the Internet on your iPhone, but if you value your privacy, you may get tired of clearing out its cache and cookies periodically. To avoid this problem, try browsing with the Privately app. Unlike Safari, Privately never stores any data in a cache or in cookies, so you can safely browse the Internet anonymously without leaving a trail behind that others can follow.

Privately *http://www .saxorama.net/*

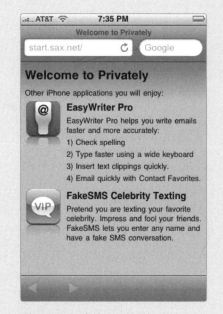

The Privately browser lets you browse the Internet without storing any personal data.

30

Copying and Pasting Text from a Web Page

When you're using your computer, you can visit your favorite web page, copy some text from it, and then paste that text into an email or word processor file. Since this can be a handy way to share or save interesting information you find on the Internet, you may want to copy text from web pages that you view on your iPhone, as well.

By copying chunks of text from a web page and pasting the text into another app, you won't have to bother bookmarking an entire site. (To learn more about copying, cutting, and pasting text, see Project 4.)

Project goal: Learn how to copy and paste text from a web page.

What You'll Be Using

To copy text from a web page on your iPhone, you need to use the following:

 The Safari application

 The Mail application

 The Notes application

Copying Text from a Web Page

Copying text from a web page involves three steps. First, you need to find a web page that contains text. (You can't copy graphics.) Second, you need to select and copy a chunk of text. Third, you need to paste that text into another app, such as Notes or Mail.

To copy text, do this:

1. From the Home screen, tap **Safari**. The Safari screen appears.
2. Navigate to a web page that contains text that you want to copy.
3. Press and hold your fingertip over the text you want to copy. Your iPhone highlights the entire paragraph, as shown in Figure 30-1. (You may need to wait until a web page completely loads before you can select text.)
4. (Optional) Drag one of the handles (the round dots) surrounding the selected text to select more or less text.
5. Tap the **Copy** button that appears next to the selected text.

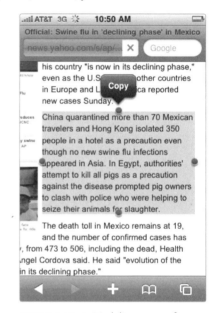

FIGURE 30-1: *Holding your fingertip over text selects that chunk of text.*

Pasting Text

After you have copied text from a web page, you can paste it into any app that allows text, such as the Notes or Mail apps. Just like a computer, your iPhone stores copied text in memory called the *Clipboard*. Once you have a chunk of copied text stored on the clipboard, you can keep pasting that text as many times as you want. But the moment you copy something new to the Clipboard, your old copied text is erased for good.

To paste text you've copied from a web page, do this:

1. Make sure you have copied text from a web page.
2. From the Home screen, tap **Notes** or **Mail** (or the icon for any other app that lets you store large amounts of text).
3. Press and hold a fingertip on the area where you want to paste your copied text. The magnifying glass appears, letting you see the details of where you placed the cursor.
4. Remove your fingertip from the screen. A Paste button appears, as shown in Figure 30-2.
5. Tap the **Paste** command. Your copied text appears.

FIGURE 30-2: *A Paste button appears after you press and hold and then remove your fingertip from the screen.*

Additional Ideas for Copying Text From a Web Page

If you copy text from a web page and store it in the Notes app, you can keep track of interesting tidbits of information that you might find handy in the future. If you copy and paste text into the Mail app, you can send off useful information to others without forcing them to access a website link and then hunt around for the text you wanted them to see. If you're only copying a short chunk of text, you can even send it as a text message.

Copying text from a web page and pasting it in another app lets you keep track of useful information without the hassle of saving an entire website as a bookmark.

With a little research and a lot of copying and pasting, you could gather enough notes to write a term paper or report on your regular computer. Now you have no excuse for not getting any work done, as long as you have an Internet connection and your iPhone.

31 Connecting to a Wi-Fi Network

You can happily browse the Internet with your iPhone through your cellular phone company's network, but doing so may be slow. For faster Internet access, latch onto a Wi-Fi network if one is in range. Many public places, such as airports and coffeehouses, now offer Wi-Fi as a free service, and there's a good chance that you may also have a Wi-Fi connection at home (or you may be in range of an altruistic neighbor's network). When you're using Wi-Fi, you'll enjoy higher speeds than you're likely to get from your cell phone network.

Project goal: Configure your iPhone to connect to a private Wi-Fi network.

What You'll Be Using

To set up a Wi-Fi connection with your iPhone, you need to use the following:

 The Settings application

Configuring an iPhone to Work with a Private Wi-Fi Connection

Wi-Fi networks are either public or private. A *public network* is free for anyone to access without a password; these are common in coffee shops and libraries. However, private, password-protected networks are also common these days. To access a *secure Wi-Fi network*, you need to know and enter the password, as shown in Figure 31-1.

To configure your iPhone to connect to a private Wi-Fi network (such as your home Wi-Fi network), do this:

1. From the Home Screen, tap **Settings**. The Settings screen appears.
2. Tap **Wi-Fi**. The Wi-Fi Networks screen appears, as shown in Figure 31-2.

FIGURE 31-1: *Before accessing a private Wi-Fi network, you must type a password.*

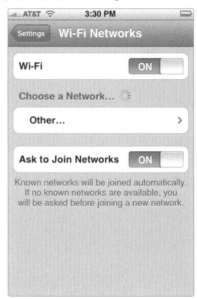

FIGURE 31-2: *The Wi-Fi Networks screen lets you turn Wi-Fi on or off.*

3. Tap the **ON/OFF** button next to Wi-Fi to turn it on. (If you turn this option off, you won't be able to access any Wi-Fi networks.)
4. (Optional) Tap the **ON/OFF** button next to Ask to Join Networks to turn it on or off. When it's turned on, a dialog will pop up asking if you want to connect

to a Wi-Fi network. When it's turned off, your iPhone will attempt to latch onto a Wi-Fi network without first asking for your permission.

5. Tap **Other** under Choose a Network. The Other Network screen appears, as shown in Figure 31-3.

6. Tap **Name** and use the virtual keyboard to type the name of your private Wi-Fi network.

7. Tap **Security**. A Security screen appears, listing the different types of wireless encryption supported by the iPhone, as shown in Figure 31-4.

8. Tap the encryption method used by your Wi-Fi network (ask the person who set it up if you don't know), and then tap **Other Network** in the upper-left corner of the screen. A Password field appears, as shown in Figure 31-5.

FIGURE 31-3: *The Other Network screen lets you define the name and security (encryption) for a Wi-Fi network.*

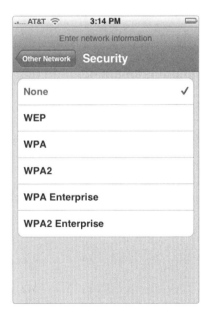

FIGURE 31-4: *The Security screen displays different encryption methods.*

FIGURE 31-5: *The Password field appears after you select an encryption method.*

9. Tap the **Password** field and enter the password for the network. (The person who set up the Wi-Fi network should be able to tell you the password to use.)

10. Tap **Join** in the lower-right corner of the screen. With this information saved, your iPhone should be able to connect to this particular Wi-Fi network in the future without your having to reenter the password.

Choosing Between Multiple Wi-Fi Networks

When your iPhone detects multiple Wi-Fi connections, it displays a Select a Wi-Fi Network dialog so you can choose the Wi-Fi network you want to use, as shown in Figure 31-6.

If you're currently connected to a Wi-Fi network but you want to switch to another one, you can choose another Wi-Fi connection by doing this:

1. From the Home Screen, tap **Settings**. The Settings screen appears.

2. Tap **Wi-Fi**. The Wi-Fi Networks screen appears, listing available Wi-Fi networks from which you can choose, as shown in Figure 31-7.

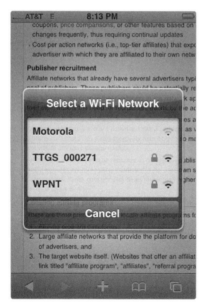

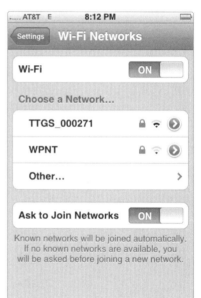

FIGURE 31-6: *When multiple Wi-Fi connections are available, your iPhone lets you choose which one to use.*

FIGURE 31-7: *The Wi-Fi Networks screen lists all available Wi-Fi networks you can use.*

3. Tap the Wi-Fi network you want. If a lock icon appears next to the network name, you'll have to type a password to access that network.

Forgetting a Wi-Fi Network

If you find your iPhone trying to latch on to a Wi-Fi network that you don't want to use, you can stop this by making it "forget" that particular network. That way, your iPhone will skip that network and try to latch on to another one instead.

To "forget" a Wi-Fi network, do this:

1. From the Home screen, tap **Settings**. The Settings screen appears.
2. Tap **Wi-Fi**. The Wi-Fi screen appears.
3. Tap the white arrow inside the blue circle that appears to the right of the network you want your iPhone to forget. The network screen appears, as shown in Figure 31-8.
4. Tap **Forget this Network**. A red Forget Network button and a Cancel button appear at the bottom of the screen.
5. Tap the red **Forget this Network** button, and then press the Home button to return to the Home screen.

FIGURE 31-8: *Forgetting a Wi-Fi network keeps your iPhone from connecting to it.*

Deleting Wi-Fi Network Information

If you decide to give away or sell your iPhone to somebody else, guess what? If you've configured your iPhone to connect to a private Wi-Fi network, your network settings will still be stored in your iPhone, which means that person can access those private networks. Since you may not want to give another person access to a private Wi-Fi network, you'll need to wipe out your network settings by resetting them and reconfiguring the settings to the factory settings.

To reset your network settings, do this:

1. From the Home screen, tap **Settings**. The Settings screen appears.
2. Tap **General**. The General screen appears.
3. Scroll down and tap **Reset** at the bottom of the screen. A Reset screen appears, as shown in Figure 31-9.
4. Tap **Reset Network Settings**. A dialog appears, telling you that your choice will delete your current network settings, as shown in Figure 31-10.

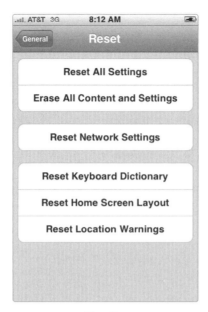

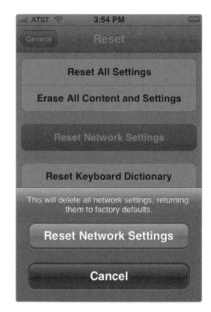

FIGURE 31-9: *The Reset screen*

FIGURE 31-10: *The dialog offers you a choice of resetting network settings or canceling.*

5. Tap **Reset Network Settings**. Your iPhone should restart, at which point you'll have to reconfigure your iPhone's Wi-Fi settings if you want to connect to a private Wi-Fi network.

Additional Ideas for Connecting to a Wi-Fi Network

Even if you don't have a Wi-Fi network of your own, you might as well take a few moments to learn how to configure a Wi-Fi network on your iPhone. This information can be handy later when you do need to connect to a private Wi-Fi network at work or at home.

A Wi-Fi network gives you faster Internet access for browsing web pages, viewing YouTube videos, or downloading apps from the App Store. In general, you'll want to use a Wi-Fi network for greater speed and rely on your cell phone company's network only if Wi-Fi is unavailable. By knowing how to configure a Wi-Fi connection and switch between connections, you'll be able to keep your iPhone connected to the Internet wherever you go.

PART 6

Using Email

32 Setting Up an Email Account

The iPhone is all about staying in touch with people, via phone calls or text messaging, for example. One of the most popular ways to communicate with others is through email messages.

You can send and receive email messages from your existing email accounts using your iPhone, but before you'll be able to do so, you'll need to configure your email account to work with your iPhone.

You can set up any type of email account to work with your iPhone. However, your iPhone already knows how to connect to the following types of email accounts, so they're the easiest to set up:

- AOL
- Gmail
- Yahoo! Mail
- Microsoft Exchange
- MobileMe

* *NOTE:* If you need to set up an email account that iPhone doesn't already support, you may need to find your Post Office Protocol (POP) or Internet Message Access Protocol (IMAP) server names. If that confuses you, ask your Internet/email service provider for help.

Project goal: Set up your email account so that you can access it from your iPhone using your email address and your account password.

What You'll Be Using

To set up an email account on your iPhone, you need to use the following:

 The Settings application

Configuring Your iPhone for Your Email Account

If you have an email account, you'll be able to set it up on your iPhone so that you don't miss any email messages. To set up an email account, do this:

1. From the Home screen, tap **Settings**. The Settings screen appears.
2. Tap **Mail, Contacts, Calendars**. The Mail, Contacts, Calendars screen appears, as shown in Figure 32-1.
3. Tap **Add Account** in the Accounts category. The Add Account screen appears, as shown in Figure 32-2.

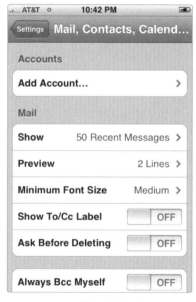

FIGURE 32-1: *The Mail, Contacts, Calendars screen lets you add a new email account.*

FIGURE 32-2: *The Add Account screen lets you choose the type of email account to set up.*

4. Tap the account type, such as AOL or MobileMe. If your email account doesn't appear in the list, tap Other. A New Account screen appears, as shown in Figure 32-3.

5. Tap the **Name** text box. A virtual keyboard appears.

6. Type the name that you want others to see associated with your email address. The name you use should be descriptive, such as your actual name or a nickname.

7. Tap the **Address** text box and type your email address.

8. Tap the **Password** text box and enter your email access password.

9. (Optional) Tap the **Description** text box and enter a brief description of your email account, such as My Work Account or Secret Account.

10. Tap **Save** in the upper-right corner of the screen.

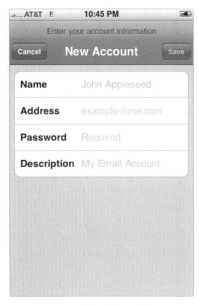

FIGURE 32-3: *The New Account screen lets you define your account information.*

If you are setting up an email account that your iPhone doesn't already recognize, another screen appears, asking for an incoming and outgoing server name, as shown in Figure 32-4. You'll need to get this information from an administrator or the company in charge of your email account.

1. Tap the IMAP or POP tab, depending on the type of email account you want to add. (If you have no idea what an IMAP or POP account is, ask your email company for help.)

2. Enter the incoming and outgoing server names (scroll down to see the outgoing server fields) and tap **Save**. If everything works correctly, your iPhone should be ready to send and receive email.

3. Press the Home button to return to the Home screen.

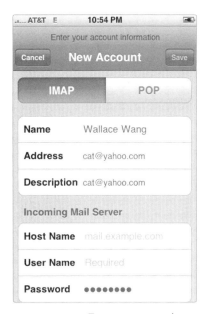

FIGURE 32-4: *For some email accounts, you may need to type the host name of the incoming mail server.*

After you've created at least one email account, you can access it at any time by pressing the Home button and then tapping the Mail icon at the bottom of the screen. If you've created multiple email accounts, you'll need to select which account to use.

Deleting an Email Account from Your iPhone

To delete an email account on your iPhone that you no longer use (or don't want to appear), do this:

1. From the Home screen, tap **Settings**. The Settings screen appears.
2. Tap **Mail, Contacts, Calendars**. The Mail, Contacts, Calendars screen appears (see Figure 32-1).
3. Tap the name of the account you want to delete. That account's screen appears.
4. Scroll down and tap **Delete Account**, as shown in Figure 32-5. Another Delete Account button appears.
5. Tap **Delete Account**.
6. Press the Home button.

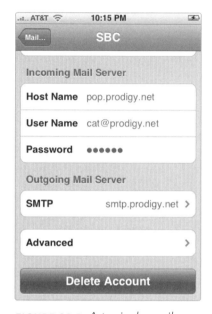

FIGURE 32-5: A typical email account screen

Additional Ideas for Setting Up Email Accounts

You can set up as many email accounts to work with your iPhone as you wish, such as a personal email account and a work account. Of course, if you create too many email accounts, you'll have a hard time keeping them all organized, but at least you can boast how important you are by linking your iPhone to multiple email accounts at once. You can also create and access multiple email accounts with different services, such as Gmail or Yahoo! Mail.

Why would you want to use multiple personal accounts? Well, if one account starts getting overrun by spam, you can kill that account, create a new one, and switch to using the new account. (Of course, you'll probably want to let your friends know when you make the change. Or maybe not.) With the ability to create and use multiple email accounts, you'll no longer have a reason not to communicate with people—unless you really just can't stand them.

33 Reading Email

With your iPhone, you can access your email no matter where you are. The next time you're expecting a message from a friend, loved one, or co-worker, you don't have to wait until you get back to your computer. Once you've set up an email account with your iPhone, you can start reading email messages right away, as long as you're within range of a Wi-Fi network or cellular phone network.

Project goal: Learn how to read email on your iPhone.

What You'll Be Using

To learn how to read email with your iPhone, you need to use the following:

 The Mail application

 The Settings application

Reading a Message

Every email account consists of multiple folders, as shown in Figure 33-1:

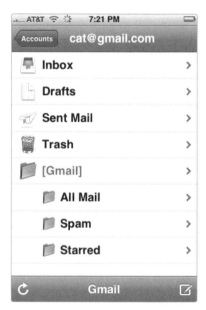

- ▶ **Inbox**   Contains new messages
- ▶ **Drafts**   Contains outgoing messages until you're ready to send them
- ▶ **Sent Mail**   Contains copies of messages you've sent
- ▶ **Trash**   Contains deleted messages that you can still read and retrieve if necessary, until you empty your trash

To read individual messages, you need to choose the email account, the folder, and the specific message that you want to read.

FIGURE 33-1: *The folder structure of a typical email account*

Choosing an Email Account

Since you can set up multiple email accounts on your iPhone, you may need to choose which email account to use by doing this:

1.   From the Home screen, tap **Mail**. The number of unread email messages appears as a white number inside a red circle at the upper-right corner of the Mail icon at the bottom of the screen, as shown in Figure 33-2.

FIGURE 33-2: *The number of unread messages appears on the Mail icon.*

2. (Optional) If a specific email account screen appears (see Figure 33-1), tap **Accounts** in the upper-left corner of the screen. The Accounts screen appears, as shown in Figure 33-3.

3. Tap the account you want to use.

Choosing a Folder and a Message

Once you've selected an email account, your next step is to select a folder (most likely the Inbox folder) and a message in that folder to read. To read an email message, do this:

1. Follow the steps in the section "Choosing an Email Account" on page 256 to display the folders of an account.

2. Tap a folder, such as the Inbox folder. A list of stored messages appears, as shown in Figure 33-4.

3. Tap a message that you want to read. The message appears on the screen.

Viewing File Attachments

Many people send files attached to an email message. If you receive a message with a file attachment, a paper clip icon appears next to the sender's name (see Figure 33-4). Unlike a regular computer, your iPhone can open and display only a limited number of file types, including Microsoft Word and Excel files, text files, PDF (Adobe Acrobat) files, and HTML (web) files.

FIGURE 33-3: *The Accounts screen displays all the email accounts set up on the iPhone.*

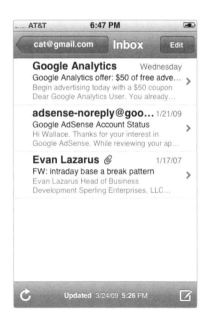

FIGURE 33-4: *Each folder can contain multiple messages.*

Since file attachments can be large, your iPhone won't waste time download-ing them until you specifically ask it to do so. To view a file attachment, do this:

1. Follow the steps in the section "Choosing a Folder and a Message" on page 257 to display a list of messages in an account.
2. Tap a message that contains a file attachment (a message that displays the paper clip icon next to the sender's name). The message appears with a downward-pointing arrow icon that represents your file attachment, as shown in Figure 33-5.
3. Tap the file attachment icion to download it. After the file is downloaded, the file attachment icon changes its appearance, as shown in Figure 33-6.

FIGURE 33-5: *A file attachment waiting to be downloaded*

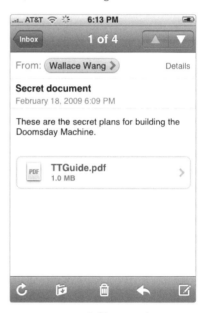

FIGURE 33-6: *A file attachment that's been downloaded*

4. Tap the file attachment icon to display it. You may need to scroll up and down to view the contents of the entire file. To view the original message that came with the file attachment, tap **Message** in the upper-left corner of the screen.

Viewing Other Email Messages

When you're viewing a message on the screen, you'll see up and down arrows in the upper-right corner and an Inbox button in the upper-left corner, as shown in Figure 33-7.

After displaying a message, you can choose from among several options to view other messages:

▶ To return to your list of messages, tap **Inbox**.

▶ To view the previous message, tap the up arrow.

▶ To view the next message, tap the down arrow.

Deleting a Message

When you delete a message, your iPhone stores the deleted message in a special Trash folder, which allows you to view that message again or move it out of the Trash folder to retrieve it. To delete messages permanently, delete them from the Trash folder.

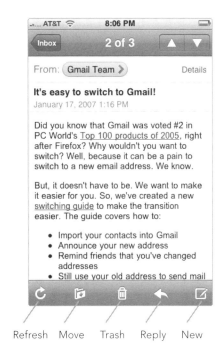

FIGURE 33-7: *Icons for navigating through your messages appear on the screen.*

Sending a Message to the Trash Folder

To delete a message stored in another folder, such as the Inbox folder, and send it to the Trash folder, do this:

1. Follow the steps in the section "Choosing an Email Account" on page 256 to display the folders of your email account.
2. Tap a folder, such as the **Inbox** folder. A list of messages stored in that folder appears (see Figure 33-4).
3. Tap the message you want to delete. The Trash icon appears at the bottom of the screen (see Figure 33-7).
4. Tap the Trash icon. The message disappears from the folder and is moved to the Trash folder.

Emptying the Trash

After you send unwanted messages to the Trash folder, they'll just pile up like a wastebasket that nobody has bothered to empty. That means all your unwanted messages are still gobbling up space, so you'll need to clean out this Trash folder periodically. To delete a message for good, you must empty the Trash by doing this:

1. Follow the steps in the section "Choosing an Email Account" on page 256 to display the folders for an account.
2. Tap **Trash**. A list of deleted messages appears.
3. Tap a message that you want to delete permanently.
4. Tap the Trash icon to delete the message.

Moving a Message

You can move messages from one folder to another, such as between the Trash folder and your Inbox folder, to retrieve a previously deleted message.

To move a message between folders, do this:

1. Follow the steps in the section "Choosing an Email Account" on page 256 to display the folders of an email account.
2. Tap a folder (such as the **Trash** folder) that contains the message you want to move. A list of messages appears.
3. Tap the message that you want to move.
4. Tap the Move icon (see Figure 33-7). A Mailboxes screen appears, listing all the available folders, as shown in Figure 33-8.
5. Tap the folder where you want to store the message, such as the Inbox. Your chosen message moves to the selected folder.

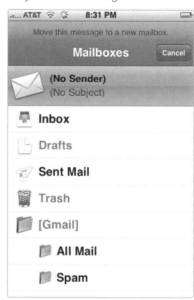

FIGURE 33-8: *The Mailboxes screen lists all your folders.*

Customizing the Appearance of the Mail Application

Since you'll be using the Mail program every time you want to read your email, you might want to take the time to modify the following settings in the Mail, Contacts, Calendars screen, as shown in Figure 33-9:

- **Show** Defines how many messages are displayed at a time

- **Preview** Defines how many lines of a message to display so you can preview the message contents

- **Minimum Font Size** Defines the font size used to display your messages

- **Show To/Cc Label** Determines whether to display the To and Cc labels on each message

- **Ask Before Deleting** Tells your iPhone to ask you whether you really want to delete a message

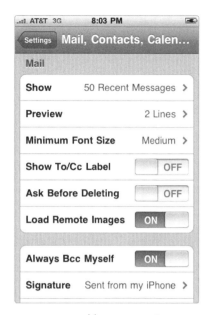

FIGURE 33-9: *You can customize the Mail program through the Mail, Contacts, Calendars screen.*

- **Always Bcc Myself** Tells your iPhone to send yourself copies of every message that you send so you can verify that the message was actually sent out

- **Load Remote Images** Lets you prevent images from loading to make your messages display faster

  To change the appearance of the Mail program, do this:

1. From the Home screen, tap **Settings**. The Settings screen appears.
2. Tap **Mail, Contacts, Calendars**. The Mail, Contacts, Calendars screen appears.
3. Scroll down to the Mail category.

4. Tap **Show**. The Show screen appears, letting you choose how many recent messages you want to display, as shown in Figure 33-10.

5. Tap an option, such as **50 Recent Messages**, and then tap **Mail** in the upper-left corner of the screen to return to the Mail, Contacts, Calendars screen.

6. Tap **Preview**. The Preview screen appears, where you can choose the number of lines in a message you want to display, as shown in Figure 33-11.

7. Tap an option, such as **5 Lines**, and then tap **Mail** to return to the Mail, Contacts, Calendars screen.

8. Tap **Minimum Font Size**. The Minimum Font Size screen appears, where you can choose how large your text will appear, as shown in Figure 33-12.

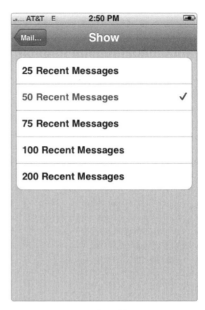

FIGURE 33-10: *The Show screen lets you define the number of messages to display.*

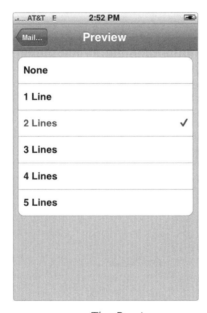

FIGURE 33-11: *The Preview screen lets you define how many lines will display from each message.*

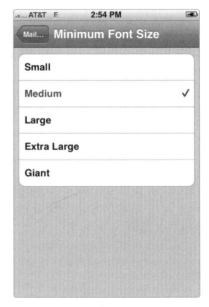

FIGURE 33-12: *The Minimum Font Size screen lets you define how large to display text.*

9. Tap an option, such as **Large**, and then tap **Mail** to return to the Mail, Contacts, Calendars screen.

10. Tap the **ON/OFF** button next to Show To/Cc Label to turn this option on or off.

11. Tap the **ON/OFF** button next to Ask Before Deleting to turn this option on or off.

12. Tap the **ON/OFF** button next to Always Bcc Myself to turn this option on or off.

13. Tap the **ON/OFF** button next to Load Remote Images to turn this option on or off.

14. Press the Home button to return to the Home screen.

Defining How Often Messages Are Retrieved

You can access email in two ways: Push and Fetch. The *Push* option works only for certain email accounts, such as MobileMe or Gmail, where the service tries to send new messages to your iPhone as soon as it receives them without your having to do anything. When messages are pushed to your phone, you should receive and be able to read messages within seconds after they're sent to you (theoretically).

The *Fetch* option works the way most email works, by periodically checking your email account for new messages. Because Fetch checks only periodically, such as every 15 minutes, the time delay between receiving a new message and it actually appearing on your iPhone can vary from a few seconds to several minutes, depending on the setting. The shorter you set this time interval, the more frequently your iPhone will check for email. (More frequent checking can slow things down on your phone, so you might try different settings to see which works best.)

To define how fast your iPhone will retrieve email data, do this:

1. From the Home screen, tap **Settings**. The Settings screen appears.

2. Tap **Mail, Contacts, Calendars**. The Mail, Contacts, Calendars screen appears.

3. Tap **Fetch New Data**. The Fetch New Data screen appears, as shown in Figure 33-13.

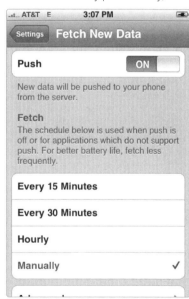

FIGURE 33-13: *The Fetch New Data screen lets you turn Push on or off and define a Fetch time interval.*

4. (Optional) Tap the **ON/OFF** button next to Push to turn it on or off.
5. (Optional) In the Fetch group, tap a time interval, such as **Every 15 Minutes**. (If you tap Manually, your iPhone will check email each time you open and view your email account.)
6. Press the Home button to return to the Home screen.

Additional Ideas for Reading Your Email

Reading email can be fun, especially when you receive messages from people you like. If you like receiving email, but you're not receiving enough messages, sign up for Google Alerts (*http://www.google.com/alerts*) or Yahoo! Alerts (*http://alerts .yahoo.com*). Both free services can send you email messages containing the latest news on any topic that you choose. You can fill up your Inbox with all sorts of information almost instantly, if that's what you would like.

Whether you enjoy tracking the latest sports, technology, or entertainment news, set up a Google or Yahoo! Alert and you'll be assured of receiving a steady supply of useful email messages every day. With an Inbox folder crammed full of messages, you'll always have interesting reading material, or just a bunch of time-wasters, to peruse whenever you have a free moment during the day. But do try to avoid that spam.

34

Writing and Sending Email

Reading email from friends, loved ones, and co-workers is nice, but you'll eventually want to respond to some of those messages. You can type email messages and send them directly from your iPhone so you can stay in touch with others whether you're at home, on the road, or stuck in traffic somewhere around town.

Project goal: Learn how to write and send email on your iPhone.

What You'll Be Using

To learn how to write and send email on your iPhone, you need to use the following:

 The Settings application   The Contacts application

 The Mail application   The Photos application

Configuring Settings for the Mail Application

When writing email messages, you may want to configure two additional settings for the Mail program:

▶ **Signature**   This setting displays text at the end of your message, such as your company name and motto. You can also choose not to display the "Sent from my iPhone" signature.

▶ **Default Account**   This setting defines the email account to use when sending email from a program other than the Mail program, such as the Contacts program.

To modify these settings, do this:

1. From the Home screen, tap **Settings**. The Settings screen appears.
2. Tap **Mail, Contacts, Calendars**. The Mail, Contacts, Calendars screen appears, as shown in Figure 34-1.
3. Tap **Signature**. A Signature screen appears, as shown in Figure 34-2.
4. Type or edit the text using the virtual keyboard, and then tap **Mail** in the upper-left corner of the screen to return to the Mail, Contacts, Calendars screen.

* **NOTE:** Signatures are a great place to put the address for your personal or company's website. Every message you send will act like a free advertisement for your site.

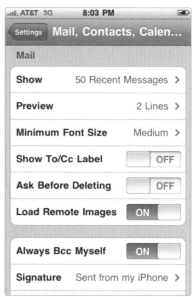

FIGURE 34-1: *You can modify the Mail settings in the Mail, Contacts, Calendars screen.*

5. Tap **Default Account**. A list of email accounts appears.
6. Tap the email account you want to set as the default account. This will be the email address that all your messages will come from.
7. Press the Home button to return to the Home screen.

Writing a New Message

A new message lets you initiate email contact with a person. To create a new email message, you can use the Mail program or the Contacts program.

The Mail program is useful for typing an email address to send your message to. The Contacts program is useful if you've already stored an email address and don't feel like typing it again.

Writing a Message from the Mail Application

The Mail program lets you either type an email address or retrieve an email address from the Contacts program. To use the Mail program to write and send a message, do this:

1. From the Home screen, tap **Mail**. The Mail screen appears. (If you have set up multiple email accounts, you may first need to select which account to use.) The New Message icon, which looks like a slip of paper with a pencil, appears in the lower-right corner of the screen, as shown in Figure 34-3.

FIGURE 34-2: *The Signature screen displays text that appears at the end of every message you send.*

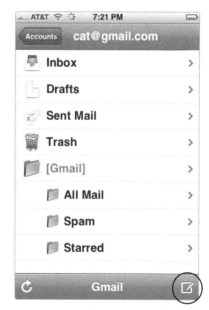

FIGURE 34-3: *Tapping the New Message icon at the bottom of the Mail screen lets you create a new message.*

2. Tap the New Message icon. The New Message screen appears, as shown in Figure 34-4.
3. Type an email address in the To text box. (If you tap the white plus sign in the blue circle that appears at the right of the To text box, the Contacts screen appears. There, you can tap a name to insert that person's saved email address automatically.)
4. Tap in the **Subject** text box and type a subject for your message.
5. When you're done typing your message, tap **Send** in the upper-right corner of the screen.

Writing a Message from the Contacts Application

FIGURE 34-4: *The New Message screen*

If you want to send a message to someone whose contact information is stored in your Contacts program, it's much easier to use that person's saved email address than type it in yourself. You can do this directly from the Contacts program. To send a message to a contact stored in your Contacts program, do this:

1. From the Home screen, tap **Contacts**. The Contacts screen appears.
2. Tap a name that contains an email address of a person to which you want to send your message. An Info screen appears, listing that person's contact information.
3. Tap the email address to which you want to send your message. A New Message screen appears (see Figure 34-4) with the recipient's email address already added.
4. Tap in the **Subject** text box and type a subject for your message.
5. When you're done writing your message, tap **Send**.

Replying to a Message

If you've received a message from someone and you want to reply to that message, do this:

1. From the Home screen, tap **Mail**. The Mail screen appears.
2. Select an email account, and then tap a folder such as the Inbox folder.
3. Tap the message to which you want to write a reply. A reply icon (a curved arrow pointing to the left) appears at the bottom of the screen, as shown in Figure 34-5.
4. Tap the reply icon. Reply and Forward buttons appear, as shown in Figure 34-6.

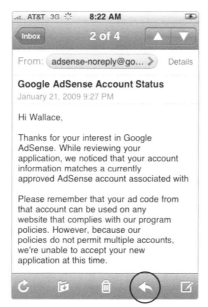

FIGURE 34-5: The reply icon appears at the bottom of the screen.

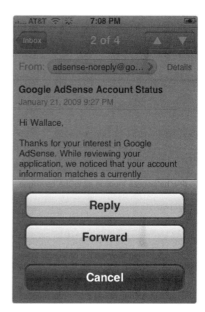

FIGURE 34-6: The Reply and Forward buttons

5. Tap **Reply**. A Message screen appears with the sender's email address already added to the To text box, a subject already added to the Subject text box, and the contents of the old message in the Message text box so the recipient can view the message to which you are replying. (If you tap **Forward**, you'll need to add an email address in the To text box.)
6. Tap **Send** when you're done typing your message.

Working with Drafts

Sometimes you may start writing a message and need to stop to do something else. Rather than wiping out your partial message and starting all over again later, you can save your message in the Drafts folder. Then you can leisurely complete your email and send it when you're ready.

Storing a Message in the Drafts Folder

The Drafts folder is meant to store all draft messages until you're ready to send them. To store a message in the Drafts folder, do this:

1. Create an email message by tapping the New Message icon in the lower-right corner of the Mail screen. Or, to reply to or forward an existing message, tap the reply icon and then tap the **Reply** or **Forward** button.
2. Tap **Cancel** in the upper-left corner of the screen. Save, Don't Save, and Cancel buttons appear at the bottom of the screen, as shown in Figure 34-7.
3. Tap **Save** to store your message in the Drafts folder. To edit it again, you'll need to open the Drafts folder and tap this message.
4. (Optional) Tap **Don't Save** to delete and discard the message.
5. (Optional) Tap **Cancel** to return to your message in the Drafts folder so you can continue typing.

FIGURE 34-7: *The Save, Don't Save, and Cancel buttons*

Sending a Message from the Drafts Folder

After you've saved an email message in the Drafts folder, you can always go back when you're ready to finish writing it. To send a message from the Drafts folder, do this:

1. Open the Drafts folder that contains the email message you want to send. A list of messages stored in the Drafts folder appears.
2. Tap the email message that you want to send. The message appears on the screen.
3. (Optional) Make changes to your message.
4. Tap **Send** in the upper-right corner of the screen.

Deleting a Message from the Drafts Folder

Sometimes you may store a message in the Drafts folder and then decide that you don't want to send it after all. To delete a message from the Drafts folder, do this:

1. Open the Drafts folder that contains the message you want to delete. A list of messages stored in the Drafts folder appears.
2. Tap **Edit** in the upper-right corner of the screen. Radio buttons appear to the left of each message, and a red Delete button appears at the bottom of the screen.
3. Tap the radio button(s) next to the message(s) you want to delete. A checkmark appears in each of the selected radio buttons, as shown in Figure 34-8.
4. Tap **Delete**. (If you tap Move, you'll be able to select a folder and move your messages there.)

FIGURE 34-8: *A checkmark appears next to each selected message.*

Sending a Photo

In a regular email program on a computer, you can attach all sorts of files to your messages, such as word processor documents, videos, and audio files. With the iPhone, the only file attachments you can send are pictures. To send a picture, do this:

1. From the Home screen, tap **Photos**. The Photo Albums screen appears.
2. Select a photo album and then scroll through your pictures until you see one that you want to send.
3. Tap the photo that you want to send. A row of icons appears at the bottom of the screen, as shown in Figure 34-9.

FIGURE 34-9: *Tapping a photo displays icons at the bottom of the screen.*

4. Tap the icon on the far left, which looks like a square with an arrow pointing to the right. A series of options pops up, as shown in Figure 34-10.

5. Tap the **Email Photo** button. A New Message screen appears with your photo attached, as shown in Figure 34-11.

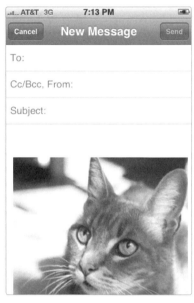

FIGURE 34-10: *Options appear to let you choose what you want to do with your photo.*

FIGURE 34-11: *An attached photo in a new message*

6. Type an email address in the To text box, a subject in the Subject text box, and your actual message above the photo.

7. Tap the **Send** button in the upper-right corner of the screen to send out your message with the photo attached.

Additional Ideas for Writing and Sending Email

If you often write and send messages to the same people, take a moment to store their email addresses in the Contacts program. That way, you can spare yourself typing each person's email address every time you want to send him or her a message. If you'd rather not use the Contacts program, just reply to your messages and let your iPhone add the recipient's email address automatically.

If you want to promote your business or your contact information, you can modify your signature. Add your name, your company name, and your website address, or add a funny saying that you want to share with everyone who reads your email messages. Since the email messages you write can express your creativity, let your imagination run wild and create a signature that uniquely reflects your personality.

By storing messages in the Drafts folder, you can take your time writing messages so you can say exactly what you mean without feeling rushed, or you can go back and spell check your email message to get rid of typos and grammatical errors.

PART 7

Business Stuff

35 Taking Notes

Have you ever had a great idea and couldn't find a pen and paper so you could write it down? Too often, we promise ourselves we'll jot down our wonderful ideas as soon as we can—and then the whole day goes by and we've not only forgotten to write down our ideas, but we've forgotten what they were in the first place.

To capture your thoughts as soon as they occur, you can type them into the Notes program on your iPhone. Not only will this let you save your ideas immediately, but it also ensures that you'll be able to find and read them instead of trying to decipher hasty scribbles on a napkin or a scrap of paper that happened to be convenient at the time.

Project goal: Learn how to type, save, and find notes stored on your iPhone.

What You'll Be Using

To type, save, and find notes on your iPhone, you need to use the following:

 The Notes application

Typing a Note

The Notes program acts like a simple word processor that lets you type a note and save it. To create and save a note, do this:

1. From the Home screen, tap **Notes**. The Notes screen appears.
2. Tap the plus sign in the upper-right corner of the screen. The virtual keyboard appears at the bottom of the New Note screen, as shown in Figure 35-1.
3. Type your note text. When you're finished, tap **Done**. The Notes screen appears again, briefly displaying a few words from each of your saved notes, as shown in Figure 35-2.

FIGURE 35-1: The virtual keyboard lets you type text to save as a note.

FIGURE 35-2: The Notes screen displays a bit of each note on a separate line.

Viewing and Editing a Note

After you've typed and stored one or more notes on your iPhone, you can view and edit them at any time by doing this:

1. From the Home screen, tap **Notes**. The Notes screen appears, showing each note on a separate line (see Figure 35-2).
2. Tap a note, and it appears, along with four icons (Previous Note, Email Note, Trash, and Next Note) at the bottom of the screen, as shown in Figure 35-3.
3. (Optional) Tap the Previous Note or Next Note icon to view a different note. (If either icon appears dimmed, that means you are already viewing the first or last note.)
4. (Optional) Tap your note if you want to edit it or type new text. The virtual keyboard appears at the bottom of the screen.
5. Tap **Done** when you're finished viewing and editing a note.

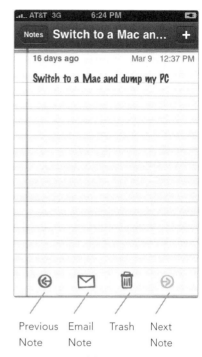

FIGURE 35-3: *Your note appears with four icons.*

＊ **NOTE:** To move the cursor, tap your fingertip over the text where you want the cursor to appear.

Deleting a Note

Notes are handy for storing information you need for a while, such as a shopping list. Eventually, you'll probably want to delete most of your notes when you don't need them anymore. To delete a note, do this:

1. From the Home screen, tap **Notes**. The Notes screen appears with a list of all your notes.
2. Tap the note you want to delete. The note appears and displays four icons (Previous Note, Email Note, Trash, and Next Note) at the bottom of the screen (see Figure 35-3).

3.   Tap the Trash icon. Two new buttons appear, as shown in Figure 35-4.

* **NOTE:** Make sure you really want to delete a note before tapping Delete Note. Once you delete a note, you cannot retrieve it.

4.   Tap **Delete Note** (or tap **Cancel** if you've changed your mind).
5.   Tap **Notes** in the upper-left corner of the screen to see a list of your saved notes.

Emailing a Note

Sometimes you may write a note that you want to send to someone else, such as a cool business idea. Rather than retype your note into an email message, you can send your note directly as an email message. To do this, you must have first set up an email account to work with your iPhone (see Project 32). Then do this:

1.   From the Home screen, tap **Notes**. The Notes screen appears, listing all of your saved notes.
2.   Tap the note you want to email. Your chosen note appears on the screen.
3.   Tap the Email Note icon. An email screen appears, displaying your note as the text in an email message.
4.   Tap the **To** field. A virtual keyboard appears at the bottom of the screen, as shown in Figure 35-5.
5.   Type an email address in the To text box. (If you tap the plus sign that appears at the far right of the To text box, you can access your Contacts list of names and email addresses.)

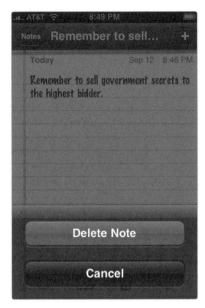

FIGURE 35-4: *Two buttons appear to let you delete the note or cancel if you've changed your mind.*

FIGURE 35-5: *The email screen displays the contents of your note as a message.*

6. (Optional) Tap the message text if you want to edit your message or add new text using the virtual keyboard.

7. Tap **Send** to send your note in an email.

Using Phone Numbers and Email Addresses in a Note

If you type a phone number or email address, Notes is smart enough to recognize it as such and underline it. If you tap an underlined phone number, your iPhone gives you the option to call that number. If you tap an underlined email address, your iPhone displays a New Message screen with the email address already in the To text box.

To see how to dial a phone number and send an email from Notes, do this:

1. From the Home screen, tap **Notes**. The Notes screen appears.

2. Tap the plus sign in the upper-right corner of the screen. The virtual keyboard appears at the bottom of the New Note screen (see Figure 35-1).

3. Type your note text. Make sure you include a real phone number and email address. When you're finished, tap **Done**. (Notice that after you tap Done, the phone number and email address both appear underlined.)

4. Tap the phone number. A dialog appears, asking if you want to Cancel or Call that number, as shown in Figure 35-6.

5. Tap **Cancel** or **Call**. If you tap Call, your iPhone dials your selected number.

FIGURE 35-6: *Tapping a phone number gives you the option of calling that number*

6. Tap the underlined email address in your note. A New Message screen appears. (Notice that it contains the email address already typed into the To text box.) Now you can type a message and tap **Send** to send the email or tap **Cancel** to discard it.

Additional Ideas for Using Notes

Notes can be handy for jotting down ideas and keeping track of your thoughts. Keep your iPhone with you, and when you have an idea, make a note of it before you forget. You can also use a note to remind yourself of things you need to do, or to help you remember your grocery list. Carry your iPhone so you can review your list at the store.

Type positive affirmations or goals into a note, and whenever you have a spare moment, take out your iPhone and review your affirmations or goals. This can help you stay focused on what you want to achieve and spare you the boredom of being stuck someplace, such as waiting in line, where you can't do anything productive.

If you want to transfer your notes to your computer, just email them to yourself. When you open that email message on your computer, your note will appear as ordinary text that you can copy and paste into another program, such as a word processor.

Notes can safely store your thoughts so you'll always be able to find them again. You'll never risk losing a good idea—unless, of course, you lose your iPhone.

Use Your iPhone to Sketch Your Ideas

The Notes app is great for jotting down ideas by typing on the virtual keyboard. However, if you prefer jotting down ideas by scribbling on a napkin, you might prefer Napkin Genius Lite. This app lets you draw on your iPhone's screen and save your images as a picture file, much like drawing on a napkin. Now you can capture your ideas in visual form.

Napkin Genius Lite   *http://www.atomicpowered.net/iphone/napkingeniuslite*

Napkin Genius Lite lets you sketch your ideas.

36 Recording Voice Memos

If you are suddenly struck with inspiration, you could type your thoughts into the Notes app to store them in print. But inspiration isn't always convenient—you may be busy driving and don't want to take the time to type out your ideas.

As an alternative to the Notes app, use the Voice Memos app, which lets you turn your iPhone into a digital audio recorder. Now if you have anything that you want to remember, you don't have to waste time typing it. Just speak it into your iPhone, and store your information as an audio file that you can play back later.

This makes it handy to save telephone numbers, email addresses, or just random thoughts by recording them. After you record your ideas, you can even email the audio file or send it as a multimedia message (see Project 16).

Project goal: Learn how to store, retrieve, and send voice memos on your iPhone.

What You'll Be Using

To record voice memos on your iPhone, you need to use the following:

 The Voice Memos application

Recording a Memo

To record a memo, follow these steps:

1. From the Home screen, tap the **Voice Memos** icon. The Voice Memos screen appears, as shown in Figure 36-1.
2. Tap the red record button in the bottom-left corner of the screen. The record button turns into a pause button, as shown in Figure 36-2.

FIGURE 36-1: *The Voice Memos screen*

FIGURE 36-2: *The pause button appears when you're recording.*

3. Start speaking to record an audio memo.
4. (Optional) Tap the pause button to temporarily stop recording. Tap the pause button a second time to resume recording again.
5. Tap the black stop button in the bottom-right corner of the screen to end your recording session.

Listening to a Memo

After you have recorded a memo, you'll probably want to listen to it. To replay a memo, do this:

1. From the Home screen, tap the **Voice Memos** icon. The Voice Memos screen appears.
2. Tap the button that appears in the bottom-right corner of the screen. The Voice Memos screen appears, as shown in Figure 36-3.
3. Tap the voice memo you want to replay. A play button (an arrow in a circle) appears to the left of your chosen voice memo, as shown in Figure 36-4.

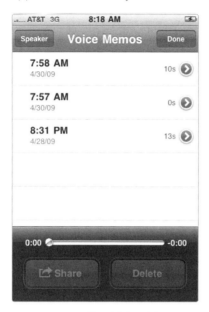

FIGURE 36-3: *The Voice Memos screen lists all your recorded memos, arranged by date and time.*

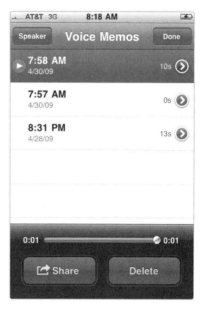

FIGURE 36-4: *After you select a voice memo, you can play, share, or delete it.*

4. Tap the play button to the left of the selected voice memo to listen to that memo.

Sharing a Memo

Voice memos are great for recording your thoughts, and you may also want to share them with others via email or text message. You can send your recorded voice memo by doing this:

1. From the Home screen, tap the **Voice Memos** icon. The Voice Memos screen appears.
2. Tap the button that appears in the bottom-right corner of the screen. The Voice Memos screen appears, listing all your recorded memos (see Figure 36-2).
3. Tap the voice memo you want to share. Share and Delete buttons appear at the bottom of the screen, as shown in Figure 36-5.
4. (Optional) Tap the **Delete** button. A red Delete Voice Memo and Cancel button appear. At this point, you can tap the red **Delete Voice Memo** button to permanently erase your voice memo, or tap **Cancel** to keep your voice memo.
5. Tap the blue **Share** button. Email Voice Memo, MMS, and Cancel buttons appear at the bottom of the screen, as shown in Figure 36-6.

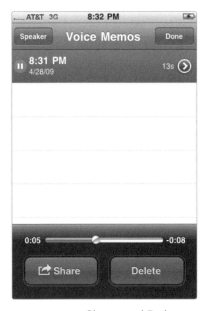

FIGURE 36-5: Share and Delete buttons appear after you select a voice memo.

FIGURE 36-6: The Email Voice Memo, MMS, and Cancel buttons

6. Tap the **Email Voice Memo** or **MMS** button. Depending on which button you tap, you'll need to type or choose an email address or mobile phone number to which you want to send an MMS (Multimedia Service message).

Editing a Memo

If you tend to take a while getting to your point when you're talking, you might want to edit your voice memos after you record them. You can either cut a memo from the beginning or the end—you cannot cut out chunks of your memo from the middle.

Besides trimming a voice memo, you can also give it a unique label or name such as *Podcast*, *Idea*, or *Lecture*. That way you can easily identify what content your voice memo contains.

To trim the beginning or end of a voice memo and give it a label, do this:

1. From the Home screen, tap the **Voice Memos** icon. The Voice Memos screen appears.
2. Tap the button that appears in the bottom-right corner of the screen. The Voice Memos screen appears, listing all your recorded memos (see Figure 36-2).
3. Tap the arrow button that appears to the far right of the voice memo you want to edit. An Info screen appears, as shown in Figure 36-7.
4. Tap the **Trim Memo** button. A slider appears along with a Trim Voice Memo button at the bottom of the screen.
5. Place your finger at the beginning or end of the slider (on the three vertical lines), and drag your finger left or right to trim the beginning or end of your voice memo, as shown in Figure 36-8.
6. Lift your fingertip off the screen when you're happy with the amount of time you've trimmed from your voice memo.
7. (Optional) Tap the play button that appears to the left of the slider to hear your trimmed voice memo.

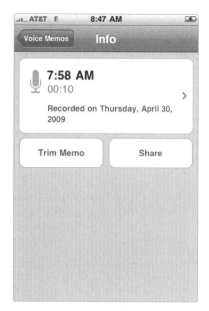

FIGURE 36-7: *The Info screen displays the Trim Memo button.*

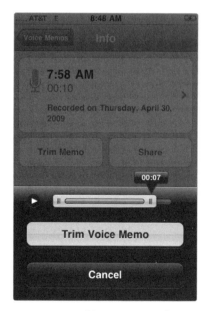

FIGURE 36-8: *You can trim the beginning or end of a voice memo.*

You may need to adjust the amount of trimming you've done.

8. Tap the **Trim Voice Memo** button when you're happy with the edited version of your voice memo. The Info screen appears again.

9. Tap the arrow that appears to the right of the time and date your voice memo was recorded. A Label screen appears, listing ways you can label your voice memo, as shown in Figure 36-9.

10. Tap a label such as **Memo** or **Interview**. (If you tap Custom at the bottom of the screen, you can use the virtual keyboard to type your own label.)

Deleting a Memo

Eventually, you'll probably want to delete some voice memos to avoid cluttering your iPhone with old recordings. You can do that by following these steps:

1. From the Home screen, tap the **Voice Memos** icon. The Voice Memos screen appears.

2. Tap the button that appears in the bottom-right corner of the screen. The Voice Memos screen appears, listing all your recorded memos (see Figure 36-2).

3. Tap the voice memo that you want to delete. A red Delete button appears at the bottom of the screen (see Figure 36-4).

4. Tap the red **Delete** button. A red Delete Voice Memo button appears at the bottom of the screen, as shown in Figure 36-10.

5. Tap the **Delete Voice Memo** button (or tap the **Cancel** button if you've changed your mind).

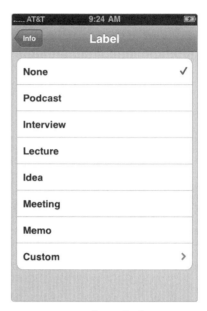

FIGURE 36-9: *The Label screen lets you give your voice memo a descriptive name.*

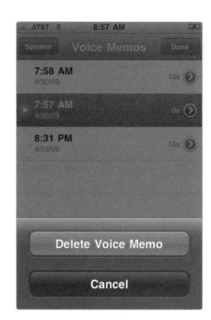

FIGURE 36-10: *A Delete Voice Memo and Cancel button appear.*

Additional Ideas for Recording Voice Memos

Voice Memos can be handy for capturing your own thoughts or the voices of others. Instead of writing down somebody's phone number or email address, just ask that person to tell you and record it in a voice memo. Then you can listen to that information later!

If you're attending a class or a meeting, use your iPhone to record a lecture or a presentation so you can replay it and review it later. If you get stopped by the police, record your interactions with them. That way, you'll have a record of everything you said to the police officers and what they said back to you.

Rather than clutter your iPhone with voice memos, send them to yourself by email, download them to your computer, and then delete them from your iPhone. Your computer probably has far more storage space than your iPhone.

The next time you go to the grocery store, record your shopping list as a voice memo. Then you can listen to your list to make sure you never forget to buy milk or eggs. With the Voice Memos app, you can throw away your old audio recorder and use your iPhone instead.

37

Storing Contact Information

Unless you're a hermit, you probably need to contact certain people occasionally, such as friends, family members, co-workers, and business associates. You could try memorizing each person's contact information—name, address, email address, and phone number—but a much simpler solution is to store this information in your iPhone so you can find it any time you need it.

To store contact information, you can use the Contacts program, which acts like a simple database, similar to a Rolodex of business cards. After you've stored important contact information, you'll be able to send email, make a phone call, or send a text message just by tapping a person's name. You can even attach a picture of each person so you'll never forget a face.

Project goal: Learn how to store contact information on your iPhone.

What You'll Be Using

To store contact information on your iPhone, you need to use the following:

 The Contacts application   The iPhone USB cable

 The Settings application

Importing Contact Data from Other Programs

If you have contact information stored in another program (such as a database program on Windows or Mac OS X), or you've stored information on a mobile phone such as a BlackBerry or Windows Mobile device, you can transfer that data to your iPhone, but it may take a few extra steps. Fortunately, you'll only have to do this once, so here's the basic idea of how it works.

To transfer contact data trapped on another mobile phone, you must first synchronize the data with your ordinary database program on your computer (such as Microsoft Outlook). After all your data is current in your computer database program, you'll have to export all the data to one of four types of files:

- ▶ **vCard**   A standard file format for storing business card data

- ▶ **LDIF**   Lightweight Data Interchange Format, a format for storing individual pieces of data

- ▶ **Tab-delimited**   A text file in which data is separated by tabs

- ▶ **Comma-separated values (CSV)**   A text file in which data is separated by commas

Most contact database programs, such as Microsoft Entourage and Outlook, can export data in either the vCard or LDIF format. Other databases or spreadsheets, such as FileMaker, MS Excel, or MS Access, can export data as tab-delimited or CSV files.

After you've exported your data from a database program, your next step is to import that data into the Address Book (Mac OS X) or Outlook (Windows). From here, you can sync your data with your iPhone by connecting your iPhone to your computer with your USB cable and using iTunes (see Project 12).

If your data is trapped in your old mobile phone, such as a BlackBerry, Palm, or Windows Mobile device, you can spare yourself much hassle by getting a program called The Missing Sync for iPhone (*http://www.markspace.com/*). Not only will The Missing Sync program transfer your contact information, but it will transfer photographs and appointment information, as well.

If your contact information is stored in Google Contacts, you can synchronize the data using the Google Sync for iPhone program (*http://www.google.com/mobile/apple/sync.html*).

Storing Names and Other Information

The Contacts program relies on you to add information. In addition to adding a person's name, you can also add his or her street address, phone number, email address, website address, and a variety of other contact information you might need. You can store different information about each person, such as the name and phone number of one person and the name and email address of another person.

The basic idea behind any database, such as the Contacts program, is that it provides blank areas, called *fields*, where you can store data. The following fields are included in the Contacts program:

▶ **Add new Phone** Add a person's phone number and label it as mobile, work, home, or another description—if someone calls you from a phone number that you've stored in the Contacts program, your iPhone will display that person's name on the screen.

▶ **Ringtone** Define a unique ringtone to play when a particular person calls you.

▶ **Add new Email** Store a contact's work, home, or other type of email address.

▶ **Add new URL** Store a contact's personal, work, or other type of website address.

▶ **Add new Address** Store a contact's home or work street address.

▶ **Add Field** Add unique information about a person, such as a birthday, a nickname, or a phonetic pronunciation of his or her name.

To add a name and contact information to your iPhone, do this:

1. From the Home screen, tap **Contacts**. (You may need to scroll to the second pane to find the Contacts icon.) The All Contacts screen appears, as shown in Figure 37-1. (If you haven't stored any names, the All Contacts screen will be blank.)

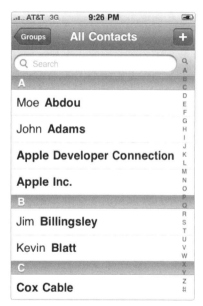

FIGURE 37-1: The All Contacts screen displays a list of saved contact names.

2. Tap the plus sign in the upper-right corner of the screen. The New Contact screen appears, as shown in Figure 37-2.

3. Tap **First Last**. The Edit Name screen appears, where you can type a person's first and last name and company, as shown in Figure 37-3.

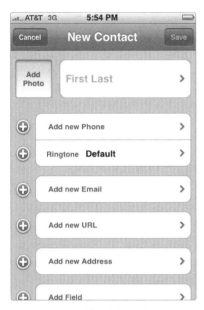

FIGURE 37-2: *The New Contact screen lets you store information about a contact.*

FIGURE 37-3: *The Edit Name screen lets you type a person's name and company information.*

4. Type a first and last name and a company name, if appropriate. Then tap **Save**. The New Contact screen appears again (see Figure 37-2).

5. Tap a button to add new contact information, such as **Add new Phone**, **Add new Email**, or **Add new Address**. An Edit screen appears, where you can type information using the virtual keyboard. For example, if you tap Add new Phone, the Edit Phone screen appears, as shown in Figure 37-4. Tap **Save** after you've entered the new contact information, and you'll see the New Contact screen. Repeat this step for each new chunk of information you want to add about a person.

6. (Optional) In the New Contact screen, tap **Add Photo**. Two buttons appear near the bottom of the screen, as shown in Figure 37-5. Tap **Take Photo**, and you can take a person's picture with your iPhone camera. Tap **Choose Existing Photo** to select a stored picture that will appear next to a person's name.

7. Tap **Save**. The Contact screen displays your newly added name.

FIGURE 37-4: *In the Edit Phone screen, you can type a phone number and choose a label for that number.*

FIGURE 37-5: *You can take a picture or choose an existing image to add to your contact information.*

Finding a Contact

The simplest way to find a name in the Contacts program is to scroll down the list of stored contacts. If you've stored a small number of contacts, this can be acceptable, but if you've stored dozens of names, scrolling to find one can be too time consuming. Instead of scrolling, you can search alphabetically or search by typing all or part of a name.

Searching Alphabetically

The right side of the All Contacts screen displays the alphabet from A to Z. If you know a person's last name, you can search for that name by doing this:

1. From the Home screen, tap **Contacts**. The All Contacts screen appears.
2. Tap the letter on the right side of the screen that corresponds to the last name of the contact you want to find. For example, if you want to find somebody whose last name begins with an *S*, tap the letter **S**. All contacts whose last names begin with the chosen letter appear on the screen.
3. Scroll up or down until you find the name you want.
4. Tap the name to view the person's contact information.

Searching by Text

Another way to search for a contact is to type all or part of the person's name or company name. To search by typing text, do this:

1. From the Home screen, tap **Contacts**. The All Contacts screen appears.
2. Tap the search text box. A virtual keyboard appears.
3. Type a partial contact or company name. As you type, a list of matching names appears above the virtual keyboard, as shown in Figure 37-6.
4. Tap the name to view the person's contact information.

Editing Contacts

After you've stored a name and contact information, you can edit that information later by changing it or adding new information. To edit contact information, do this:

1. From the Home screen, tap **Contacts**. The All Contacts screen appears.
2. Tap the name of the contact you want to edit. An Info screen appears, listing all your stored information.
3. Tap **Edit**. Two types of circles appear to the left of various fields, allowing you to add or edit information, as shown in Figure 37-7.
4. (Optional) Tap the white minus sign inside a red circle that appears next to saved information. A Delete button appears; tap **Delete** to delete the currently saved data.

FIGURE 37-6: *As you type part of a name, you'll see a list of matching names.*

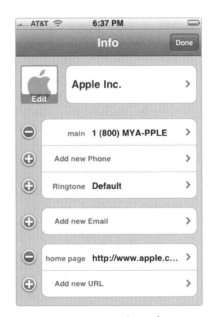

FIGURE 37-7: *From the Info screen, you can edit information about a saved contact.*

5. (Optional) Tap the white plus sign inside a green circle next to a field. The green circle means you haven't stored data in this particular field. A new screen appears, where you can type information to save.

6. Tap **Done** when you're finished adding or deleting information. Tap **All Contacts** in the upper-left corner of the screen to view the Contacts screen again.

Sharing Contacts

Chances are good that you have a phone number and address for someone stored on your iPhone that someone else wants to have. While you could read this information aloud and let the other person type it into their mobile phone, this method is slow, tedious, and prone to error. To make things easier, you can send contact information in an email or MMS message.

To share contact information, do this:

1. From the Home screen, tap **Contacts**. The All Contacts screen appears.

2. Tap the name of the contact whose information you want to share. An Info screen appears, listing all your stored information for that person.

3. Tap **Share Contact**. (You may need to scroll down to find this option on the screen.) **Email**, **MMS**, and **Cancel** buttons appear, as shown in Figure 37-8.

4. Tap **Email** or **MMS**. If you tap Email, you'll need to choose an email address to send the information to. If you tap MMS, you'll need to choose a mobile phone number to send the information to.

FIGURE 37-8: *You can share contact information by sending it in an email or MSS.*

Deleting Contacts

Rather than delete individual fields for a stored contact name, you might want to delete an entire contact altogether. To delete a contact name and all information saved with that name, do this:

1. From the Home screen, tap **Contacts**. The All Contacts screen appears.

2. Tap the name of the contact you want to delete. An Info screen appears, listing all your stored information.

3. Tap **Edit** in the upper-right corner of the screen.
4. Scroll down until you see the red Delete Contact button at the bottom of the screen, as shown in Figure 37-9.
5. Tap **Delete Contact**. Another Delete Contact button and a Cancel button appear, as shown in Figure 37-10.
6. Tap **Delete Contact** to delete the information (or tap **Cancel** if you've changed your mind). The All Contacts screen appears, and the deleted name is nowhere in sight.

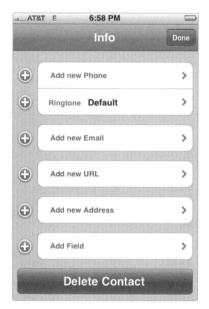

FIGURE 37-9: *The Delete Contact button appears at the bottom of the Info screen.*

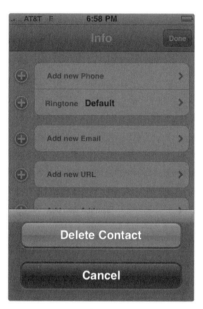

FIGURE 37-10: *You can choose to delete the contact or cancel the action if you've changed your mind.*

Customizing the Contacts Application

By default, the Contacts program displays each contact's first name followed by the last name. However, you can switch this order if you want. When sorting names, the Contacts program sorts according to the contact's last name followed by the first name. If you'd rather sort by first name, you can switch this around, too.

The *sort order* determines how your iPhone arranges names. So if you choose Last, First as your sort order, all your names appear sorted alphabetically by last name.

The *display order* determines how your iPhone actually displays names. So if you choose Last, First as your display order, all your names appear with the last name first such as Smith, John.

To change the sort and/or display order, do this:

1. From the Home screen, tap **Settings**. The Settings screen appears.
2. Tap **Mail, Contacts, Calendars**. The Mail, Contacts, Calendars screen appears.
3. Scroll down until you see the Contacts options, as shown in Figure 37-11.
4. Tap **Sort Order**. The Sort Order screen appears, as shown in Figure 37-12.

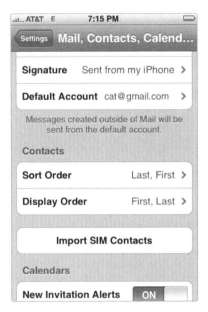

FIGURE 37-11: *The Contacts options allow you to change the sort and display orders of contact names.*

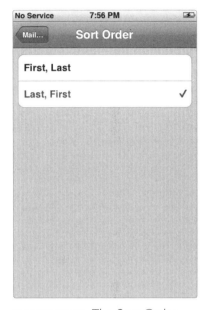

FIGURE 37-12: *The Sort Order screen lets you define how to sort contact names.*

5. Tap **First, Last** or **Last, First**, and then tap **Mail** in the upper-left corner of the screen to return to the Mail, Contacts, Calendars screen.
6. Tap **Display Order**. The Display Order screen appears.
7. Tap **First, Last** or **Last, First**, and then tap **Mail** in the upper-left corner of the screen to return to the Mail, Contacts, Calendars screen.

Additional Ideas for Storing Contacts on Your iPhone

Everyone can think of friends and family members whose contact information can be saved in the Contacts program, but another handy use for the Contacts database is to store crucial information, such as toll-free numbers you need to call if your credit cards are stolen, or your insurance company's name and phone number and policy numbers so you can find this information quickly if you need to file a claim.

If you're not careful, the Contacts program can soon become as cluttered as most people's closets, so it's a good idea to take time periodically to weed out unnecessary contact names. That way, you can save only important names and get rid of people you'll never contact again in a million years (such as some of your relatives).

Use Your iPhone to Store Contact Information from Business Cards

Typing in someone's contact information can be painfully slow, especially if you try to type it directly in your iPhone using the virtual keyboard. For a faster way, use the CardLasso app.

Just take a picture of a business card using your iPhone's built-in camera, upload the picture to CardLasso, and you'll receive the contact information in a spreadsheet or email format so you can easily import it into your Contacts database.

You'll need to pay a monthly fee that varies, depending on how many business cards you need to store each month. But the cost is minimal, especially if you'd rather not spend your time typing in data from business cards.

CardLasso   *http://www.lasso2go.com/*

CardLasso lets you take pictures of business cards to store that information.

38

Keeping Track of Appointments

Everyone needs to be in different places at specific times, but it's often too easy to forget crucial appointments, especially when you start getting overwhelmed by all your work and personal commitments. To help you stay organized and on time, the iPhone offers a Calendar application.

The Calendar application lets you store your appointments in a single location and provides reminders to alert you when a specific appointment is coming up. By using automatic calendar alerts, you can ensure that you'll never miss a crucial appointment again (unless you really want to).

Project goal: Learn how to save, view, and edit appointment information on your iPhone's Calendar application.

What You'll Be Using

To save, view, and edit appointment information on your iPhone, you need to use the following:

 The Calendar application

Importing Appointment Data from Other Programs

If you've been using a computer or another mobile phone to keep track of your appointments, you've already stored appointment information there. If you haven't stored too much information, you might find it easy to retype it into your iPhone's Calendar application. However, if you have dozens of stored appointments, retyping all this information would probably be too much trouble. Fortunately, there is a simple solution.

Your iPhone syncs with iCal or Entourage (Mac OS X) or Outlook (Windows). If you want to synchronize data with a different program, you may need to get special synchronization software that works with your program. Whatever program you've used to store current appointments, the data can be exported to a comma-separated values (CSV) file and then imported into iCal or Outlook. From there, you can sync your data with your iPhone by connecting your iPhone to your computer with your USB cable and using iTunes (see Project 12).

If your appointment data is trapped on another mobile phone, buy The Missing Sync for iPhone (*http://www.markspace.com/*) and make your life easier. If you use Google, you can synchronize your Google calendar information using the free Google Sync for iPhone program (*http://www.google.com/mobile/apple/sync.html*).

Setting an Appointment

Every appointment involves a time and a location. In addition to defining a starting time, you can also define an ending time and indicate whether you want your iPhone to alert you ahead of time and whether you want to schedule the appointment to repeat at particular times.

To create an appointment, do this:

1. From the Home screen, tap **Calendar**. If you have already created appointments, they'll be listed in the Calendars screen, as shown in Figure 38-1, which shows how appointments look in the list view. If you haven't created any appointments, this screen will be blank.

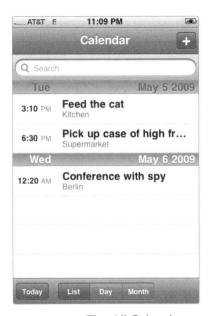

FIGURE 38-1: *The All Calendars screen displays appointment dates and times.*

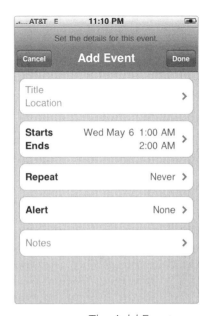

FIGURE 38-2: *The Add Event screen lets you define an appointment.*

2. Tap the plus sign in the upper-right corner of the screen. An Add Event screen appears, as shown in Figure 38-2.

3. Tap **Title Location**. A Title & Location screen appears, as shown in Figure 38-3.

4. Tap the **Title** text box and type a description of your appointment.

5. Tap the **Location** text box and type a location for your appointment.

6. Tap **Done** in the upper-right corner of the screen. The Add Event screen appears again with your appointment title and location displayed.

FIGURE 38-3: *The Title & Location screen lets you type a description of your appointment and a location.*

7. Tap **Starts Ends**. The Start & End screen appears, where you can define a starting and ending time, as shown in Figure 38-4.

8. Tap **Starts** and scroll the time wheels up or down to specify a date, hour, minute, and AM or PM.

9. Tap **Ends** and scroll the time wheels up or down to specify a date, hour, minute, and AM or PM.

10. (Optional) Tap the **ON/OFF** button next to All-day to switch it on or off. When this button is set to ON, the appointment takes up your entire day.

11. Tap **Done** in the upper-right corner of the screen. The Add Event screen appears with your appointment starting and ending times displayed.

12. Tap **Notes**. A Notes screen appears with a virtual keyboard. Type a brief description or additional information about your appointment, as shown in Figure 38-5.

13. Tap **Done**. The Add Event screen appears again.

14. Tap **Done** in the upper-right corner of the screen to view your calendar.

Viewing a Calendar

Once you've created and stored one or more appointments, you can view your calendar to see your schedule. You have the option of viewing a calendar in List, Day, or Month view, as shown in Figure 38-6.

▶ List

▶ Day

▶ Month

FIGURE 38-4: The Start & End screen lets you specify times by scrolling wheels up and down.

FIGURE 38-5: The Notes screen lets you type information about your appointment.

FIGURE 38-6: *You can view calendars in three ways: list view, day view, and month view.*

To view a calendar of appointments, do this:

1. From the Home screen, tap **Calendar**. The Calendars screen appears.
2. Tap **List**, **Day**, or **Month**. The calendar screen shows appointments in your chosen view.
3. (Optional) Tap **Today** to view today's appointments.

Editing an Appointment

After you've created an appointment, you may need to edit it to modify information or change the starting or ending time. To edit an appointment, do this:

1. From the Home screen, tap **Calendar**. The Calendars screen appears.
2. Tap the appointment you want to edit. An Event screen appears, as shown in Figure 38-7.
3. Tap **Edit** in the upper-right corner of the screen. The Edit screen appears.

FIGURE 38-7: *The Event screen shows your appointment information.*

4. Tap the data you want to modify, edit your text, or choose a different starting or ending time.
5. (Optional) Tap **Delete Event** at the bottom of the screen. When another Delete Event button appears, tap it to confirm the deletion.
6. Tap **Done** when you're finished.

Creating a Recurring Appointment

A *recurring appointment* is an appointment that occurs regularly at a fixed time interval, such as every day, every week, or every month. Instead of forcing you to type separate appointment information for every instance of a recurring appointment, the Calendar program lets you type recurring appointment information once and specify how often you want that appointment to repeat.

You can define a recurring appointment when you first create the appointment, or you can edit an existing appointment and turn it into a recurring one. To edit an appointment to make it a recurring appointment, do this:

1. From the Home screen, tap **Calendar**. The All Calendars screen appears.
2. Tap the appointment you want to edit. The Event screen appears (see Figure 38-7).
3. Tap **Edit** in the upper-right corner of the screen. The Edit screen appears, as shown in Figure 38-8.
4. Tap **Repeat**. A Repeat Event screen appears, as shown in Figure 38-9.

FIGURE 38-8: *The Edit screen lets you modify or delete an appointment.*

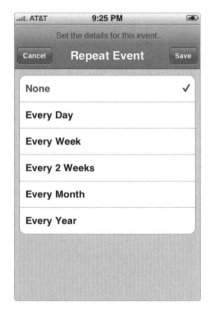

FIGURE 38-9: *The Repeat Event screen lets you define how often a recurring appointment should repeat.*

5. Tap an option such as **Every Day** or **Every Month**, and then tap **Save** in the upper-right corner of the screen.
6. Tap **Done** in the upper-right corner of the screen. The Event screen appears.
7. Tap the date button in the upper-left corner of the screen to view your calendar.

Setting a Reminder for an Appointment

Setting an appointment is useless if you forget about it. To make sure you don't miss an appointment, you can set an alert so your iPhone will vibrate, make a sound, or display the appointment at a set time prior to your appointment. To make your iPhone alert you with sound and vibration, do this:

1. From the Home screen, tap **Settings**. The Settings screen appears.
2. Tap **Sounds**. The Sounds screen appears.
3. (Optional) Tap the **ON/OFF** button next to Vibrate to turn vibration on or off.
4. (Optional) Slide the Volume slider left or right to adjust the volume at which your iPhone will alert you.
5. Tap the **ON/OFF** button next to Calendar Alerts. (You may need to scroll down the Sounds screen to find this option.)

When a calendar alert goes off, it displays a dialog, as shown in Figure 38-10.

✳ **NOTE:** You can set multiple alerts for a single appointment. That way, you can set an alert to remind you early in the day, another alert an hour before your appointment, and then a third alert five minutes before your appointment.

FIGURE 38-10: A reminder message displays on the screen.

To set an alert for an appointment, do this:

1. From the Home screen, tap **Calendar**. The All Calendars screen appears.
2. Tap an appointment you want to edit. The Event screen appears (see Figure 38-7).
3. Tap **Edit** in the upper-right corner of the screen. The Edit screen appears (see Figure 38-8).
4. Tap **Alert**. An Event Alert screen appears, as shown in Figure 38-11.
5. Tap a time, such as **1 hour before** or **On date of event**. Then tap **Done**. The Edit screen appears.
6. Tap **Done** again. The Event screen appears.
7. Tap the date button in the upper-left corner of the screen to view your calendar.

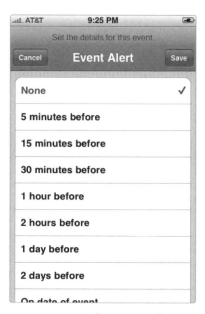

FIGURE 38-11: *The Event Alert screen lets you set an event reminder.*

Additional Ideas for Storing Appointments on Your iPhone

In addition to storing obvious appointments, such as doctor's appointments, Little League practices, or hot dates, you can use the Calendar program as a reminder system to help you complete tasks that you might otherwise forget about.

If you've set a goal, such as losing weight or stopping smoking, set a recurring appointment every day that will alert you and display a friendly reminder about your goal. If you need to take medication at a certain time of day, set a reminder for that, too. If you always forget to take out the garbage on trash pickup day, set another reminder so you'll never be stuck with a pile of trash for an extra week.

The Calendar program helps you keep track of your schedule. Now you just need a reason to be in a particular place at a certain time.

Use Your iPhone to Get More from Your Calendar

If you already store appointments in Google Calendar, you can sync it with the Calendar app on your iPhone. However, if you want a more powerful alternative to the built-in calendar, skip the Calendar app and consider using GooSync. GooSync provides advanced features, such as the ability to use data from Google Calendar and label each appointment by a priority number, a classification, a busy status, and even map coordinates. By switching to GooSync, you now have a more powerful alternative to the Calendar app that comes with your iPhone.

GooSync   *http://www.goosync.com/*

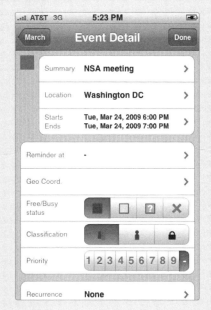

GooSync provides additional ways to classify an appointment.

39

Viewing Maps

We've all gotten lost in an unfamiliar neighborhood. In the old days, we asked strangers for directions or used a mobile phone to call for help. To prevent this dilemma, many people now print out maps before they venture out toward a new or unfamiliar part of town, but maps can be easy to lose and useless if you don't know where you are to begin with. For a better solution, you can use the Maps application on your iPhone.

Project goal: Learn how to view maps on your iPhone.

What You'll Be Using

To view maps on your iPhone, you need to use the following:

 The Maps application

Viewing a Map

The Maps program relies on the Internet to retrieve maps and directions, so you'll find that the program runs faster when you're connected to a Wi-Fi network. If you aren't able to connect to a Wi-Fi network, your iPhone will access your cellular telephone company's network, but the Maps program will run much slower.

Of course, having a map is pretty useless unless you know where you are on that map to begin with. You can use Maps to find out where you are. To view a map of your current location, do this:

1. From the Home screen, tap **Maps**. The Maps screen appears.
2. Tap the crosshair icon in the lower-left corner of the screen. The screen displays a map with a blue dot highlighting your current location, as shown in Figure 39-1.
3. (Optional) Press your fingertip anywhere on the map and slide your finger up, down, left, or right on the screen to view different parts of the map.
4. (Optional) Pinch two fingers on the screen and then spread them apart to zoom in. Close the two fingers on the screen to zoom out.

✳ **NOTE:** If you're driving a car or riding a bus as you're viewing a map, you'll see the blue dot move to display your location as you travel. Your iPhone uses various cellular network towers to triangulate your location, so if you find yourself in an area without any cellular phone coverage, the Maps program won't be able to show your current location.

FIGURE 39-1: The map displays a blue dot to identify your current location.

Viewing Different Types of Maps

Normally, the Maps screen displays a simplified map, which makes it easy to identify roads and highways. However, your iPhone offers three different types of map
views, as shown in Figure 39-2:

▶ **Map**   Displays roads and highways in a simplified map

▶ **Satellite**   Displays a satellite photograph of roads and highways, along with
buildings and other physical features

▶ **Hybrid**   Displays a simplified map superimposed over a satellite
photograph

FIGURE 39-2: *Three types of map views are available: Map, Satellite, and Hybrid.*

To change the way the Maps screen displays a map, do this:

1. From the Home screen, tap **Maps**. The Maps screen appears.
2. Tap the Options icon (which looks like a page with a corner curling back) in
    the lower-right corner of the screen. The lower-right corner of the map curls
    back, revealing several options, as shown in Figure 39-3.

3. Tap **Map**, **Satellite**, or **Hybrid** at the bottom of the screen.

* *NOTE:* If you tap List, you'll see a list of all the companies responsible for creating your iPhone's maps.

4. Tap the Options icon to cover up the options and view the map again.

Checking Traffic

If you need to drive somewhere in a hurry, Maps can not only help you figure out how to get there, but by display-ing real-time traffic data, your iPhone can also show you how to avoid traffic bottlenecks. Your iPhone draws green lines to show you where traffic is flowing smoothly on the highways. Yellow lines are used to show routes where traffic is slowing down, and red lines show routes where traffic is at a standstill. By knowing the locations of traffic jams and avoiding those areas, you can get to your destina-tion as quickly as possible.

FIGURE 39-3: *Tapping the Options icon causes the map to curl back and reveal addi-tional options for customizing the map.*

* *NOTE:* Traffic data appears only for major highways, not for side streets.

To view real-time traffic data on a map, do this:

1. From the Home screen, tap **Maps**. The Maps screen appears.
2. Tap the crosshair icon in the lower-left corner of the screen.
3. Tap the Options icon in the lower-right corner of the screen. The lower-right corner of the map curls back, revealing several options (see Figure 39-3).

4. Tap **Show Traffic** in the middle of the screen. The map displays green, yellow, and red lines to reveal traffic congestion information for several highways, as shown in Figure 39-4.

＊ *NOTE:* **To turn off traffic data, tap the Options icon, and then tap Hide Traffic.**

Additional Ideas for Viewing Maps

Maps are always handy whenever you're lost in an unfamiliar neighborhood. Instead of pulling into a gas station to buy a map or asking a stranger for directions, you can use Maps to help you navigate to your current location so you'll know where you're at and where you want to go.

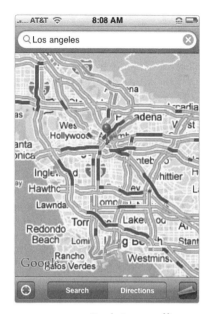

FIGURE 39-4: *Real-time traffic data can help you avoid traffic jams.*

Maps can also be a fun way to study geography. From the Maps screen, type the name of a major city in the search text box at the top of the screen, and then tap **Search** at the bottom of the screen. If you slide your finger to move the map view left, right, up, or down, you can view different areas. This can be a fun way to keep bored children amused and get them interested in studying maps and learning about other parts of the world.

With a cellular phone connection and your iPhone, you'll always know where you are. Now you just need to worry about where you want to go.

Use Your iPhone to Find a Restaurant

A map is useless if you don't know what you're looking for. In case you're looking for something to eat, use the Urbanspoon app. This app displays a slot machine–like interface of three reels that identify a location, a type of cuisine (such as Mexican or Indian), and a price.

You can lock one or two of these reels in case you only want to find Chinese restaurants in a certain neighborhood, and then shake your iPhone to set the reels spinning. Your iPhone will display a restaurant that matches your criteria. Just tap the **Map** field to view a map of the restaurant's location, and you can go get something to eat. Urbanspoon and your iPhone can help you find the best restaurants wherever you happen to be, so you won't have to rely on locals to give you recommendations.

Urbanspoon   *http://www.urbanspoon.com/*

Urbanspoon can help you find a restaurant near you.

Finding a Location and Getting Directions

Looking at a map, you may have no idea where a favorite restaurant or sports bar might be. On a traditional paper map, you can mark a big X on a spot to help you quickly identify a specific location. That makes it easy to find that place again.

While you can't write directly on an iPhone map, you can place a cartoon push pin on the map to identify a favorite place, so you'll always be able to find your favorite sushi restaurant or the cheapest gas station every time you glance at your iPhone map. Better yet, your iPhone can give you driving, walking, and mass transit directions to help you get where you want to go.

Project goal: Learn how to find the most direct route to any location on a map displayed on your iPhone.

What You'll Be Using

To get locations and directions using your iPhone, you need to use the following:

 The Maps application

Getting Directions

The Maps program can give you directions to help you get from one place to another through the magic of GPS (Global Positioning System) technology. Before you can get directions, you need to define your starting and ending destinations by doing one of the following:

▶ Type in a street address.

▶ Use your current location.

▶ Use a previously saved location.

To find directions with a starting and ending destination, do this:

1. From the Home screen, tap **Maps**. The Maps screen appears.
2. Tap **Directions** at the bottom of the screen. The Directions screen appears and displays Start and End text boxes at the top of the screen. By default, the Start text box contains your current location using GPS, as shown in Figure 40-1.
3. (Optional) Tap the swap icon (the wavy double-sided arrow) to switch the current location from the Start text box to the End text box.

FIGURE 40-1: The Directions screen lets you choose starting and ending locations.

4. (Optional) If you want to clear the contents of a text box, tap in the Start or End text box to display an *X*, as shown in Figure 40-2. Tap the *X* to clear that text box.

5. Tap the **Start** text box and type a street address (including the city and state). Or, if you tap the Bookmarks icon that appears to the right of the field, the Bookmarks screen appears, listing all previously saved locations; choose a location by tapping its name.

6. Tap the **End** text box and type a street address (including the city and state). Or, if you tap the Bookmarks icon that appears to the right of the field, the Bookmarks screen appears, listing all previously saved locations; choose a location by tapping its name. After you've chosen an ending location, a blue Route button appears in the lower-right corner of the screen.

FIGURE 40-2: *You can clear the contents of a destination text box.*

7. Tap **Route**. The iPhone map highlights a route and displays car, bus, and walking icons at the top of the screen, as shown in Figure 40-3.

FIGURE 40-3: *Three different types of direction icons appear at the top of the screen; you can choose to display driving, transit, or walking directions.*

8. To get driving directions, tap the car icon. To get mass transit directions, tap the bus icon. To get walking directions, tap the walking icon.

9. Tap **Start**. The screen displays a map with directions telling you which way to go, along with the number of screen directions and the current screen you're looking at (such as 1 of 10), as shown in Figure 40-4.

10. Tap the left and right arrow buttons in the upper-right corner to view each screen of instructions that will get you closer to your destination.

Finding Businesses on a Map

Having a map is useless if you don't know where anything is. To help you out, your iPhone lets you type in a description of a place you want to find. The map then displays pins that highlight those locations. For example, if you want to find a nearby coffeehouse, just type *coffee* into your iPhone. If you want to find the closest sushi restaurant, type *sushi*.

To find a specific type of business on a map, do this:

1. From the Home screen, tap **Maps**. The Maps screen appears.

2. Tap the **Search** button at the bottom of the screen.

3. Tap in the search text box at the top of the screen. The virtual keyboard appears at the bottom of the screen.

4. Type a description of a business you want to find, such as *gas station* or *pizza*, and tap the **Search** button in the lower-right corner of the screen. Your iPhone displays red push pins at the locations of relevant businesses, as shown in Figure 40-5.

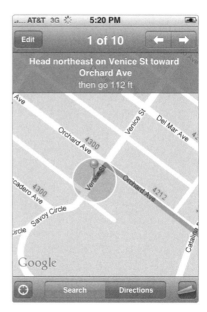

FIGURE 40-4: *The Maps program displays travel directions.*

FIGURE 40-5: *Red push pins identify multiple businesses that match your search criteria.*

5.   (Optional) Tap a red push pin to display the name of the business repre-
     sented. Then tap the white arrow in the blue circle to view the phone number
     and address of the business. You can also tap the Directions To Here button
     to get directions to this business.

Marking a Location on a Map

If you find a location on a map that you want to save, you can place a virtual push
pin on that spot, called a *dropped pin*. After placing the pin, you can move it
around until it appears exactly where you want it. Then give it a distinctive name so
you'll always be able to find a specific location, such as the site of a favorite park or
hiking trail, which may not have a specific street address. You can also delete a pin
from a map later if you want.

Dropping a Pin on a Map

When you drop a pin on a map, the pin appears in purple. The purple color means
that you can move the pin around, because you haven't yet given it a descriptive
name. The moment you name the pin location, the color of the pin changes to red.
     To place a pin on a map, do this:

1.   From the Home screen, tap **Maps**.
     The Maps screen appears.
2.   Tap the Options icon in the
     lower-right corner of the screen
     (it looks like a corner of a page
     curling back). The lower-right
     corner of the map curls back,
     revealing several options.
3.   Tap **Drop Pin** in the middle of the
     screen. The map now displays a
     purple pin floating above your
     map, as shown in Figure 40-6. This
     pin probably won't appear exactly
     where you want it, so you'll have to
     move it.
4.   Press and hold your fingertip on
     the pin until it appears to lift off the
     map. (You may find it easier to "lift"
     the pin off the map if you press
     your fingertip near the bottom of
     the pin image.)
5.   Lift your finger off the screen when
     the pin is exactly where you want it.
     The pin appears to drop and stick
     in the map.

FIGURE 40-6: *A purple pin lets
you mark a specific location on
a map.*

❋ *NOTE:* Only one purple pin can appear on the map at a time.

Naming a Pin Location

After you've placed the pin on a map, you'll probably want to name it; otherwise, the pin won't represent anything obvious. To give a pin a name, do this:

1. Tap the white arrow in the blue circle that appears above the purple pin on the map. The Info screen appears, as shown in Figure 40-7.
2. Tap **Add to Bookmarks**. An Add Bookmark screen appears with the virtual keyboard, so you can type a descriptive name for the pin's location, as shown in Figure 40-8.

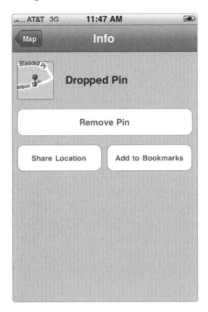

FIGURE 40-7: *The Info screen lets you bookmark your pin location.*

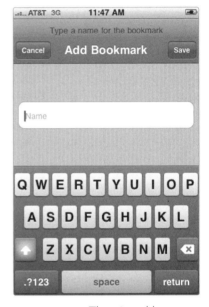

FIGURE 40-8: *The virtual keyboard lets you type a descriptive name for your chosen location.*

3. Type a descriptive name and tap **Save**. The Info screen appears again.
4. Tap **Map** in the upper-left corner of the screen. Notice that the pin color has changed to red, and your descriptive name appears in the dialog directly above the pin.

＊ **NOTE:** **Although you can have only one purple pin on the map at a time, you can have as many red pins on the map as you want.**

Finding a Pin Location

After you've placed multiple red pins on a map, you may want to find a specific location in a hurry. To find a location identified by a pin, do this:

1. From the Home screen, tap **Maps**. The Maps screen appears.
2. Tap **Search**. The Search or Address text box appears at the top of the screen.
3. Tap the Bookmarks icon that appears in the text box. (If the Bookmarks icon does not appear, tap the close button.) The Bookmarks screen appears, as shown in Figure 40-9.
4. (Optional) If the Bookmarks screen does not appear, tap **Bookmarks** at the bottom of the screen.
5. Tap the location you want to find. The Maps screen appears, displaying a red pin on the map that represents the location you chose.
6. (Optional) Tap the white arrow in the blue circle. The Info screen appears. Now you can tap Directions To Here or Directions From Here to get directions for your chosen location.

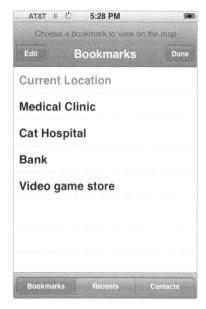

FIGURE 40-9: *The Bookmarks screen lets you choose a specific location.*

Viewing Google Street View

When viewing maps of major cities, you can often view actual photographs of your desired location using Google Street View, a feature of Google Maps. Basically, Google hired cars with 360-degree cameras mounted on their roofs to drive around major streets of the United States and take pictures. By using Google Street View, you can see how your destination looks before you get there. That way, you'll be familiar with the building you want to find.

To use Google Street View, you must first identify a specific location with a red pin. Then you can check whether Google Street View is available for that location by doing this:

1. From the Home screen, tap **Maps**. The Maps screen appears.
2. Find a red pin by following the steps in "Finding a Pin Location" on page 323.
3. Tap the red pin to display a description dialog.

4. Look for an orange circle with a white silhouette of a man that appears to the left of the red pin's descriptive dialog, as shown in Figure 40-10. This orange circle identifies street addresses that can be seen through Google Street View.

* *NOTE:* **Not all streets have Google Street View photographs available for you to view.**

5. Tap the orange circle. Google Street View for that address appears, as shown in Figure 40-11.
6. Slide your finger across the screen to swivel the view. (You can rotate the iPhone to view the street horizontally or vertically on the screen.)
7. Tap the screen to display a blue Done button in the corner. Tap **Done** to exit street view.

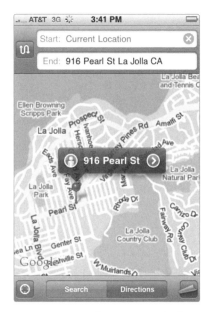

FIGURE 40-10: *An orange circle with a white silhouette identifies Google Street View.*

FIGURE 40-11: *Google Street View displays a street address view in 360 degrees.*

Deleting a Pin

After you've placed pins on a map, you'll eventually want to delete at least some of them to keep them from cluttering up your map. To delete a pin, do this:

1. From the Home screen, tap **Maps**. The Maps screen appears.
2. Tap the Bookmarks icon in the Search or Address text box. (If the Bookmarks icon does not appear, tap the close icon.) The Bookmarks screen appears (see Figure 40-9). (If the Bookmarks screen does not appear, tap **Bookmarks** at the bottom of the screen.)
3. Tap **Edit** in the upper-left corner of the screen. A white minus sign inside a red circle appears to the left of all your bookmarked pin locations.
4. Tap the white minus sign inside the red circle to display a red Delete button, as shown in Figure 40-12.
5. Tap **Delete**, and the bookmarked pin location disappears.
6. Tap **Done** twice. The map reappears, and the selected pin has been removed.

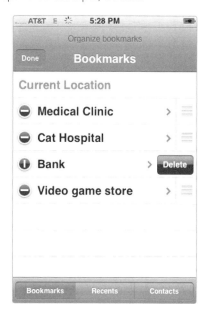

FIGURE 40-12: A red Delete button lets you delete a bookmarked pin from the map.

Finding a Recent Search

If finding a certain location was important to you once, chances are it will be important for you to find it again. Each time you search for a location, the Maps program stores that search in a Recents list, which you can view. So instead of typing the same address over and over again, you can browse the Recents list of past location searches, tap the one you want, and view the location right away.

To view and choose from a list of recent searches, do this:

1. From the Home screen, tap **Maps**. The Maps screen appears.
2. Tap the Bookmarks icon. The Bookmarks screen appears (see Figure 40-9).

3. Tap **Recents** at the bottom of the screen. The Recents screen appears, listing past location searches, as shown in Figure 40-13.

4. Tap a location. The Maps screen displays a pin identifying that location or route.

5. (Optional) Tap **Clear** in the upper-left corner of the screen to clear your list of past searches. Tap the **Clear All Recents** button to clear your list, or tap **Cancel** if you change your mind, as shown in Figure 40-14.

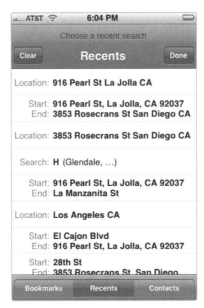

FIGURE 40-13: The Recents screen shows your previous searches.

FIGURE 40-14: Tapping Clear All Recents erases your list of previous searches.

Additional Ideas for Getting Directions

Whenever you're lost, use the Maps program to get your current location so you'll know where you're at and where you need to go. Check out your current location the next time you're riding in a taxi. Turn on your iPhone, look at a map, and you can tell whether the cab driver is taking the shortest route possible or driving you all over town to increase your cab fare.

If you're traveling to an unfamiliar location, check Google Street View to scope out the area. This can help you identify potential parking spots or recognize the building when you get close to it. Using Maps on your iPhone, you should be able to navigate through many new places without getting lost.

Use Your iPhone to Find Cheap Gas

Getting directions from your current location to a destination may be nice, but if you're driving, you may need to stop for gas somewhere along the way. Most people just stop at the first gas station they find, but if you'd rather look for the lowest prices around, use the Cheap Gas! app.

This app uses your current location and ties it into a constantly updated database of the lowest gas prices in a neighborhood. At the touch of a button, you'll be able to find which gas stations offer the cheapest gas closest to you.

Cheap Gas! *http:// davidjhinson.wordpress .com/cheap-gas/*

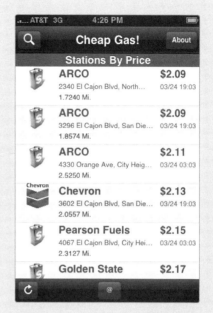

The Cheap Gas! app locates the gas stations closest to you with the lowest prices.

PART 8

Fun Stuff

41 Taking Pictures

Few of us carry a camera everywhere we go, but we may regret it when we see something worth capturing, such as Sasquatch or a UFO. To avoid this problem, the iPhone includes a built-in camera. Since you usually always carry your iPhone with you, its built-in camera means you'll always have a camera available when you really need one.

Of course, the built-in iPhone camera isn't nearly as good as a real digital camera. The iPhone's camera offers only 2-megapixel resolution, while most digital camera models offer 7-megapixel resolution or higher. In addition, the iPhone camera doesn't allow you to zoom in, so unless you're close enough to capture the image detail, you'll be out of luck if that's what you're looking for. Despite these limitations, the iPhone camera can be handy for capturing quick images at the spur of the moment.

In addition to capturing images around you, you can also use your iPhone to capture images that appear on your iPhone's screen. Capturing such images can be handy for showing people how to use different features of the iPhone (such as the screenshots in this book) or for capturing error messages or quirky iPhone behavior that you want to show to others to verify that something strange really did happen and wasn't just your imagination.

Project goal: Learn how to take pictures and capture screenshots with your iPhone.

What You'll Be Using

To take pictures and capture screenshots with your iPhone, you need to use the following:

 The Camera application

 The Photos application

Taking and Viewing Pictures

The iPhone's camera lens is on the back of the iPhone near the Sleep/Wake button. The lens looks like a little hole, so make sure your finger doesn't accidentally cover it when you take a picture. After you take a picture, you'll probably want to view it, so this section shows you how to do that, too.

⁎ **NOTE:** When you capture pictures using the iPhone camera, your iPhone saves them in the JPEG file format. When you capture screen images, your iPhone saves them in the PNG file format.

Taking Pictures

To take a picture, you need to run the Camera program by doing this:

1. From the Home screen, tap **Camera**. The Camera screen appears and displays a dialog asking if you want to tag the photo with your current location, as shown in Figure 41-1.
2. Tap **OK** or **Don't Allow**. After a few seconds, the screen will appear to open and whatever image you're aiming at with the lens will appear.

FIGURE 41-1: The Camera screen is blank before the lens engages.

3.   Point the camera at an object and tap the camera icon at the bottom of the screen to take the picture. The picture is automatically stored in the Camera roll.

4.   Press the Home button to return to the Home screen, or stick with the Camera screen if you want to view your image.

Viewing Pictures on the Camera Screen

Immediately after you take a picture, you can look at it to see if it's worth keeping or if you need to take another picture right away. To view your pictures without exiting the Camera screen, do this:

1.   With the Camera screen displayed on your iPhone, tap the thumbnail icon in the lower-left corner of the screen. The Camera Roll screen appears, displaying the last image you captured, as shown in Figure 41-2.

2.   (Optional) Scroll left or right to view all the images stored on your iPhone. Tap the Trash icon in the lower-right corner if you don't like the image you just captured. When a dialog appears asking if you really want to delete the currently displayed photograph, tap **Delete**.

3.   Tap the **Done** button in the upper-right corner of the screen. You'll then return to the camera screen so you can take more pictures.

FIGURE 41-2: *Viewing your recently captured image*

✱ **NOTE:** You may notice a lag while you're taking photos with your iPhone. To minimize it, you can tap and hold your finger on the camera button as you set up your shot; then simply release your finger when you're ready to take a picture.

Viewing Pictures on the Photo Albums Screen

After you've exited the Camera screen, you can view your stored pictures through the Photo Albums screen, which you can open by doing this:

1.   From the Home screen, tap **Photos**. The Photo Albums screen appears, as shown in Figure 41-3.

2. Tap **Camera Roll**. The Camera Roll screen appears, showing thumbnail images of all your captured photographs.
3. Tap the image you want to view.
4. (Optional) Tap the Trash icon in the lower-right corner if you don't like the image you just captured. When a dialog appears, asking if you really want to delete the currently displayed photograph, tap **Delete**.
5. (Optional) Tap the screen once to display navigation buttons along the bottom. By tapping the left and right arrows, you can view additional photographs. Or slide your finger left or right across the screen to view the previous or next picture, respectively.

FIGURE 41-3: *The Photo Albums screen displays all your stored photo albums.*

Capturing Screenshots

Anything you see on your iPhone screen can be captured and stored as a digital file. This can be handy for creating iPhone tutorials or for showing someone the neat features of your iPhone so he can feel inadequate about his own ancient mobile phone that already looks like a relic from the dustbins of history.

To capture screenshots of anything that appears on your iPhone screen, hold down the Sleep/Wake button and then press the Home button. The screen should flash white briefly to signal that you have just captured a screenshot. Now release both buttons. The screenshot is saved to the Camera Roll.

To view your screenshots, you'll need to open the Photo Albums screen, as explained in "Viewing Pictures on the Photo Albums Screen" on page 333.

Additional Ideas for Taking Pictures with Your iPhone

A camera can come in handy at the most unusual times. If you are involved in an accident, take pictures of the scene for evidence. If you see Bigfoot or a UFO, whip out your iPhone and capture a picture to provide solid photographic evidence once and for all.

Take pictures of your friends, family members, and loved ones so you'll always have their pictures stored on your iPhone. Then if you go on a long trip away from home, you can still see their smiling faces on your iPhone whenever you miss them.

Capturing screenshots can be useful when you're trying to show someone how to use an iPhone or if you're having problems using your iPhone yourself. Take a screenshot and show someone what they should do to accomplish a particular task. If you see a strange error message, capture that screenshot and show the geniuses at the Apple Store what happened so they can help troubleshoot problems on your iPhone.

Your iPhone can double as a simple camera when you don't have a real digital camera with you. Have fun, take pictures, and erase any that you don't like. Now you can experiment with photography without buying an expensive camera to do it.

Use Your iPhone to Draw on Your Photos

Taking pictures can be fun, but to keep yourself even more amused, use the Photo Brush Lite program, which lets you modify any pictures stored on your iPhone. Take pictures of your friends and draw mustaches on them. Capture pictures of landmarks or scenery and draw cartoon space aliens and monsters running around. By using your existing photographs as a starting point, you can exercise your creativity by finger painting on your iPhone.

Photo Brush Lite   *http://bobbysoftware.com/BobbySoftware/Home.html*

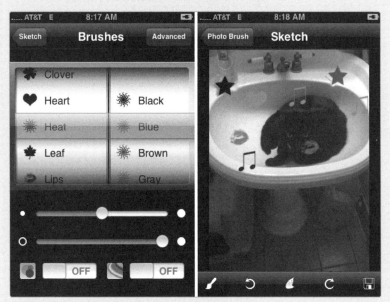

Photo Brush Lite lets you modify pictures.

42

Viewing Stored Pictures

Whether you capture pictures with your iPhone or copy them from your computer, you'll probably want to view your images on your iPhone. You can turn your iPhone into a slideshow viewer and cycle through your pictures, or you can look at pictures individually (and delete them if you don't need them any more). By using your iPhone to store and view pictures, you can turn your iPhone into a portable digital picture frame so you can take along your favorite pictures wherever you go.

Project goal: Learn different ways to view pictures stored on your iPhone.

What You'll Be Using

To view pictures with your iPhone, you need to use the following:

 The Settings application

 The Photos application

Viewing Pictures as a Slideshow

Since you can store literally thousands of photographs on your iPhone, you might find it most convenient to view them in a slideshow, where each picture appears on the screen for a few seconds before automatically switching to a new picture. By viewing pictures as a slideshow, you won't have to switch pictures manually.

Defining Your Slideshow

When defining your slideshow, you can modify four options:

▶ How long each slide appears on the screen

▶ The transition time between each slide

▶ Whether or not to repeat the entire slideshow

▶ Whether to display pictures in order or at random

To customize a slideshow, do this:

1. From the Home screen, tap **Settings**. The Settings screen appears.
2. Scroll down and tap **Photos** near the bottom of the screen. The Photos screen appears, as shown in Figure 42-1.
3. Tap **Play Each Slide For**. The Play Each Slide For screen appears, where you can choose a duration to display each picture, as shown in Figure 42-2.

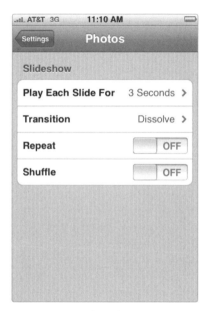

FIGURE 42-1: The Photos screen lets you customize your slideshow.

4.   Tap a time duration, such as **2 Seconds** or **10 Seconds**. Then tap **Photos** in the upper-left corner of the screen. The Photos screen appears again.

5.   Tap **Transition**. The Transition screen appears, as shown in Figure 42-3.

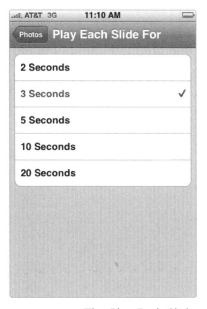

FIGURE 42-2: *The Play Each Slide For screen lets you define a time duration to display each picture.*

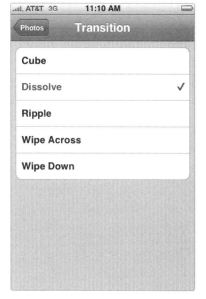

FIGURE 42-3: *The Transition screen lets you choose a visual effect between each image.*

6.   Tap a transition, such as **Cube** or **Ripple**, and then tap **Photos** in the upper-left corner of the screen to return to the Photos screen. (The *Cube* transition rotates pictures as if they appear on the face of a cube, and the *Dissolve* transition makes pictures seem to disappear slowly. The *Ripple* transition makes pictures look like water ripples. The *Wipe Across* and *Wipe Down* transitions make it appear as if a picture is sliding out of the way to reveal another one.)

7.   Tap the **ON/OFF** button next to Repeat. If turned on, your iPhone will play the slideshow continuously until you press the Home button. If turned off, your iPhone will play your slideshow only once, until every picture has been displayed exactly one time.

8.   Tap the **ON/OFF** button next to Shuffle. If turned on, your iPhone will display pictures in random order. If turned off, your iPhone will display pictures in the order that you stored them.

Viewing a Slideshow

Whenever you want to view your stored pictures in a slideshow, do this:

1. From the Home screen, tap **Photos**. The Photo Albums screen appears.
2. Tap the album that contains the photos you want to view, such as **Camera Roll**. Thumbnail images of all your stored pictures appear, along with a play button at the bottom of the screen, as shown in Figure 42-4.
3. Tap the play button. Your slideshow runs exactly as you defined it in the preceding section.
4. Press the Home button to stop your slideshow and return to the Home screen.

FIGURE 42-4: *The play button appears at the bottom of the screen.*

Viewing Pictures Manually

As an alternative to viewing your pictures as a slideshow, you can view them manually. This lets you choose a specific picture to view and control when to view the next picture.

To view individual pictures manually, do this:

1. From the Home screen, tap **Photos**. The Photo Albums screen appears.
2. Tap the album that contains the photos you want to view, such as **Camera Roll**. Thumbnail images of all your stored pictures appear, along with a play button at the bottom of the screen (see Figure 42-4).
3. Scroll up or down until you find a picture you want to view.
4. Tap the picture you want to view. The picture fills the iPhone screen.
5. Tap the screen. Navigation buttons appear along the bottom, as shown in Figure 42-5.
6. (Optional) Tap the left or right arrow button, or press your fingertip on the screen and slide your finger to the left or right to view the previous or next picture, respectively.
7. (Optional) Tap the button that contains the name of your current photo album in the upper-left corner of the screen to view thumbnail images of all your stored pictures.

* NOTE: When viewing pictures stored in the Camera Roll album, a Trash icon appears in the lower-right corner of the screen. Tapping the Trash icon lets you delete a picture. Note that you cannot delete a picture from any other photo albums except the Camera Roll album.

8. Press the Home button to stop viewing your pictures and return to the Home screen.

Sharing Pictures

Viewing a picture can be nice, but you may want to do more than just browse through your pictures. If you have a favorite picture, you can use it as your wallpaper, email it to a friend, or assign the picture to a saved name in your Contacts program.

To share a picture, do this:

1. From the Home screen, tap **Photos**. The Photo Albums screen appears.
2. Tap the album that contains the photos you want to view, such as **Camera Roll**. Thumbnail images of all your stored pictures appear, along with a play button at the bottom of the screen (see Figure 42-4).
3. Scroll up or down until you find a picture you want to view.
4. Tap the picture you want to view. The picture fills the iPhone screen.
5. Tap the option icon (the rectangle with the right-pointing arrow) that appears in the lower-left corner of the screen (see Figure 42-5). A dialog appears with several buttons, as shown in Figure 42-6.

FIGURE 42-5: *Tapping the screen displays navigation buttons at the bottom.*

FIGURE 42-6: *The list of options for sharing a picture*

6.   (Optional) Tap **Use As Wallpaper**. A Move and Scale screen appears, as shown in Figure 42-7. Move the picture and pinch the screen to zoom in or out to adjust the picture. Then tap **Set Wallpaper**. To see your wallpaper, turn your iPhone off and then on again and your chosen picture will appear.

7.   (Optional) In the dialog, tap **Email Photo**. The New Message screen appears, as shown in Figure 42-8. Tap the **To**, **Subject**, and **Message** text boxes and use the virtual keyboard to type an email address, subject, and message. When you're done, tap **Send**.

FIGURE 42-7: *The Move and Scale screen lets you move and adjust the size of a picture.*

FIGURE 42-8: *You can send photos to friends via email.*

✳ *NOTE:* Sending a picture by email works only if you've already set up an email account to work with your iPhone (see Project 32).

8.   (Optional) In the dialog, tap **Assign to Contact**. An All Contacts screen appears. Tap a name. In the Move and Scale screen, tap **Set Photo** to assign the picture to that person's name.

9.   (Optional) In the dialog, tap **Send to MobileMe**. A MobileMe Albums screen appears, letting you choose in which album to store your picture.

10. Press the Home button to return to the Home screen.

Additional Ideas for Viewing Pictures on Your iPhone

Since you can assign pictures to names stored in your Contacts program, you can take a picture of a certain animal and associate that picture with someone you don't like. Take vacation pictures and send them to your friends and family members back home so they can see what a wonderful time you're having without waiting for you to return and bore them with a typical vacation slideshow later.

If you're the type who forgets shopping lists and doesn't like writing things down, take a picture of the inside of your refrigerator. Then, at the store, you can see at a glance what you're missing and what you need. They say that a picture is worth a thousand words, so feel free to experiment with different uses for pictures. As long as you have your iPhone with you, you'll always have a photographic memory.

43 Checking the Weather Forecast

Almost everyone needs to check a weather forecast once in a while to plan for a visit or an outdoor excursion. To see a current temperature and a weather forecast for the next six days for a particular place, you can use the iPhone's Weather application. As long as you have Internet access through a Wi-Fi network or your cellular telephone network, you can get the latest forecast for nearly any city in the world.

Project goal: Learn how to view weather conditions and the latest forecast on your iPhone.

What You'll Be Using

To learn how to view weather conditions and the latest forecast on your iPhone, you need to use the following:

 The Weather application

Defining a City for a Forecast

Before you can view a weather forecast, you must first define one or more cities for which you want to display weather information. First, you'll probably want to add the city where you live. You can also add other cities so you'll be able to view multiple weather forecasts for different areas at the same time.

Adding a City

To add a city to your weather forecast list, do this:

1. From the Home screen, tap **Weather**. The Weather screen appears, as shown in Figure 43-1. (Until you define a location, your iPhone will simply display the default city, Cupertino, where Apple headquarters is located.)
2. Tap the information (**i**) button in the lower-right corner of the screen.
3. The Weather screen displays a list of default cities as well as any cities that you've added, as shown in Figure 43-2.

FIGURE 43-1: *The Weather screen displays the current temperature and the forecast for a pre-selected city.*

FIGURE 43-2: *The Weather screen displays a list of cities.*

4. Tap the plus sign button in the upper-left corner of the screen. The virtual keyboard appears.
5. Type a ZIP Code or a name of a city. If you start typing a city name, a list of matching city names appears, as shown in Figure 43-3.
6. Tap the name of the city you want to add. The Weather screen appears again, including your newly added city.
7. (Optional) Tap **°F** or **°C** to display temperatures in Fahrenheit or Celsius, respectively.
8. Tap the **Done** button in the upper-right corner to view the weather forecast screen.

Deleting a City

If you no longer want to view forecasts for a particular city, you can remove it from your weather forecast list by doing this:

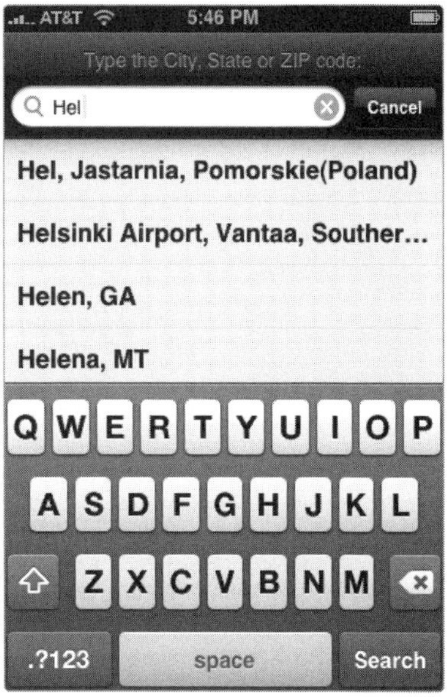

FIGURE 43-3: The iPhone tries to guess what city you're typing.

1. From the Home screen, tap **Weather**. The Weather screen appears (see Figure 43-1).
2. Tap the information (**i**) button in the lower-right corner of the screen. The Weather screen displays a list of cities currently stored on your iPhone (see Figure 43-2).
3. Tap the white minus sign inside a red circle to the left of the name of the city you want to remove from the list. A red Delete button appears.
4. Tap **Delete**. The city disappears from the forecast list.
5. Tap the **Done** button in the upper-right corner to view the weather forecast screen.

Viewing a Forecast

If you defined only one city in your forecast list, tapping Weather from the Home screen will always display weather information for that city. If you have defined two or more cities, you can view forecasts for each of those cities by doing this:

1. From the Home screen, tap **Weather**. The Weather screen appears. Dots appear at the bottom of the weather screen to show you how many city forecasts are available.

2. Slide your finger to the left or right on the Weather screen to display the previous or next forecast, respectively, as shown in Figure 43-4. If you have added more than one or two cities, keep sliding until you see the forecast for the city you want.

3. Press the Home button to return to the Home screen.

Additional Ideas for Checking the Weather Forecast

If you plan to travel to multiple cities, take a moment to add each of those cities to your forecast list. That way, you'll be able to prepare for the weather in those areas without running into any nasty surprises such as extreme heat or cold.

In addition to checking the weather for a destination, you might also want to check the latest events happening in that city. If you have the time and the weather is nice, you can attend events unique to that particular area, such as a museum event. To view the latest cultural events in a city on your forecast list, do this:

1. From the Home screen, tap **Weather**. The Weather screen appears.

2. Tap the Yahoo! icon in the lower-left corner of the screen. A Yahoo! web page appears.

3. Scroll down to view the weather forecast and a list of events occurring in that city today, as shown in Figure 43-5.

4. Tap an event to view more information.

5. Press the Home button to return to the Home screen.

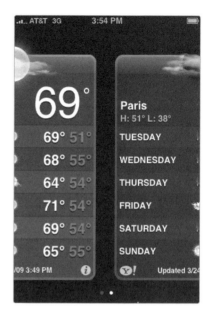

FIGURE 43-4: *Slide your finger left or right to reveal additional forecasts.*

FIGURE 43-5: *Yahoo! can display a weather forecast along with a list of events.*

Get Detailed Weather Information on Your iPhone

The Weather app included with your iPhone can provide a simple forecast of the weather in a particular area, but if you crave more detailed information, grab a copy of the Weather Channel's iPhone app. This app lets you see a map of an area, view ten-day forecasts, and even view videos so you can see weather conditions for yourself. If you need to know the absolutely latest news about the weather, let the Weather Channel app turn your iPhone into your up-to-date weather forecasting source.

Weather Channel   *http://www.weather.com/mobile/pda/iphone*

The Weather Channel provides comprehensive forecasts.

44 Watching the Stock Market

Many people invest in the stock market. While some people buy stocks and forget about them, many more actively enjoy watching a stock's price go up (hopefully) or down. By carefully tracking the price of your stocks, you can decide the best time to buy or sell.

In the old days, you'd check a stock listing in the newspaper or visit a financial website and type in the stock name to view current prices. If you were following several stocks, typing and retyping stock symbols could get annoying; your iPhone lets you type the symbols of the stocks you want to track once, and then you can view the latest prices at any time as often as you want. From the convenience of your iPhone, you can check to see if you've made or lost money in the stock market.

Project goal: Learn how to store and retrieve stock quotes on your iPhone.

What You'll Be Using

To view stock quotes on your iPhone, you need to use the following:

 The Stocks application

Defining Stocks to Watch

To retrieve stock quotes, you must first define which stocks you want to watch. To do this, you must identify the stock symbol for each stock, which is usually a one- to four-letter acronym, such as *T* for AT&T, *TM* for Toyota Motor Company, *RHT* for Red Hat Software, or *AAPL* for Apple, Inc. To find a symbol for a stock, you'll need to visit a financial website and look up the symbol—simply type the name of the company to see the specific stock symbol for that company. Two popular financial websites that offer symbol lookups are the New York Stock Exchange (*http://www.nyse.com/*) and NASDAQ (*http://www.nasdaq.com/*).

After you've identified the symbol for each stock that you want to track, you can open the Stocks program, delete stock symbols you don't want to track, and add stock symbols that you do want to track.

Deleting a Stock

The Stocks application includes several sample stock quotes, just so you can see how the program works. You might not care about these sample stock quotes, so you can delete them to make room for stocks that you do care about.

To delete a stock, do this:

1. From the Home screen, tap **Stocks**. The Stocks screen appears, as shown in Figure 44-1.
2. Tap the information (**i**) button in the lower-right corner of the screen. The Stocks screen displays a list of stocks currently chosen, as shown in Figure 44-2.

FIGURE 44-1: *The Stocks screen initially shows sample stock quotes.*

3. (Optional) Tap the **%** or **Numbers** button at the bottom of the screen. The % button lets you view stock quote changes as a percentage of the stock's price, such as +1.82%. The Numbers button lets you see the actual price rise or drop in a stock, such as -0.68.

4. Tap the red circle with the white minus sign next to the stock you want to remove. A red Delete button appears to the right of the stock name, as shown in Figure 44-3.

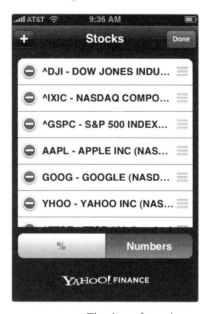

FIGURE 44-2: The list of stocks

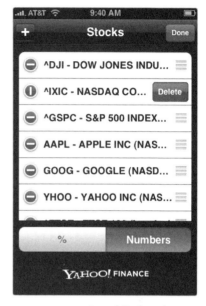

FIGURE 44-3: A red Delete button appears so you can remove a stock quote from the Stocks screen.

5. Tap **Delete**. The stock disappears from your list.
6. Tap **Done**.

Adding a Stock

To view the stocks that you care about, you'll need to add them to the Stocks screen by doing this:

1. While running the Stocks program, tap the information (**i**) button in the lower-right corner of the screen. The Stocks screen displays a list of stocks currently chosen.
2. Tap the plus sign in the upper-left corner of the screen. The virtual keyboard appears.

3. Type the stock symbol name. A list of matching stock names appears as you type, as shown in Figure 44-4.

4. Tap the name of the stock symbol that you want to add. The Stocks screen appears again, including your chosen stock.

5. Tap **Done**.

Viewing Your Stock Listings

After you've customized the Stocks screen to display only the stock quotes that you care about, you can check on your stocks at any time.

✳ **NOTE:** Stock quotes are delayed by approximately 20 minutes, so what you'll see on the Stocks screen are "historical" prices, not real-time prices.

To view your stock quotes, do this:

1. From the Home screen, tap **Stocks**. The Stocks screen appears, displaying your stock symbols and quotes. (You may need to scroll down to view all your stocks.)

2. Tap a stock. The bottom half of the screen shows a chart for your selected stock, as shown in Figure 44-5.

FIGURE 44-4: The virtual keyboard lets you type a stock symbol.

FIGURE 44-5: You can view charts of each stock.

3. (Optional) To change the time frame of the chart, tap a different time, ranging from 1d (1 day) to 2y (2 years).

4. (Optional) Tap the Yahoo! icon in the lower-left corner of the screen to view a Yahoo! web page containing additional information about your selected stock, as shown in Figure 44-6.

5. Press the Home button to return to the Home screen.

FIGURE 44-6: *You can visit Yahoo! to view additional information about a stock.*

Additional Ideas for Viewing Stock Quotes

The Stocks application can help you track your stock portfolio so you can see how much money you've made (or lost) that day. Even if you don't own any stocks, you might want to track stock prices of a few popular companies just to be aware of their financial health.

For example, compare the stock prices of Apple (AAPL) with Microsoft (MSFT), and you can get a rough idea which company seems to have a brighter future. Do the same with search engine rivals Google (GOOG) and Yahoo! (YHOO), and you can see which company is financially stronger. By watching stocks on your iPhone, you can see if you have what it takes to make (or lose) money consistently in the stock market.

Use Your iPhone to Play the Stock Market
with Virtual Cash

Playing the stock market can be like a game, but if you don't know how to play intelligently, you could lose a good chunk of money. Before you risk buying and selling stock with real cash, try the Virtual Stock Market app, which lets you paper trade with an imaginary portfolio of $100,000.

By playing this game, you can test out different stock trading strategies and track your results. If you're the competitive type, you can even compete against others to see who can generate the highest score by making the most money in the stock market. Once you feel comfortable paper trading, you can make that step into risking real money.

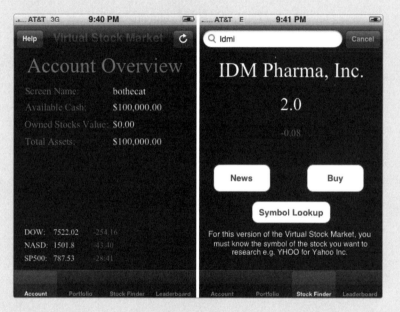

The Virtual Stock Market app lets you paper trade with real stock data.

45

Using Your iPhone as a Clock, Alarm Clock, Stopwatch, and Timer

In addition to making telephone calls, you can use your iPhone to view the time. Rather than wear a watch, many people glance at their iPhone for the current time. And in addition to acting like a watch, it can also function as an alarm clock, stopwatch, and timer.

If you need to know the correct time, or you need to keep track of time, let your iPhone do the work so you can do something else and have fun instead.

Project goal: Learn how to view, measure, and set the time on your iPhone.

What You'll Be Using

To work with time on your iPhone, you'll need the following:

 The Clock application   The Settings application

Viewing the Time

When you need to know the time, do one of the following:

▶ If your iPhone is in sleep mode, press the Sleep/Wake button or the Home button to display the current date and time on the screen along with a slider that lets you access your iPhone, as shown in Figure 45-1.

▶ If your iPhone is currently running, press the Home button to view the Home screen. The current time appears at the top of the screen, as shown in Figure 45-2.

FIGURE 45-1: *Waking an iPhone from sleep mode displays the current time and date on the screen.*

FIGURE 45-2: *The current time appears at the top of the Home screen.*

Sometimes you may want to know both the current local time and the time in another time zone. For example, if you live in Los Angeles but need to call London or Tel Aviv on a regular basis, you'll need to know the current time in those cities.

Rather than force you to perform mental calculations when you need to know the current time in another time zone, your iPhone World Clock can show you the time in major cities around the world.

Adding Time Zones to the World Clock

To add a time zone to your iPhone's World Clock, do this:

1. From the Home screen, tap **Clock**. The Clock screen appears.
2. Tap **World Clock**. The World Clock screen appears, as shown in Figure 45-3. The World Clock always displays the current time for your local area on top.
3. Tap the plus sign in the upper-right corner of the screen. The virtual keyboard appears.
4. Type the name of a major city in the time zone that you want to track. As you type, a list of cities appears, as shown in Figure 45-4.
5. Tap the city name you want. The World Clock screen displays your newly added time zone, as shown in Figure 45-5.

FIGURE 45-3: The World Clock screen shows current local time.

FIGURE 45-4: Type part of a name to display a list of possible cities.

FIGURE 45-5: The World Clock screen can display information for multiple time zones.

Deleting Time Zones from the World Clock

If you no longer need to track time in another time zone, you can remove it from the World Clock screen by doing this:

1. From the home screen, tap **Clock**. The Clock screen appears.
2. Tap **World Clock**. The World Clock screen appears.
3. Tap **Edit** in the upper-left corner of the screen. A white minus sign inside a red circle appears to the left of each time zone, as shown in Figure 45-6.
4. Tap the white minus sign inside a red circle next to the time zone you want to remove. A red Delete button appears, as shown in Figure 45-7.

FIGURE 45-6: *Remove a time zone from the World Clock by tapping the white minus sign inside a red circle that appears next to its name.*

FIGURE 45-7: *A red Delete button appears so you can remove a time zone.*

5. Tap **Delete**. Your chosen time zone disappears.
6. Tap **Done**.

Setting an Alarm

To help you stay on schedule, you can set an alarm. That way, you'll know when it's time to get up or get ready for your next appointment. When setting an alarm, you can choose four options:

▶ **Repeat** Sets an alarm to occur regularly at the same time on a certain day of the week

▶ **Sound** Defines a sound to alert you to the alarm

▶ **Snooze** Defines whether to allow the snooze function so you can temporarily dismiss an alarm

▶ **Label** Sets a descriptive label for your alarm

Adding an Alarm

To set an alarm, do this:

1. From the Home screen, tap **Clock**. The Clock screen appears.
2. Tap **Alarm**. The Alarm screen appears.
3. Tap the plus sign in the upper-right corner of the screen. An Add Alarm screen appears, as shown in Figure 45-8.
4. (Optional) Tap **Repeat**. The Repeat screen appears, as shown in Figure 45-9. Tap one or more buttons to define the day or days to activate the alarm, and then tap **Back** when you're done.

FIGURE 45-8: Create alarm settings in the Add Alarm screen.

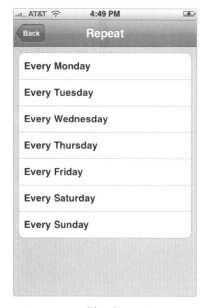

FIGURE 45-9: The Repeat screen lets you choose one or more days to use an alarm.

5. (Optional) Tap **Sound**. The Sound screen appears, where you can choose a sound to play when your alarm activates, as shown in Figure 45-10. Tap a sound, and then tap **Back** when you're done.

6. (Optional) Tap the **ON/OFF** button next to Snooze to enable or disable the snooze feature.

7. (Optional) Tap **Label**. A Label screen appears, where you can type a description for your alarm, as shown in Figure 45-11. Type a description for your alarm, such as *Meet with Charlie*, or *Lunch meeting with stupid boss*, and then tap **Back** when you're done.

8. Scroll the hour, minute, and AM/PM wheels at the bottom of the Add Alarm screen to choose a time for your alarm.

9. Tap **Save**. The Alarm screen displays all your current alarms, as shown in Figure 45-12.

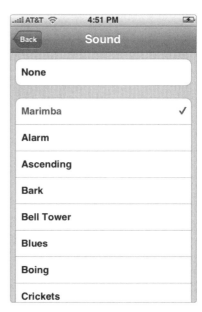

FIGURE 45-10: *The Sound screen lets you choose a sound for your alarm.*

FIGURE 45-11: *The Label screen lets you type a description for your alarm.*

FIGURE 45-12: *The Alarm screen displays all active alarms.*

Responding to an Alarm

When an alarm goes off, your iPhone will vibrate (as long as you haven't turned the vibrate feature off) and play your chosen sound to alert you. The alarm's description will appear on the screen, as shown in Figure 45-13.

When an alarm goes off, tap **Snooze** or **OK**. If you tap Snooze, the alarm temporarily turns off but pops up again until you eventually tap OK. If you tap OK, the alarm turns off. If this is a recurring alarm, it will be automatically set to go off again at its designated time.

Editing an Alarm

You can change the alarm's message, time and date, sound, or whether it remains on or off. To edit an alarm, do this:

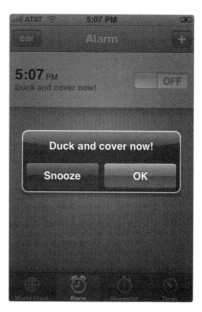

FIGURE 45-13: An alarm displays a message on the screen.

1. From the Home screen, tap **Clock**. The Clock screen appears.
2. Tap **Alarm**. The Alarm screen appears, listing all alarms that you've defined.
3. (Optional) Tap the **ON/OFF** button next to an alarm that you want to turn on or off.
4. Tap **Edit**. A white minus sign inside a red circle appears next to each alarm.
5. Tap the alarm you want to edit. (Do *not* tap the minus sign button!) The Edit Alarm screen appears.
6. Make changes to your alarm and tap **Save**.

Deleting an Alarm

Eventually, you will need to delete an alarm, since you probably won't need it forever. To delete an alarm, do this:

1. From the Home screen, tap **Clock**. The Clock screen appears.
2. Tap **Alarm**. The Alarm screen appears, listing all alarms that you've defined.
3. Tap **Edit**. A remove button appears next to each alarm.
4. Tap the white minus sign inside a red circle next to the alarm that you want to delete. A red Delete button appears next to that alarm.
5. Tap **Delete**. Your chosen alarm disappears.

Using the Stopwatch

If you need to measure time, such as timing how fast someone can run a mile or swim a lap, you can use the stopwatch feature of your iPhone. To turn your iPhone into a stopwatch, do this:

1. From the Home screen, tap **Clock**. The Clock screen appears.
2. Tap **Stopwatch**. The Stopwatch screen appears, as shown in Figure 45-14.
3. Tap **Start** to start the stopwatch. The Stopwatch screen displays a red Stop button along with a gray Lap button.
4. (Optional) Tap **Lap** if you're timing laps, as shown in Figure 45-15.
5. Tap **Stop** to stop the stopwatch.
6. Tap **Reset** to reset the stopwatch time.

FIGURE 45-14: *The Stopwatch screen lets you start and stop the stopwatch.*

FIGURE 45-15: *The Stopwatch can time laps.*

Setting a Timer

If you've ever thrown food in an oven, you've probably turned on a timer to alert you when the time is up and the food is cooked. The iPhone timer works in a similar way. You define the amount of time you want, and when that time limit is reached, your iPhone will play a sound to alert you.

To set the timer, do this:

1. From the Home screen, tap **Clock**. The Clock screen appears.
2. Tap **Timer**. The Timer screen appears, as shown in Figure 45-16.
3. Scroll the hours and minutes wheels to define how long you want to set the timer.

* **NOTE:** If your iPhone drifts into sleep mode while your timer is running, the timer will still count down and alert you when the time is up.

4. (Optional) Tap **When Timer Ends**. A When Timer Ends screen appears, listing different sounds from which you can choose. Tap the sound to play when the timer ends and then tap **Set**.
5. Tap **Start**. The Timer screen starts counting down. (You can tap Cancel to stop the timer.) A Timer Done dialog appears when the timer is done, as shown in Figure 45-17.
6. Tap **OK**.

FIGURE 45-16: *The Timer screen lets you scroll wheels to set the timer.*

FIGURE 45-17: *A Timer Done dialog appears to let you know when the timer is finished.*

Setting the Time

Most likely, your iPhone has already accessed your cellular phone network to find the correct time and date. However, if you let your battery die and you happen to be out of range of cellular phone coverage, or if you just like setting your clock five minutes ahead so you'll never be late, you may need to set the date and time manually. To set the time, do this:

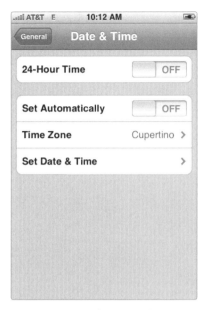

FIGURE 45-18: *The Date & Time screen lets you set the correct time on your iPhone.*

1. From the Home screen, tap **Settings**. The Settings screen appears.
2. Tap **General**. The General screen appears.
3. Scroll down the General screen and tap **Date & Time**. The Date & Time screen appears, as shown in Figure 45-18.
4. (Optional) Tap the **ON/OFF** button next to 24-Hour Time. When this is set to off, your iPhone identifies time with AM/PM designations, such as 2:49 PM or 9:10 AM. When this button is set to on, your iPhone displays times in *24-hour time*, with morning times shown as usual (such as 9:10) and afternoon times shown in 24-hour time—so, for example, 2:29 PM would appear as 14:29).
5. (Optional) Tap the **ON/OFF** button next to Set Automatically. If the button is set to on, your iPhone will set the correct time by itself. If your iPhone is displaying the wrong time, you'll need to set the time manually by continuing with the remaining steps.
6. Turn Set Automatically off. A Time Zone and Set Date & Time button appear on the screen. (If Set Automatically is on, the Time Zone and Set Date & Time buttons do not appear.)
7. Tap **Time Zone**. A Time Zone screen appears, as shown in Figure 45-19.
8. Using the virtual keyboard, type the name of the largest city closest to your current location. As you type, the iPhone displays the names of cities it recognizes.

9. Tap the name of the city closest to your location. The Date & Time screen appears again.

✳ **NOTE:** After defining the correct time zone, you can turn Set Automatically on so your iPhone will identify the correct time in your time zone. Otherwise, you can set the time manually by continuing with the following steps.

10. Tap **Set Date & Time**. A Date & Time screen appears, as shown in Figure 45-20.
11. Tap the button displaying the time. Scroll wheels appear displaying hours and minutes, as shown in Figure 45-21.
12. Scroll the wheels up and down until they display the correct time, and then tap **Date & Time** in the upper-left corner of the screen.
13. Press the Home button.

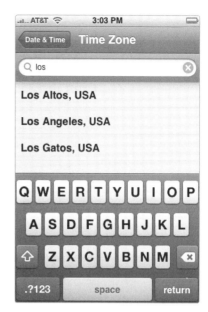

FIGURE 45-19: *The Time Zone screen lets you type the name of a city in your time zone.*

FIGURE 45-20: *The Date & Time screen lets you define the current date.*

FIGURE 45-21: *The Date & Time screen lets you define the current time.*

Additional Ideas for Using the Clock Application

With so many ways to play with time, your iPhone can replace a watch, an alarm clock, a stopwatch, and a timer. If you're on a blind date and want an escape route if the date isn't going well, set an alarm for a time that will occur in the middle of your date. When the alarm goes off, you can pretend it's an important phone call and excuse yourself from your date.

Run Multiple Timers on Your iPhone

For a more practical application, set time limits for different tasks, such as reminding yourself that you need to clean out the garage or exercise on a treadmill for an hour. Then use the timer on your iPhone to let you know when your time is up. With your iPhone as your constant companion, you should never lose track of time again—unless, of course, you forget to recharge your iPhone. The iPhone's timer is handy for measuring time, but it can only display one timer at a time. If you want to keep track of multiple times, you'll need the Chronology app, which lets you display up to twelve timers on the screen simultaneously.

Chronology offers multiple timers.

Now you can measure time, such as how fast someone can run a fixed distance while also counting down from a specified time (such as 20 minutes) so you can tell when you need to do something, such as pulling a pot roast out of the oven or making an important phone call.

Chronology *http://treeness.com/*

PART 9

Safety and Privacy

<table>
<tr><td>

46

</td><td>

Protecting Your iPhone with a Passcode

</td></tr>
</table>

If you lose or temporarily misplace your iPhone, anyone can pick it up, turn it on, and start making phone calls at your expense. To protect yourself from unauthorized users, you can protect your iPhone with a four-digit passcode.

This passcode forces anyone (including you) to type a four-digit number every time you turn on your iPhone or wake it up from sleep mode. If someone (including you) can't type the proper four-digit passcode, your iPhone remains securely locked to prevent unauthorized access.

Project goal: Learn how to protect your iPhone with a passcode.

What You'll Be Using

To protect your iPhone with a passcode, you need to use the following:

 The Settings application

Setting a Passcode

To set a passcode, you must choose a four-digit number that will be easy for you to remember but difficult for someone else to guess. For example, a passcode of *1234* might be easy to remember, but it's also way too easy for someone to guess.

Ideally, choose a four-digit number that means something to you and that no one else will know about. For example, use the first four numbers of your Social Security number or the year that your favorite sports team last won a major championship (such as 1997).

When you've decided on a four-digit passcode, follow these steps:

1. From the Home screen, tap **Settings**. The Settings screen appears.
2. Tap **General**. The General screen appears.
3. Tap **Passcode Lock**. The Set Passcode screen appears, as shown in Figure 46-1.
4. Type your four-digit number on the numeric keypad that appears on the screen. A second Set Passcode screen appears, asking you to re-enter your four-digit passcode.
5. Type your four-digit number again. The Passcode Lock screen appears, as shown in Figure 46-2.
6. (Optional) Tap **Require Passcode**. The Require Passcode screen appears, as shown in Figure 46-3.
7. Tap the **Passcode Lock** button in the upper-left corner of the screen. The Passcode Lock screen appears again.
8. (Optional) Tap the **ON/OFF** button next to Erase Data.
9. Press the Home button to return to the Home screen.

FIGURE 46-1: *The Set Passcode screen lets you enter a four-digit number.*

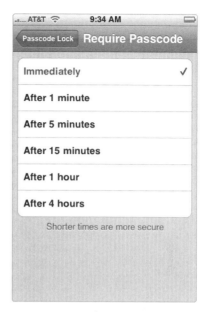

FIGURE 46-2: *The Passcode Lock screen lets you modify your passcode settings.*

FIGURE 46-3: *The Require Passcode screen lets you define how much time can elapse before requiring a passcode.*

Modifying Your Passcode

At any time, you can modify your passcode to change the four-digit code or change the time limit before your passcode locks down your iPhone.

Changing Your Passcode

For security reasons, it's a good idea to change your four-digit passcode periodically. That way, if someone has guessed or stolen your passcode, you can change it to lock that person out of your iPhone. To change your passcode, follow these steps:

1. From the Home screen, tap **Settings**. The Settings screen appears.
2. Tap **General**. The General screen appears.
3. Tap **Passcode Lock**. The Enter Passcode screen appears.
4. Type your current four-digit passcode on the numeric keypad that appears on the screen. The Passcode Lock screen appears.
5. Tap **Change Passcode**. The Change Passcode screen appears.
6. Type your new four-digit passcode. A second Set Passcode screen appears, asking you to re-enter your new four-digit passcode.
7. Type your new four-digit code again. The Passcode Lock screen appears.
8. Press the Home button to return to the Home screen.

Changing Your Passcode Time Limit

The default time limit is Immediately, which means as soon as your iPhone goes to sleep, you'll need to type your passcode to wake it up. If this gets to be too annoying, you can choose a delayed time limit, such as After 5 minutes. Choosing a longer time limit lets you wake up your iPhone within this time limit without having to type your passcode. Although this makes it convenient for you to turn your iPhone on and off while you're using it, it can also give others a chance to use your iPhone within this time limit.

To choose a different time limit for your passcode, follow these steps:

1. From the Home screen, tap **Settings**. The Settings screen appears.
2. Tap **General**. The General screen appears.
3. Tap **Passcode Lock**. The Enter Passcode screen appears.
4. Type your four-digit passcode. The Passcode Lock screen appears.
5. Tap **Require Passcode**. The Require Passcode screen appears (see Figure 46-2).
6. Tap a time limit, such as **After 15 minutes** or **After 1 minute**.
7. Press the Home button to return to the Home screen.

Disabling Passcode Protection

Although a passcode can help secure your iPhone, it can also make your iPhone less convenient to use. If you want to turn off the passcode feature altogether, follow these steps:

1. From the Home screen, tap **Settings**. The Settings screen appears.
2. Tap **General**. The General screen appears.
3. Tap **Passcode Lock**. The Enter Passcode screen appears.
4. Type your current four-digit passcode. The Passcode Lock screen appears.
5. Tap **Turn Passcode Off**. The Turn Off Passcode screen appears.
6. Type your four-digit passcode. The General screen appears again.
7. Press the Home button to return to the Home screen.

Additional Ideas for Protecting Your iPhone

Passcodes can help prevent your iPhone from being accessed by unauthorized users, but the best way to keep others from using your iPhone is to make sure you never lose or misplace it. Consider buying a protective carrying case that you can attach to your belt. This will help keep your iPhone with you at all times, although there's still the risk of misplacing it or losing it to a skilled pickpocket.

Passcodes can also come in handy for parents who buy their children an iPhone. If your kids misbehave, you can passcode-protect their iPhone with a four-digit number that they'll never guess in a million years. This effectively renders their iPhone useless until you're ready to grant them iPhone privileges again.

Ultimately, the best protection for your iPhone is knowing where it is at all times and keeping it tucked out of sight whenever possible. Since using your iPhone will alert a potential thief, always make sure you have a secure way to carry your iPhone whenever you're in a public area.

For the truly paranoid, do what street-savvy New Yorkers do with their wallets: Carry a "disposable" wallet with a little cash in it while hiding your real wallet somewhere safe. If a mugger wants your wallet, you can give him this disposable wallet. Adapting this technique, find a secure place to store your iPhone and keep a "dead" iPhone look-alike nearby. If someone wants to steal your iPhone, they may take the useless iPhone look-alike instead.

Ultimately, the best security for your iPhone is to keep an eye on it at all times, but consider using passcodes as an additional layer of defense to protect your iPhone from unauthorized users.

47 Making an iPhone Kid Friendly

If you have children, they may want to share your iPhone or even use one of their own. Although you could punish your kids by forcing them to use a clumsier, more frustrating mobile phone, you might decide that torturing your children with other phones is too cruel. While giving a child an iPhone may be the ultimate in parental benevolence, you may not want your child using certain features. If you're worried about outside media corrupting your child, take some time to make the iPhone kid friendly.

Making an iPhone kid friendly involves restricting access to certain features, including playing video with explicit content, browsing the Internet, watching YouTube videos, using iTunes, or installing new iPhone applications.

Project goal: Learn how to restrict access to certain iPhone features to make the iPhone kid friendly.

What You'll Be Using

To restrict access to certain iPhone features, you need to use the following:

 The Settings application

Blocking iPhone Features

To restrict access to certain iPhone features, you need to use a four-digit passcode. The only way someone (including you) can access these blocked features is by first typing the correct four-digit passcode.

You can block the following features of your iPhone to make it more kid friendly:

▸ Watching video or listening to audio labeled as *Explicit*

▸ Accessing the Internet with the Safari web browser

▸ Watching YouTube videos

▸ Listening to music through iTunes

▸ Installing iPhone applications

▸ Taking pictures with the built-in camera

▸ Tagging pictures with your current location

When you purchase video or audio files through iTunes, certain files may be tagged as *Explicit* due to their violent or sexual nature. It's important to note that your iPhone can block only explicit video and audio files that were purchased though iTunes. So, for example, if you load an R-rated movie or adult-content audio file to your iPhone that you received from a source other than iTunes, your iPhone won't recognize the file as explicit, and you won't be able to block access to it.

Blocking access to the Internet serves two purposes: First, it can keep your child from using the iPhone to access pornographic sites. Second, blocking Internet access can also keep your child from running up huge bills by spending too much time on the Internet if you don't have a flat-rate data usage plan.

You may want to block access to YouTube videos, too—not necessarily because they may contain adult content, but because you may not want your child wasting time watching music videos or silly homemade videos of someone getting hit in the crotch.

Besides blocking YouTube video and Internet access, you may also want to block iTunes access. This can keep your child from spending too much time listening to music and not paying attention to doing anything else (like studying, doing homework, or showing up to school every day).

Blocking access to installing additional iPhone applications can also be a good idea. It can keep your kids from installing a bunch of useless applications that clutter up your iPhone. Or you may not want your kids downloading iPhone applications that cost money to buy. Finally, you may not want your kids to download and install the multitude of iPhone games available, which will give them an excuse to waste time playing with their iPhone instead of doing something perhaps a bit more productive.

To block access to one or more of these features, follow these steps:

1. From the Home screen, tap **Settings**. The Settings screen appears.
2. Tap **General**. The General screen appears.
3. Tap **Restrictions**. A Restrictions screen appears, as shown in Figure 47-1. Notice that all the ON/OFF buttons appear dimmed, since you cannot restrict access until you first enable restrictions.
4. Tap **Enable Restrictions**. The Set Passcode screen appears.
5. Type a four-digit number on the numeric keypad that appears on the screen. A second Set Passcode screen appears, asking you to re-enter your four-digit passcode. Be sure to choose a passcode you will remember.
6. Type your four-digit code again. The Restrictions screen appears again, allowing you to tap the ON/OFF buttons of different features, as shown in Figure 47-2.
7. (Optional) Tap the **ON/OFF** button next to Safari, YouTube, iTunes, Installing Apps, Camera, or Location.
8. Press the Home button to return to the Home screen.

* *NOTE:* **When you turn off a feature, such as YouTube or Safari, the icon for that feature disappears from your Home screen.**

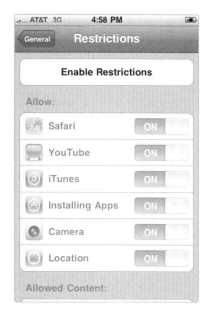

FIGURE 47-1: The Restrictions screen lets you selectively block access.

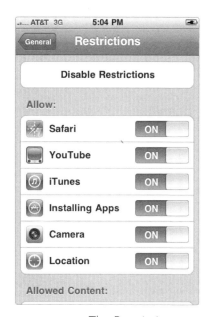

FIGURE 47-2: The Restrictions screen lets you turn different features on or off.

Restricting Content

In addition to blocking access to certain features, your iPhone can also block access to certain content with ratings, such as movies, TV shows, or music. Just remember that your iPhone can only block content that comes from the iTunes Store. If you download content from another source, it probably won't be tagged with a rating or label, so your iPhone won't know to block it.

To block access to certain content, do this:

1. From the Home screen, tap **Settings**. The Settings screen appears.
2. Tap **General**. The General screen appears.
3. Tap **Restrictions**. An Enter Passcode screen appears.
4. Type your four-digit passcode. The Restrictions screen appears.
5. Scroll down to see the Allowed Content section, as shown in Figure 47-3.
6. (Optional) Tap the **ON/OFF** button next to In-App Purchases. This will allow or block apps that can send you additional data for a fee without making you go through the iTunes Store.
7. (Optional) Tap the **Ratings For** button. A Ratings For screen appears, letting you choose your specific country so your iPhone knows that country's ratings system.

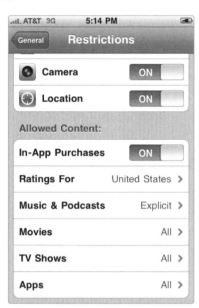

FIGURE 47-3: *The list of content you can block on an iPhone*

8. (Optional) Tap the **ON/OFF** button next to Music & Podcasts. A Music & Podcasts screen appears, letting you tap an **ON/OFF** button for Explicit. Tap this switch and then tap the **Restrictions** button in the upper-left corner of the screen.

9. (Optional) Tap **Movies**, **TV Shows**, or **Apps** to reveal a screen that lets you choose a restriction limit—for example, choosing NC-17 as a movie rating that you do not want to be allowed on your iPhone (see Figure 47-4).
10. Tap the **Restrictions** button in the upper-left corner.

Disabling Restrictions

By tapping the ON/OFF buttons, you can selectively disable certain iPhone features. However, if you want to remove restrictions altogether, follow these steps:

1. From the Home screen, tap **Settings**. The Settings screen appears.
2. Tap **General**. The General screen appears.
3. Tap **Restrictions**. An Enter Passcode screen appears.
4. Type your four-digit passcode. The Restrictions screen appears (see Figure 47-2).
5. Tap **Disable Restrictions**. A Turn Off Passcode screen appears.
6. Type your four-digit passcode on the numeric keypad that appears on the screen.
7. The Restrictions screen appears again (see Figure 47-1).
8. Press the Home button to return to the Home screen.

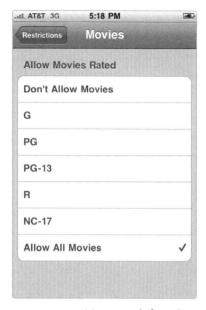

FIGURE 47-4: *You can define the rating for acceptable content on your iPhone.*

Additional Ideas for Using Restrictions on Your iPhone

The main purpose of restricting access to certain iPhone features is to keep your kids from wasting time and corrupting their minds watching explicit video or listening to adult-content audio. However, you may also want to restrict your own access to certain features to avoid the temptation to waste time.

For example, suppose you're addicted to the Internet, and you're spending way too much time surfing when you should be working. You can simply restrict access to Safari and/or YouTube and remove the temptation from your Home screen.

To make this even more effective, have someone else type in a passcode to restrict your access to certain features. Now you won't be tempted to turn off these features, since even you won't have the proper four-digit passcode. (Just make sure that you trust the person restricting your access to your own iPhone, or else you may never gain access to those features again without completely resetting your iPhone.)

PART 10

Cool Things You Can Do with Apps

48

Keeping Up with the News

Many people love keeping up with the latest news, whether it's international events, political or business news, or just mindless entertainment and celebrity gossip. If it's something different and fresh, people want to learn about it as quickly as it they can.

To help you keep up with the latest news, major news networks offer special apps that let you tap into their news whenever you need a quick update (or just need something to distract you from the boredom of waiting in line or sitting at your desk at work).

Project goal: Learn how to retrieve the latest news on your iPhone from multiple sources.

What You'll Be Using

To get and read the latest news, you need to use the following:

 iTunes (on your Mac or PC)   The iPhone USB cable

 The App Store application   The NYTimes application

 The BBCReader application   The Variety application

 The SCI FI Wire application

Getting News Apps

Many of the major news networks have already developed an app for the iPhone, and many more are sure to do so in the future. Some of the more popular news apps that you can download and install include:

▶   **NYTimes**   News from *The New York Times*, one of the most respected daily newspapers in the world

▶   **BBCReader**   The latest news from the BBC

▶   **Variety**   The most recent Hollywood news

▶   **SCI FI Wire**   News about the latest movies, TV shows, books, and games related to science fiction

Finding Apps in iTunes

To get these apps, you'll have to search for them in the iTunes Store or the App Store. To use iTunes to find these apps, follow these steps:

1.   Open iTunes on your computer.
2.   Click **iTunes Store** under the STORE category in the left pane of the iTunes Store screen.
3.   Click in the **Search iTunes Store** search field in the upper-right corner of the iTunes screen and type `NYTimes`, `BBCReader`, `Variety`, or `SCI FI Wire` and press RETURN. Your chosen app's icon appears in the iTunes window.
4.   Click the **Get App** button to download the app. You'll need to synchronize and install these apps to your iPhone by following the instructions in Project 12.

Finding Apps in the App Store

If you'd rather download and install these apps directly to your iPhone without the hassle of downloading and synchronizing them through a computer, follow these steps:

1. From the Home screen, tap **App Store**. The App Store screen appears.
2. Tap the **Search** icon at the bottom of the screen. The Search screen appears.
3. Tap in the search text box at the top of the screen. The virtual keyboard appears.
4. Type `NYTimes`, `BBCReader`, `Variety`, or `SCI FI Wire` and then tap the blue **Search** button in the lower-right corner of the screen. The app's icon appears.
5. Tap the app's icon. An Info screen appears.
6. Tap the **FREE** button. The FREE button turns into a green INSTALL button.
7. Tap the **INSTALL** button.

Using the NYTimes App

Each time you run the NYTimes app, you'll see five icons at the bottom of the screen:

▸ **Latest**   Displays the latest news

▸ **Popular**   Displays the most popular news stories people have emailed to others

▸ **Saved**   Lists your saved news stories—if you haven't saved any news stories, this area will be empty

▸ **Search**   Lets you type on the virtual keyboard to search for a particular topic or story

▸ **More**   Displays categories of news stories (Business, Politics, Sports, Movies, and so on) so you can search for a specific type of story

To view a news story, do this:

1. From the Home screen, tap **NYTimes**. You may need to slide your Home screen to the left or right, depending on where you stored the NYTimes icon. The New York Times screen appears, as shown in Figure 48-1.

FIGURE 48-1: *Viewing a list of stories from The New York Times*

2. Tap the **Latest**, **Popular**, **Search**, or **More** icons at the bottom of the screen to view a list of stories. Then tap the story you want to read. Your chosen story appears, as shown in Figure 48-2

3. Slide your finger up or down the screen to scroll through the news story. You may also want to tap the font decrease/increase buttons (T-/T+) at the bottom of the screen to change the way text appears.

4. (Optional) Tap the email icon in the lower-left corner of the screen to display a virtual keyboard so you can type an email address and send an article to someone. (If you tap the plus sign in the To text box, you can view a list of email addresses stored in the Contacts program.)

5. (Optional) Tap **Save** in the lower-right corner of the screen to save your article. You'll be able to view all saved news stories by tapping the Saved icon at the bottom of the screen.

FIGURE 48-2: *Reading a New York Times news story*

Using the BBCReader App

One problem with most news sources in the United States is that they tend to ignore anything happening in other countries. In case you want to know important news from other parts of the world, grab the BBCReader app, which displays five icons at the bottom of its screen:

▶ **News**   Displays the latest news

▶ **Pictures**   Displays photographs from popular news headlines

▶ **History**   Lists all the news stories you've viewed—if you haven't viewed any news stories, this area will be empty

▶ **Info**   Lets you modify the way the BBCReader app works

▶ **More**   Displays news stories organized by categories and by geographic location (Middle East, Europe, Technology, Entertainment, and so on)

To use the BBCReader, do this:

1. From the Home screen, tap **BBCReader**. You may need to slide your Home screen to the left or right, depending on where you stored the BBCReader icon. The BBCReader screen appears, as shown in Figure 48-3.
2. Tap the **News front page**, **UK**, or **Americas** button at the top of the screen to read the latest news or news related to the United Kingdom (UK) or North America (Americas).
3. (Optional) Tap the **Pictures**, **History**, or **More** button at the bottom of the screen to view photographs, previously viewed news stories, or stories organized by different categories.
4. Press the Home button to return to the Home screen.

FIGURE 48-3: *Reading the BBC News headlines*

Using the Variety App

For those who love keeping track of show business, the Variety app can make you feel like you're part of the Hollywood scene without having to actually live in Los Angeles. The Variety app displays five icons at the bottom of the screen:

▶ **News** Displays the latest entertainment news

▶ **Reviews** Displays reviews of the latest movies and TV shows

▶ **Photos** Displays photographs from major entertainment news stories

▶ **Videos** Displays movie trailers so you can see if an upcoming film might interest you

▶ **Search** Displays the virtual keyboard so you can search for a word or phrase in a news story

To use the Variety app, do this:

1. From the Home screen, tap **Variety**. You may need to slide your Home screen to the left or right, depending on where you stored the Variety icon. The Variety screen appears, as shown in Figure 48-4.

2. Tap the **News**, **Reviews**, **Photos**, **Videos**, or **Search** icons at the bottom of the screen to view different information.

3. Press the Home button to return to the Home screen.

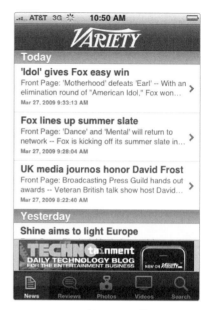

FIGURE 48-4: *Variety offers major entertainment news stories.*

Using the SCI FI Wire App

If you enjoy science fiction, horror, fantasy, the supernatural, or anything dealing with alternate realties, then you might enjoy staying up to date with the latest news from the SCI FI Wire app, which offers three icons at the bottom of its screen:

▸ **Latest News** Displays the latest news stories involving science fiction, fantasy, or horror

▸ **Sections** Displays news stories organized into sections such as Animation, Games, Music, Comics, and TV

▸ **Video** Displays trailers for upcoming movies or clips from TV shows

To use the SCI FI Wire app, do this:

1. From the Home screen, tap **SCI FI Wire**. You may need to slide your Home screen to the left or right, depending on where you stored the SCI FI Wire icon. The SCI FI Wire screen appears, as shown in Figure 48-5.

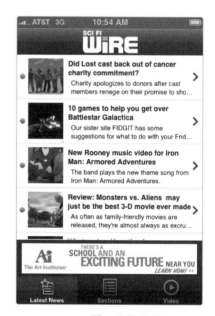

FIGURE 48-5: *The SCI FI Wire app offers news stories based on fantasy and science fiction.*

2. Tap the **Latest News**, **Sections**, or **Video** icons at the bottom of the screen to view different information.
3. Press the Home button to return to the Home screen.

Additional Ideas for Keeping Up with the News on Your iPhone

Browse through the News category in the App Store and you're sure to find news apps from other major news sources such as the Associated Press, USA Today, or even your local news stations and newspapers. With print newspapers scaling back or cutting printing altogether, the future of news is digital. By reading news from your favorite app, you can see just what you want to read and get it faster than any newspaper or magazine could ever provide.

By keeping up to date with the latest news, you can keep yourself amused the next time you're waiting at a doctor's office or bored at work. The more news you read, the better informed you will be. Maybe you'll even begin to challenge your way of thinking or expose yourself to different points of view.

49 Storing Reference Material

Nobody likes lugging around heavy books if they don't have to. If you're carrying reference books, you probably look at them only occasionally anyway.

To eliminate the need to carry multiple reference books around, use your iPhone to store apps that contain reference materials in digital format. Now you can carry as many reference books as you need without ever lifting anything heavier than your iPhone.

Project goal: Learn how to view reference materials on your iPhone from multiple sources.

What You'll Be Using

To get and read the latest news, you need to use the following:

 iTunes (on your Mac or PC)

 The App Store application

 The AllCountries application

 The iThesaurus application

 The iPhone USB cable

 The Bible application

 The Dictionaire application

Getting Reference Apps

Four of the most popular reference apps are:

▸ **Bible**   Displays text from multiple versions of the Bible

▸ **AllCountries**   Provides basic information about every country in the world

▸ **Dictionaire**   Lets you look up definitions of words

▸ **iThesaurus**   Lets you look up synonyms for words

Finding Apps in iTunes

To get these apps, you'll have to search for them in the iTunes Store or the App Store. To use iTunes to find these apps, follow these steps:

1. Open iTunes on your computer.
2. Click **iTunes Store** under the STORE category in the left pane of the iTunes Store screen.
3. Click in the **Search iTunes Store** search field in the upper-right corner of the iTunes screen and type `Bible`, `All the Countries`, `Dictionaire`, or `iThesaurus` and press RETURN. Your chosen app's icon appears in the iTunes window.
4. Click the **Get App** button to download the app. You'll need to synchronize and install these apps to your iPhone by following the instructions in Project 12.

Finding Apps in the App Store

If you'd rather download and install apps directly to your iPhone without the hassle of downloading and synchronizing them through a computer, follow these steps:

1. From the Home screen, tap **App Store**. The App Store screen appears.
2. Tap the **Search** icon at the bottom of the screen. The Search screen appears.

3. Tap in the search text box at the top of the screen. The virtual keyboard appears.
4. Type **Bible**, **AllCountries**, **Dictionaire**, or **iThesaurus** and then tap the blue **Search** button in the lower-right corner of the screen. The app's icon appears.
5. Tap the app's icon. An Info screen appears.
6. Tap the **FREE** button. The FREE button turns into a green INSTALL button.
7. Tap the **INSTALL** button.
8. Press the Home button.

Using the Bible App

By downloading and installing the Bible app, you can read the Bible anywhere you take your iPhone. The five icons displayed at the bottom of the app's screen include:

▸ **Read**   Displays text from the Bible

▸ **Search**   Lets you type on the virtual keyboard to search for a particular passage in the Bible

▸ **Daily Read**   Displays passages suitable for reading each day

▸ **Bookmarks**   Lists your saved bookmarked passages—if you haven't saved any passages, this area will be empty

▸ **More**   Displays options for customizing the app

To read the Bible on your iPhone, do this:

1. From the Home screen, tap **Bible**. You may need to slide your Home screen to the left or right, depending on where you stored the Bible icon. The Bible screen appears, as shown in Figure 49-1.
2. (Optional) Tap the button at the top of the screen that displays the current version of the Bible you're reading, such as American Standard Version. A Translations screen appears, as shown in Figure 49-2. Tap the translation you want to read and tap **Done** in the upper-right corner of the screen.

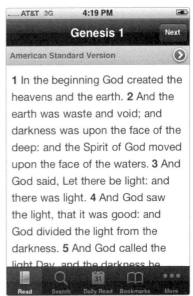

FIGURE 49-1: Viewing the Bible

3. (Optional) Tap a passage to highlight it. Three buttons appear, giving you the option to email, bookmark, or view more information about the selected passage, as shown in Figure 49-3. Tap one of these buttons to choose an option.

4. Press the Home button to return to the Home screen.

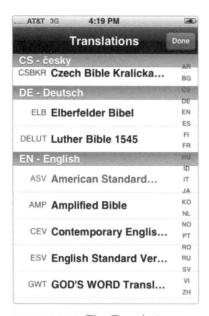

FIGURE 49-2: *The Translations screen lets you choose a specific translation of the Bible.*

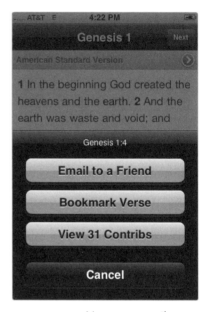

FIGURE 49-3: *You can email or bookmark a passage.*

Using the AllCountries App

Since many Americans are curious about the world beyond the United States, an app like AllCountries can come in handy. This app lets you select a country and view facts such as the population, official language, or official currency.

To use the AllCountries app, do this:

1. From the Home screen, tap **AllCountries**. You may need to slide your Home screen to the left or right, depending on where you stored the AllCountries icon. The Countries screen appears, as shown in Figure 49-4.

2. Tap a country name. Information about that country appears on the screen, as shown in Figure 49-5. You may need to scroll down to view all the information about a particular country.

3. Press the Home button to return to the Home screen.

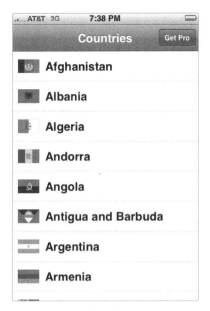

FIGURE 49-4: *The Countries screen displays a list of every country in the world.*

FIGURE 49-5: *You can view detailed information about a specific country.*

Using the Dictionaire App

The Dictionaire app lets you type in all or part of a word and then view a list of words containing the same letters that you typed. This can help you find a word when you can't quite spell the whole thing.

To use the Dictionaire app, do this:

1. From the Home screen, tap **Dictionaire**. You may need to slide your Home screen to the left or right, depending on where you stored the Dictionaire icon. The Dictionaire screen appears, along with the virtual keyboard at the bottom of the screen.
2. Type all or part of a word that you want to find. As you type, words that begin with the same letters appear in a list, as shown in Figure 49-6.
3. Tap a word on the list or tap the blue Search button in the lower-right corner of the screen. The definition for your chosen word appears at the bottom of the screen, as shown in Figure 49-7.
4. Press the Home button to return to the Home screen.

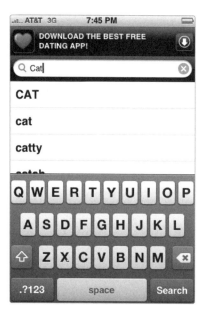

FIGURE 49-6: *The Dictionaire app tries to guess the word you might be trying to find.*

FIGURE 49-7: *Displaying a definition of a word*

Using the iThesaurus App

The iThesaurus app can be handy when you know what you want to say, but don't quite know the right word to use. The next time you're writing an email or text message, use iThesaurus and dazzle your friends with your mastery of language.

To use the iThesaurus app, do this:

1. From the Home screen, tap **iThesaurus**. You may need to slide your Home screen to the left or right, depending on where you stored the iThesaurus icon. The iThesaurus screen appears, as shown in Figure 49-8.

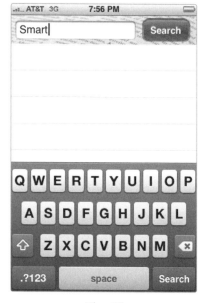

FIGURE 49-8: *The iThesaurus app displays a virtual keyboard.*

2. Type a word in the search text box at the top of the screen and tap **Search**. A list of similar words appears, as shown in Figure 49-9.
3. Tap a word to view its definition, as shown in Figure 49-10.
4. Press the Home button to return to the Home screen.

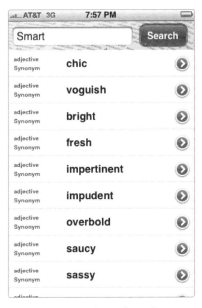

FIGURE 49-9: A list of similar words

FIGURE 49-10: Viewing the definition of a chosen word

Additional Ideas for Storing Reference Materials on Your iPhone

The App Store contains dozens of other reference apps that let you view everything from the United States Constitution to pictures of space captured by NASA. If you need a particular reference material, there's a good chance that someone will eventually write an app for displaying it on your iPhone.

Load your favorite references on your iPhone and use them to prove a point, win an argument, or annoy people with just how much better your iPhone is than their standard cell phone.

50 Traveling with Your iPhone

Most people take their iPhone with them whenever they travel. Dealing with transportation issues is one of the greatest hassles of traveling, but you can use your iPhone to watch out for speed traps, reserve a cab, or check your flight number so you'll never miss a flight again. The next time you go somewhere, take your iPhone along to help you travel without the hassles.

Project goal: Learn how to get driving and flying information through your iPhone.

What You'll Be Using

To get some travel-related apps, you need to use the following:

 iTunes (on your Mac or PC)

 The App Store application

 The Taxi Magic application

 The iPhone USB cable

 The Trapster application

 The Flight Sites application

Getting Travel Information Apps

You can use the following apps to obtain travel information:

▸ **Trapster**   Identifies speed traps and fixed traffic cameras

▸ **Taxi Magic**   Lets you call a taxi in most major cities in America

▸ **Flight Sites**   Displays flight information for different airlines

Finding Apps in iTunes

To get these apps, you'll have to search for them in the iTunes Store or the App Store. To use iTunes to find these apps, follow these steps:

1. Open iTunes on your computer.
2. Click **iTunes Store** under the STORE category in the left pane of the iTunes Store screen.
3. Click in the **Search iTunes Store** search text box in the upper-right corner of the iTunes screen and type `Trapster`, `Taxi Magic`, or `Flight Sites` and press RETURN. Your chosen app's icon appears in the iTunes window.
4. Click the **Get App** button to download the app. You'll need to synchronize and install these apps to your iPhone by following the instructions in Project 12.

Finding Apps in the App Store

If you'd rather download and install these apps directly to your iPhone without the hassle of downloading and synchronizing them through a computer, follow these steps:

1. From the Home screen, tap **App Store**. The App Store screen appears.
2. Tap the **Search** icon at the bottom of the screen. The Search screen appears.
3. Tap in the search text box at the top of the screen. The virtual keyboard appears.

4. Type **Trapster**, **Taxi Magic**, or **Flight Sites** and then tap the blue **Search** button in the lower-right corner of the screen. The app's icon appears.
5. Tap the app's icon. An Info screen appears.
6. Tap the **FREE** button. The FREE button turns into a green INSTALL button.
7. Tap the **INSTALL** button.
8. Press the Home button.

Using the Trapster App

Trapster is meant to help you find speed traps and locations of cameras that could catch you running a red light or speeding. By knowing where these traffic traps are located, you can avoid them or just drive carefully as you get closer to them. With multiple users reporting on the location of various speed traps, Trapster can display an updated map to alert other motorists.

To use Trapster, do this:

1. From the Home screen, tap **Trapster**. You may need to slide your Home screen to the left or right, depending on where you stored the Trapster icon. The Trapster screen appears, as shown in Figure 50-1.
2. Tap the **Traps** button to view a list of potential speed traps near you, as shown in Figure 50-2.

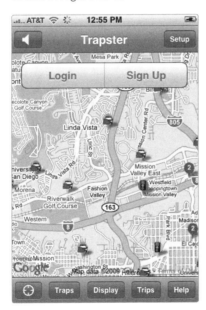

FIGURE 50-1: *Viewing a map of potential speed traps and cameras*

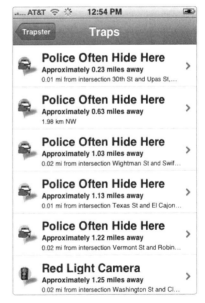

FIGURE 50-2: *Displaying a list of potential speed traps*

3. Tap a speed trap to view additional information about that trap.

4. (Optional) Tap the **Display** button to hide or display icons on the map that represent speed traps, cameras, or traffic incidents.

5. (Optional) Tap the **Trips** button to store information about a trip.

6. Press the Home button to return to the Home screen.

Using the Taxi Magic App

It's tough to find a cab in a strange city. Taxi Magic lets you view a list of cab companies you can call to arrange a ride, as shown in Figure 50-3. Just tap the cab company you want to use and the app automatically dials its phone number.

FIGURE 50-3: *The Taxi Magic app uses your current location to find nearby taxi cab companies.*

Using the Flight Sites App

If you need to get information about a particular airline or flight, you could use Safari to search for that airline's website. However, a faster and more convenient solution is to use the Flight Sites app.

To use the Flight Sites app, do this:

1. From the Home screen, tap **Flight Sites**. You may need to slide your Home screen to the left or right, depending on where you stored the Flight Sites icon. The Flight Sites screen appears, as shown in Figure 50-4.

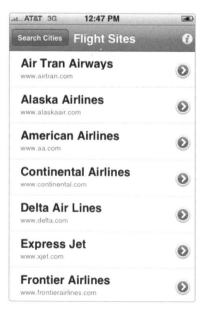

FIGURE 50-4: *Flight Sites shows you a list of airlines to choose from.*

2. Tap the name of an airline company. A screen appears, displaying additional information, such as flight status or check-in information, as shown in Figure 50-5.
3. Press the Home button to return to the Home screen.

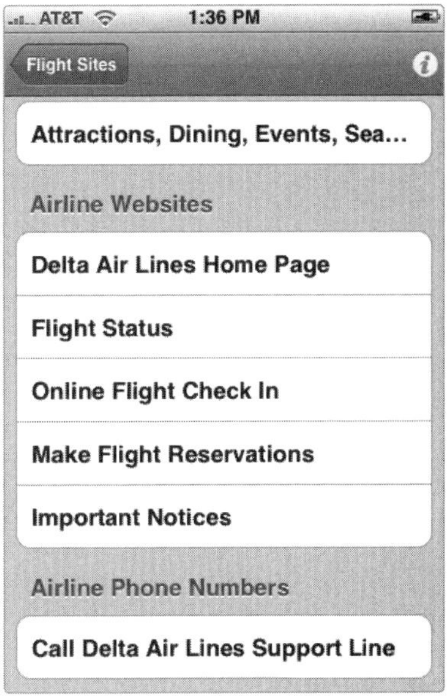

Additional Ideas for Using Your iPhone While Traveling

Your iPhone can be more than just a mobile phone; it can also be a handy source of information the next time you need taxi or airline information but don't want to waste time searching the Internet.

If you join Trapster (for free), you can even help report speed traps and notify your fellow motorists of potential traps. The more people are aware of the police, the more carefully they'll drive, which is the whole purpose of monitoring traffic in the first place (other than generating revenue for the city).

By letting your iPhone take away the hassle of traveling, you can focus on the fun part of traveling by sight-seeing, meeting new people, or just enjoying your freedom from a nine-to-five job (until you have to go back, that is).

FIGURE 50-5: *The Flight Sites app provides airline information at your fingertips.*

51

Playing Games

Since many people like to play games on their desktop or laptop computers, it's no surprise that many people use their iPhones to play games as well. There are plenty of games you can purchase, including old arcade games (like Space Invaders or Castle Wolfenstein) and modern games made especially for the iPhone.

To entice you into buying games, many companies offer a free version that gives you a taste of how the game works. Since everyone's idea of an appealing game is different, this chapter shows how to find and play some classic games that never go out of style, such as chess, checkers, and others.

Project goal: Learn how to find and play classic games on your iPhone.

What You'll Be Using

To find and play games on your iPhone, you need to use the following:

 iTunes (on your Mac or PC)

 The iPhone USB cable

 The App Store application

 The iChess application

 The Checkers Free application

 The Sudoku application

 The WordSearch Unlimited Lite application

Getting Game Apps

Some people like classic board games, while others like puzzles. Whatever your taste, there's sure to be one classic game that you'll enjoy playing on your iPhone, such as:

▶ **iChess**   Play chess against your iPhone or a human opponent.

▶ **Checkers Free**   Play checkers against your iPhone or a human opponent.

▶ **Sudoku**   Solve a Sudoku puzzle.

▶ **WordSearch Unlimited Lite**   Search for words hidden in a jumble of letters.

Finding Apps in iTunes

To get these apps, you'll have to search for them in the iTunes Store or the App Store. To use iTunes to find these apps, follow these steps:

1. Open iTunes on your computer.
2. Click **iTunes Store** under the STORE category in the left pane of the iTunes Store screen.
3. Click in the **Search iTunes Store** search field in the upper-right corner of the iTunes screen, type `iChess`, `Checkers Free`, `Sudoku`, or `WordSearch`, and press RETURN. Your chosen app's icon appears in the iTunes window.
4. Click the **Get App** button to download the app. You'll need to synchronize and install these apps to your iPhone by following the instructions in Project 12.

Finding Apps in the App Store

If you'd rather download and install these apps directly to your iPhone without the hassle of downloading and synchronizing them through a computer, follow these steps:

1. From the Home screen, tap **App Store**. The App Store screen appears.
2. Tap the **Search** icon at the bottom of the screen. The Search screen appears.

3. Tap in the search text box at the top of the screen. The virtual keyboard appears.
4. Type **iChess**, **Checkers Free**, **Sudoku**, or **WordSearch**. and then tap the blue **Search** button in the lower-right corner of the screen. The app's icon appears.
5. Tap the app's icon. An Info screen appears.
6. Tap the **FREE** button. The FREE button turns into a green INSTALL button.
7. Tap the **INSTALL** button.
8. Press the Home button.

Using the iChess App

The iChess app lets you play chess against your iPhone or against another person by turning your iPhone into a chess board, as shown in Figure 51-1. Just drag a piece around the board with your finger to move it to a new location.

If you want to customize the iChess app, just tap the icon in the lower-right corner of the screen, which resembles two gears. This displays the iChess screen, where you can choose the color you want to control (black or white), define the difficulty level of the game, change the appearance of the board, display a clock to time your moves, and show you statistics about your games, as shown in Figure 51-2.

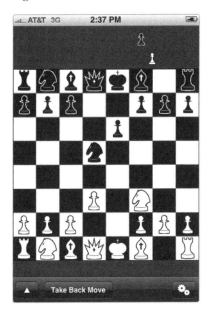

FIGURE 51-1: *The iChess board*

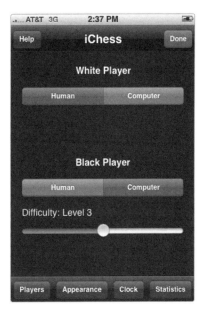

FIGURE 51-2: *Customizing the iChess app*

Using the Checkers Free App

The Checkers Free app lets you play against your iPhone or a human opponent. When you first run the game, as shown in Figure 51-3, you can tap the Options button to change whether players are forced to make jumps.

In case you make a mistake while playing against the iPhone or a human opponent, you can undo moves and learn from your mistakes. Just tap the Undo button in the upper-right corner of the screen, as shown in Figure 51-4.

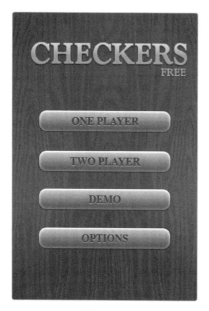

FIGURE 51-3: The opening screen for Checkers Free

FIGURE 51-4: Playing the Checkers Free game

Using the Sudoku App

Sudoku is a deceptively simple game that involves aligning rows and columns of numbers between one and nine so that no two numbers appear in the same row or column, as shown in Figure 51-5. When you play Sudoku on your iPhone, you can choose different difficulty levels and keep track of your fastest times for solving the puzzle.

Using the WordSearch Unlimited Lite App

WordSearch Unlimited Lite is a free version of a commercial program that displays words hidden within a matrix of seemingly random letters. Your job is to find words that are hidden horizontally, vertically, or diagonally. The game displays a list of words to find, and then it's up to you to drag your finger across letters to spell out those words (see Figure 51-6).

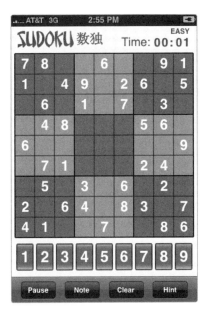

FIGURE 51-5: *The Sudoku app*

FIGURE 51-6: *Searching for words in the WordSearch Unlimited Lite game*

Additional Ideas for Playing Games on Your iPhone

The iPhone apps for chess, checkers, Sudoku, and wordsearch let you enjoy time-tested games that nearly everyone understands and can play. Obviously, these aren't the only types of games available. With the iPhone's motion detection features, many games even let you tilt the iPhone to control the movement of characters and objects.

Load up your iPhone with some free games and play them the next time you get stuck in line somewhere. Play a game on a long airplane trip, while waiting for a train or bus, or anywhere you need to take a mental break.

Games can help keep you mentally sharp and active. Then again, you're already pretty smart if you own an iPhone.

52 Communicating for Free

You can stay in touch with friends and family by making phone calls or sending text messages. Of course, your calling plan may limit you to a fixed number of minutes or text messages. Once you exceed those limits, every call or message will cost extra.

Here's a way to avoid this problem and stay in touch with everyone for free. By connecting to a Wi-Fi network (such as your home network or a free one in a coffeehouse), you can send messages and even make phone calls without paying anything extra.

Project goal: Learn ways to communicate for free with your iPhone.

What You'll Be Using

To learn how to communicate for free, you need to use the following:

 iTunes (on your Mac or PC)   The iPhone USB cable

 The App Store application   The Skype application

 The AIM application   The TwitterFon application

 The Twitter Trend application

Getting Free Communication Apps

Not only do these communication apps let you talk or chat for free, it doesn't cost anything to get them in the first place. While there are always new communication apps being developed, you can get started with these four popular apps:

▶ **Skype**   Lets you make free phone calls to other Skype users and low-cost calls to non-Skype users

▶ **AIM**   Lets you chat using the AOL Instant Messenger network

▶ **TwitterFon**   Lets you read and post messages to Twitter

▶ **Twitter Trend**   Displays the most popular words people are currently using on Twitter

Finding Apps in iTunes

To get these apps, you'll have to search for them in the iTunes Store or the App Store. To use iTunes to find these apps, follow these steps:

1. Open iTunes on your computer.
2. Click **iTunes Store** under the STORE category in the left pane of the iTunes Store screen.
3. Click in the **Search iTunes Store** search text box in the upper-right corner of the iTunes screen and type `Skype`, `AIM`, `TwitterFon`, or `Twitter Trend` and press RETURN. Your chosen app's icon appears in the iTunes window.
4. Click the **Get App** button to download the app. You'll need to synchronize and install these apps to your iPhone by following the instructions in Project 12.

Finding Apps in the App Store

If you'd rather download and install these apps directly to your iPhone without the hassle of downloading and synchronizing them through a computer, follow these steps:

1. From the Home screen, tap **App Store**. The App Store screen appears.
2. Tap the **Search** icon at the bottom of the screen. The Search screen appears.

3. Tap in the search text box at the top of the screen. The virtual keyboard appears.
4. Type **Skype**, **AIM**, **TwitterFon**, or **Twitter Trend** and then tap the blue **Search** button in the lower-right corner of the screen. The app's icon appears.
5. Tap the app's icon. An Info screen appears.
6. Tap the **FREE** button. The FREE button turns into a green INSTALL button.
7. Tap the **INSTALL** button.
8. Press the Home button.

Using Skype

Skype lets you make free phone calls through the Internet, but only if you're connected to a Wi-Fi network. (Skype can't make free calls through your cellular phone network.) To use Skype, you need to create a Skype account (*http://www.skype.com/*). Creating an account involves defining a username and password.

﹡ *NOTE:* You can also use Skype to call mobile or landline phone numbers. The only difference is that when you call a non-Skype number, you need to pay per minute.

After you tap Skype from the Home screen, you'll see five icons at the bottom of the screen:

▶ **Contacts**   Displays a saved list of phone numbers and usernames

▶ **Chats**   Displays any incoming or outgoing instant messages

▶ **Call**   Lets you type a phone number or Skype username to make a call

▶ **History**   Displays a list of all recent calls

▶ **My Info**   Displays options for customizing your profile

Customizing Your Profile

Before making a call, you may want to take some time to customize your profile, which can display additional information along with a picture of yourself or a visual image that you want to associate with yourself (such as a picture of a flower or a sports car). To add information about yourself or to add a picture for others to see, do this:

1. From the Home screen, tap **Skype**. You may need to slide your Home screen to the left or right, depending on where you stored the Skype icon.
2. Tap the **My Info** icon at the bottom of the screen. Your info screen appears, as shown in Figure 52-1.
3. Tap the Camera icon in the upper-left corner of the screen. Buttons appear at the bottom of the screen, giving you the option of capturing a picture through your iPhone's camera or using a picture already stored on your iPhone, as shown in Figure 52-2.

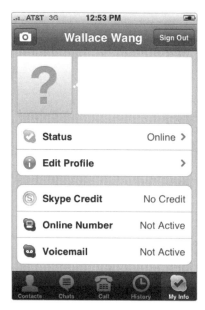

FIGURE 52-1: *The Info screen lets you modify information about yourself.*

FIGURE 52-2: *You can take a photo or choose an existing photo to use to represent yourself.*

4. Tap **Take Photo** or **Choose Existing Photo** to select a picture that other people will see.
5. Tap **Edit Profile** to open a screen where you can add information about your age, gender, or city.
6. Tap the **Status** button if you want to change your status to Online, Offline, or Do Not Disturb.

Making a Call to Another Skype User

You can make free, unlimited phone calls to other Skype users, but you'll need to know their unique Skype name. Make a call to another Skype user by doing this:

1. From the Home screen, tap **Skype**. You may need to slide your Home screen to the left or right, depending on where you stored the Skype icon.
2. Tap the **Contacts** icon at the bottom of the screen. The Contacts screen appears, listing the usernames of all your saved Skype contacts.

3. Tap a username to call that contact. A Profile screen appears for that user, as shown in Figure 52-3.

4. Tap the **Call** or **Chat** button. (If you tap the Chat button, you'll be able to send instant messages to another Skype user, which you can do over a cellular phone connection.)

If you know someone's Skype username but haven't yet stored it in the Contacts list, you can still retrieve it from the Skype directory by doing this:

1. From the Home screen, tap **Skype**. You may need to slide your Home screen to the left or right, depending on where you stored the Skype icon.

2. Tap the **Contacts** icon at the bottom of the screen. The Contacts screen appears.

3. Tap the plus sign that appears in the upper-right corner of the screen. Three buttons appear at the bottom of the screen, as shown in Figure 52-4:

▶ **Search Skype Directory** Lets you search for a user in the Skype directory, which contains all usernames on Skype

▶ **Add Phone Number** Lets you store a non-Skype number such as a mobile or landline phone

▶ **Import from iPhone** Lets you import a Skype or telephone number stored in the iPhone's Contacts application

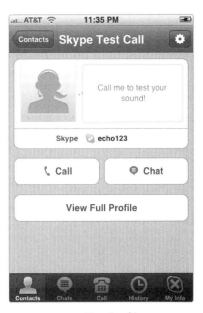

FIGURE 52-3: *The Profile screen*

FIGURE 52-4: *Three options for contacting users*

4. Tap **Search Skype Directory**. The Skype Directory screen appears along with the virtual keyboard.

5. Type the name of a person that you want to call and tap the **Search** button in the lower-right corner of the screen. The Skype Directory screen displays matches for your search.

6. Tap a name. The screen displays that person's Skype information, as shown in Figure 52-5.

7. Tap **Call** to talk or tap **Chat** to send an instant message.

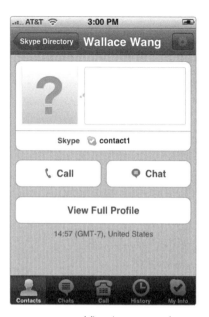

FIGURE 52-5: *Viewing a user's Skype information*

Using AIM

You can send instant messages through Skype to another Skype user, but when most people use instant messages, they usually use a dedicated messaging service such as AOL Instant Messenger (AIM). AOL offers two versions of AIM, a free, ad-supported version and a paid version without any ads. Both work identically.

Perhaps the biggest advantage of AIM is that you can send text messages to mobile phone numbers. That way, if you get charged for text messages or go over your text message limit, you can just use AIM to send text messages for free.

To use AIM, you need a MobileMe account (which you need to pay for) or a free AOL or AIM account. (You can set up an AIM account at *http://www.aim.com/.*) When you tap the AIM icon from the Home screen, you'll see five icons at the bottom of the screen:

▶   **Buddy List**   Displays a list of AIM contacts, including bots that provide information such as movie theatre showtimes

▶   **Favorites**   Displays a list of your favorite contacts for quick access

▶   **Contacts**   Displays the names and information stored in the iPhone's Contacts program

▶   **My Info**   Displays options for customizing your profile and account settings

▶   **IMs**   Lists all sent and received messages

✳ **NOTE:** The main difference between Contacts and the Buddy List is that you can access your Buddy List whenever you run AIM, whether it's on your computer at home, at work, or on your iPhone. Contacts just lets you access names stored in the Contacts application on your iPhone.

Sending a Message by Typing a Screen Name or Phone Number

To send a message through AIM by typing a screen name or mobile phone number, do this:

1. From the Home screen, tap **AIM**. You may need to slide your Home screen to the left or right, depending on where you stored the AIM icon.
2. Tap **IMs** at the bottom of the screen. The Active IMs screen appears, as shown in Figure 52-6.
3. Tap the New Message icon that appears in the upper-right corner of the screen. The virtual keyboard and a new message screen appear so you can type an AIM screen name or mobile phone number to send a text message to. Then you can type a message and tap the Send button to send your message on its way.

Adding a Contact to Your Buddy List

If you find yourself sending messages to someone regularly, you might want to store that person's name in your Buddy List by doing this:

1. From the Home screen, tap **AIM**. You may need to slide your Home screen to the left or right, depending on where you stored the AIM icon.
2. Tap **Buddy List** at the bottom of the screen.
3. Tap **Edit** in the upper-right corner of the screen. A plus sign appears in the upper-left corner of the screen, as shown in Figure 52-7.

FIGURE 52-6: *The Active IMs screen*

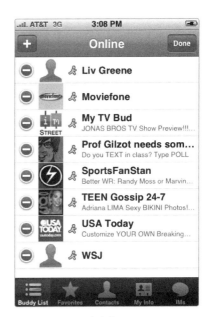

FIGURE 52-7: *Adding a name to your Buddy List*

4. Tap the plus sign in the upper-left corner of the screen. An Add Buddy screen appears, as shown in Figure 52-8.
5. Type the user's screenname, nickname, and tap the Group where you want to store this name (such as in the Family or Co-Workers group).
6. Tap **Save** in the upper-right corner of the screen.
7. Tap **Done** in the upper-right corner of the screen.

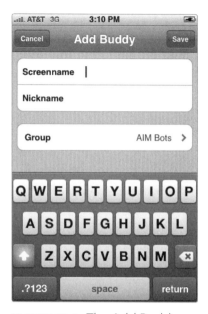

FIGURE 52-8: *The Add Buddy screen*

Sending a Message Using the Buddy List or Favorites

After you have stored screen names in your Buddy List, you can just tap that person's screen name when you want to contact them instead of typing out a name. You can send a message to a saved contact by doing this:

1. From the Home screen, tap **AIM**. You may need to slide your Home screen to the left or right, depending on where you stored the AIM icon.
2. Tap **Buddy List** or **Favorites** at the bottom of the screen. (If you tap Buddy List, you may need to dig through various Buddy List groups, such as Co-Workers or Family, until you find the screen name you want to use.)
3. Tap a screen name. The virtual keyboard and a new message screen appear so you can type a message.
4. Tap **Send** in the lower-right corner of the screen.

Sending a Message from Your Contacts List

If you've already stored someone's AIM screen name or mobile phone number in the Contacts application (see Project 37), you may find it easier to choose a name by doing this:

1. From the Home screen, tap **AIM**. You may need to slide your Home screen to the left or right, depending on where you stored the AIM icon.
2. Tap **Contacts**. The Contacts screen appears.
3. Tap a name to display that person's mobile phone or AIM screen name.
4. Tap a mobile phone number or AIM screen name. The virtual keyboard and a new message screen appear so you can type a message.
5. Tap **Send** in the lower-right corner of the screen.

Using TwitterFon and Twitter Trend

TwitterFon is a free app that lets you connect to Twitter so you can read and send tweets (updates that all your Twitter followers can read). You'll need to set up a Twitter account first (*http://www.twitter.com/*). Twitter Trend is a free app that lets you spot the words people are using most often in their tweets.

Reading and Sending Tweets Through TwitterFon

If you want to read what other people are doing, or want to send a tweet of your own, do this:

1. From the Home screen, tap **TwitterFon**. You may need to slide your Home screen to the left or right, depending on where you stored the TwitterFon icon.
2. Tap **Friends** at the bottom of the screen. The Friends screen lists all tweets from your friends (or strangers who call themselves your Twitter friends), as shown in Figure 52-9.
3. Tap the New Message icon in the upper-right corner of the screen. A New Tweet screen appears, as shown in Figure 52-10.

FIGURE 52-9: *TwitterFon displays your friends' tweets.*

FIGURE 52-10: *The New Tweet screen*

4. Type your tweet, and then tap **Send** in the upper-right corner of the screen when you're done.

Monitoring the Most Popular Words on Twitter

With so many people using Twitter, you may be curious to see what they're all talking about. To find out, do this:

1. From the Home screen, tap **Twitter Trend**. You may need to slide your Home screen to the left or right, depending on where you stored the Twitter Trend icon. The Twitter Trend screen appears, as shown in Figure 52-11.
2. Tap **Hot**, **Rising**, or **Emerging** at the top of the screen. The Hot category lists those words that are currently most popular. The Rising category lists those words that are growing in popularity, usually because of a major news story. The Emerging category lists those words that aren't the most popular, but are steadily growing anyway.

FIGURE 52-11: *The Twitter Trend screen*

Additional Ideas for Communicating for Free

By using Skype, AIM, or TwitterFon, you can stay in touch with your friends without ever paying a penny (not including the money you spent to buy your iPhone and pay your phone bill). With so many different ways to communicate, get your friends to stick to one method, such as Skype or AIM. Then everyone will know which program to use for the best way to reach others.

For a more radical approach to talking for free, use one of the apps mentioned in this chapter to arrange a time to meet in person. Then you can actually talk to a real person, which may seem like a revolutionary form of communication.

The Next Step

Between the creation of new apps and updates from Apple, you'll always have something new to learn about your iPhone. No book can teach you everything there is to know, but this book gave you a solid foundation so you can feel comfortable using your iPhone every day. After you get comfortable using your iPhone for basic tasks, you'll be ready to learn more about how to use it for more specific endeavors.

Then again, you don't have to learn everything about your iPhone as long as you know how to do the things you need to get done. The iPhone comes packed with more features than most people will ever need or use, so you don't need to waste time learning some feature just because it's there. Use your iPhone as a tool to do something useful, and then get on with the rest of your life.

Think of this book as a gentle push in the right direction; now that you've started on your journey, it's time for you to take off on your own. Don't be afraid of making mistakes, and don't be afraid to experiment. The iPhone is a forgiving tool, and if you make a mistake and find yourself looking at a screen you don't understand, just turn off your iPhone or press the Home button to get back to the familiar comfort of your Home screen icons again.

As long as you're having fun and being productive, it doesn't really matter how much or how little you know about your iPhone. All you really need is something that will help you throughout the day, and for most people, that something will be their constant companion: the iPhone.

INDEX

Updates

Visit *http://www.nostarch.com/newiphone.htm*
for updates, errata, and bonus projects
covering the latest iPhone features.

My New iPhone is set in Avenir. The book was printed and bound at Malloy Incorporated in Ann Arbor, Michigan. The paper is Glatfelter Spring Forge 60# Smooth Eggshell, which is certified by the Sustainable Forestry Initiative (SFI). The book uses a RepKover binding, which allows it to lay flat when open.